THE CATHOLIC UNIVERSITY OF AMERICA
CANON LAW STUDIES
NUMBER 58

The Appointment OF Parochial Adjutants AND Assistants

A DISSERTATION

Submitted to the Faculty of Canon Law of the Catholic University of America in Partial Fulfillment of the Requirements for the Degree of

DOCTOR OF BOTH LAWS

by

CLEMENT VINCENT BASTNAGEL

Priest of the Diocese of Indianapolis

THE CATHOLIC UNIVERSITY OF AMERICA
WASHINGTON, D. C.
MCMXXX

Nihil Obstat:

JACOBUS HUGO RYAN, PH.D., S.T.D., LL.D., LITT.D.,
Rector Magnificus Universitatis, Censor Deputatus.
Washingtonii, D. C., die XII Maii, 1930.

Imprimatur:

✠ JOSEPHUS CHARTRAND, D.D.,
Episcopus Indianapolitanus.
Indianapoli, die XV Maii, 1930.

COMPOSED BY
MONOTYPE COMPOSITION CO., INC.
BALTIMORE, MD.

TABLE OF CONTENTS

PART I

HISTORICAL CONSPECTUS

CHAPTER I

CHAPTER II

CHAPTER III

CHAPTER IV

CHAPTER IV

PART II

PRESENT LEGISLATION

CHAPTER V

CHAPTER VI

CHAPTER VI

CHAPTER VII

ABBREVIATIONS

AAS—*Acta Apostolicae Sedis.*
AER—*The American Ecclesiastical Review.*
AkKR—*Archiv für katholisches Kirchenrecht.*
Anal. Eccles.—*Analecta Ecclesiastica.*
Anal. Jur. Pont.—*Analecta Juris Pontificii.*
Apoll.—*Apollinaris.*
ASS—*Acta Sanctae Sedis.*
c.—canon seu caput (iuris antiqui).
cc.—canones seu capita (iuris antiqui).
can.—canon (novi Codicis).
cans.—canones (novi Codicis).
Canones et Decreta—*Canones et Decreta Sacrosancti Oecumenici Concilii Tridentini.*
Cath. Ency.—*Catholic Encyclopedia.*
Collectanea—*Collectanea Sacra Congregationis de Propaganda Fide.*
Coll. Lac.—*(Collectio Lacensis) Acta et Decreta Sacrorum Conciliorum Recentiorum.*
CV—*(Corpus Vindobonense) Corpus Scriptorum Ecclesiasticorum Latinorum.*
D.—Digesta vel Distinctio.
Fontes—*Codicis Iuris Canonici Fontes.*
Greg.—*Gregorianum.*
Hardouin—Hardouin, J., *Acta Conciliorum et Epistolae Decretales ac Constitutiones Summorum Pontificum.*
Hartzheim—Hartzheim, Jos., *Concilia Germaniae.*
HPR—*The Homiletic and Pastoral Review.*
IER—*The Irish Ecclesiastical Record.*
Jus Pont.—*Jus Pontificium.*
kath.—*katholisches.*
KR—*Kirchenrecht.*
LQS—*(Linzer Quartalschrift) Theologisch-praktische Quartalschrift.*
MGH—*Monumenta Germaniae Historica.*
MPG—(Migne, *Patrologia Graeca*) Migne, Jacques Paul, *Patrologiae Cursus Completus—Series Graeca.*
MPL—(Migne, *Patrologia Latina*) Migne, Jacques Paul, *Patrologiae Cursus Completus—Series Latina.*
NRT—*Nouvelle Revue Théologique.*
Periodica—*Periodica de Re Canonica et Morali Utili praesertim Religiosis et Missionariis.*

Pont. Com. Int.—Pontificia Commissio ad Codicis Canones Authentice Interpretandos.
RSE—*Revue des Sciences Ecclésiastiques.*
S. C. C.—Sacra Congregatio Concilii.
S. C. Consist.—Sacra Congregatio Consistorialis.
S. C. Ep. et Reg.—Sacra Congregatio Episcoporum et Regularium.
S. C. S. Off.—Sacra Congregatio Sancti Officii.
S. R. C.—Sacrorum Rituum Congregatio.
S. R. R.—Sacra Romana Rota.
Thesaurus Resolutionum—*Thesaurus Resolutionum Sacrae Congregationis Concilii.*
TQS—*(Tübinger Quartalschrift) Theologische Quartalschrift.*
TR—*Theologische Revue.*
Th Gl—*Theologie und Glaube.*
Wilkins—Wilkins, David, *Concilia Magnae Britanniae et Hiberniae.*
ZkT—*Zeitschrift für katholische Theologie.*

FOREWORD

The chapter of the Code of Canon Law which treats of parochial vicars presents a discipline in the historical development of which are to be found numerous variations and repeated changes, until it reaches its present expression in the general legislation of the Church. While this is true, in general, regarding all the classes of parochial vicars, it is especially obvious with regard to parochial adjutants and assistants. This evolution of the law resulted chiefly from two factors—the long continued absence of any general legislation on this topic in the earlier centuries and the gradual formation of custom in superseding the specific laws of the Council of Trent.

Of the various regulations of the Church touching upon parochial adjutants and assistants, the discipline concerning the mode of their appointment offers the greatest variety of development in its evolution through the agencies of written and customary law. The reason for this seems inherent in the fact that the rule regulating the manner of their assignment constituted the primary factor by the application of which the law could drive its opening wedge for the adaptation of other legal measures determining their status, their rights and their duties. Hence, although the present study has for its distinct objective the investigation of the evolution of the law and its current discipline concerning the appointment of parochial adjutants and assistants, it will be understood, nevertheless, that a subsidiary discussion of the position occupied by these agencies of help in parochial ministrations can serve a useful purpose by way of illustrating the motives underlying the legal norm of appointment.

Part I of this dissertation presents an historical conspectus. It is quite evident that, in days when means of communication and contact with distant persons and places involved considerable difficulties, much of the disciplinary legislation which now emanates from the center of the Christian world originated during the earlier centuries in the dioceses and provinces where the need of it was felt. This consideration explains the existence of the various forms of legislation in the different countries at one and the same time, or in the same countries at different times. It also helps to demonstrate the historical fact that laws of apparent contradiction could nevertheless enjoy a contemporaneous existence because of the limited extent and individual application of their legal force within separate, restricted territories.

Moreover, the possibility of a continued evolution in the norm of appointment regarding parochial adjutants and assistants was not absolutely precluded even after the enactment of a general law by the Council of Trent. The dioceses of Freising and of Salzburg in Austria offer evidences of an impending change in the manner of appointing assistant vicars as early as the seventeenth century. In France a similar change of discipline became current from the time of the French Revolution. Thereafter the general law of the Council of Trent fell into desuetude in other countries also. At the beginning of this century there existed only a few countries which had not appropriated for local ordinaries the right of appointment which by the law of the Council of Trent had been accorded to pastors.

Part II of this dissertation is concerned with the present legislation on appointment. Canons 475 §1 and 476 §§3-4 grant the exclusive right and competence of appointing and approving parochial adjutants and assistants to the local ordinary. Again, canons 475 §1 and 476 §4 establish a certain and definite right of presentation for the religious superior. Finally, canon 476 §§3-4 vindicates for the actual pastoral incumbent the right of being consulted by the local ordinary when he appoints, and by the religious superior when he presents for approval, a prospective candidate for a parochial assistancy. All of these acts of consultation, presentation, approval and appointment are to be executed only then when the proper conditions occasion the need of their application. The definite decision concerning the actual existence of the requisite conditions rests with the local ordinary.

The writer avails himself of the present opportunity to manifest his sincere gratitude to his esteemed bishop, the Rt. Rev. Joseph Chartrand, D.D., for the privilege of advanced studies, and for the encouragement lent by his personal interest; to the distinguished members of the Faculty of Canon Law for their untiring assistance and stimulating direction in the preparation of this study; to the librarians of the University Library for their repeated acts of helpfulness and courtesy; and to all who aided him in the final preparation of this text for their liberal co-operation.

PART I

Historical Conspectus

CHAPTER I

EARLY HISTORY OF PARISH DISCIPLINE

ART. I. PRELIMINARY REMARKS

To present an outline of the history of the Church's legislation touching on temporary parochial vicars necessitates a preparatory study of the development of her laws on parishes and parish priests. There was a time when the vicarial clergy were regarded not so much as the *public* ministers of the *common* welfare in the Church *universal,* but rather as the *private* servants of the parish priest's *personal* accommodation in the Church *parochial.*[1] The bonds of inter-relationship were thus very closely drawn. To investigate the rights and the duties of the parochial vicar without knowing the claims and obligations of the parochial pastor would prove a bootless task. Although this relationship between parish priests and parish assistants has been appreciably altered by the Church's changed viewpoint of the bond that unites them, the fundamental idea of *parish priests* and *parish churches* will ever remain the legal basis on which rests the canonical concept of an *auxiliary parochial clergy.*

Precisely for this reason it becomes imperative to devote a chapter of this study to a summary review of the Church's initial development of parish life and parish rule. Both the ante-Nicene and post-Nicene periods will bear investigation on this point.

After the Church had won her glorious struggle with the persecutors of a pagan Empire and had gained the prestige of a public recognition from the first Christian Emperor, she could look forward to a brighter future in the work of organizing her clerical forces for the conversion of the world. This second period, then, with even more intimate reason than that which

[1] Cf. Lindner, *Die Anstellung der Hilfspriester,* p. 110.

preceded it, calls for a historical review, in order that a study of the parochial vicars, who make their appearance in the organization of the Church in this era of her life, may be set in its proper perspective.

ART. II. ANTE-NICENE PERIOD

The terms *parish* and *parish priest* in the light of their present canonical conception were alien to the terminology of the earliest Christian centuries. The city or territory over which the bishop ruled was not yet apportioned into smaller districts where ecclesiastics of non-episcopal rank permanently exercised the care of souls. The bishop, singly and alone, remained the pastor of the diocese. He alone enjoyed the fundamental right and authority to preach the truths of salvation and to dispense the mysteries of grace. All other clerics of the diocese, irrespective of their higher or lower rank beneath the episcopal dignity, were totally dependent upon his individual authorization for the performance of any spiritual and ecclesiastical functions. This can be plainly gathered from the 39th canon of the *Canones Apostolorum:* "Let priests and deacons do nothing without the direction *(sententia)* of the bishop; it is he to whom the people of God have been entrusted, and from whom the account of their souls is required." [2]

In the primitive era the bishopric was conterminous with the urban center wherein it existed. Clinging to the Apostolic tradition,[3] the successors of the Apostles established their Christian Congregations in towns and cities where they could hope to gain more numerous conversions to the Christian faith than in the rural districts. Thus, each urban congregation enjoyed its own bishop, and every city with a resident Christian community constituted a bishopric for its episcopal pastor.[4]

---

[2] Funk, *Didascalia et Constitutiones Apostolorum*, I, 577.

[3] "For this cause I left thee in Crete, that thou shouldst set in order the things that are wanting, and shouldst ordain priests in every city, as I also appointed thee."—Titus, I, 5.

[4] Cf. Thomassinus, *Vetus et Nova Ecclesiae Disciplina*, P. I, lib. II, cap. 21, n. 1 ss.; Augustine, *Rights and Duties of Ordinaries* (Introduction), pp. i-iv; Coady, *The Appointment of Pastors*, pp. 5-6; Lindner, *Die Anstellung der Hilfspriester*, p. 2.

This condition of things postulated the reception of the sacraments by the faithful from their own bishop and their attendance at the sacred services in his cathedral church, as St. Ignatius clearly testifies.[5] This usage extended into the later centuries,[6] and still obtained when the Christian faith had been disseminated in rural districts.[7]

In spite of the periodic persecutions that raged against them, the early Christian congregations soon outgrew the conveniences that the single cathedral church could offer them. Pagan

[5] In his letters written to the churches of Asia Minor the Martyr Bishop bears abundant testimony to this practice. Cf. *Ad Ephes.*, cap. 4: ". . . Illud vero digne nominandum et Deo dignum, presbyterium ita cooptatum sit episcopo, quomodo chordae in cithara colligatae."—Funk, *Patres Apostolici*, I, 215; *MPG*, V, 648. *Ad Magnes.*, cap. 7, 1-2: ". . . Sicut ergo Dominus sine Patre nihil facit, . . . sic etiam et vos sine episcopo, sive presbyter, seu diaconus, sive laicus. Non ergo aliquid rationabile vobis videtur extra ipsius sententiam; tale etenium iniquum est et Deo inimicum. . . . Omnes adunati ad templum Dei concurrite, sicut ad unum altare."—Funk, *op. cit.*, I, 235; *MPG*, V, 668. *Ad Trall.*, cap. 2, 2: ". . . ut sine episcopo nihil agatis . . ."—Funk, *op. cit.*, I, 242; *MPG*, V, 676. *Ad Phil.*, cap. 7: ". . . sed Spiritus annuntiavit dicens ita; sine episcopo nihil facite . . ."—Funk, *op. cit.*, I, 268; *MPG*, V, 701. *Ad Smyr.*, cap. 8, 1: ". . . Separatim ab episcopo nemo quidquam faciat eorum quae ad ecclesiam spectant. Valida eucharistica habeatur illa, quae sub episcopo peragitur, vel sub eo cui ipse concesserit."—Funk, *op. cit.*, I, 282; *MPG*, V, 713. *Ibid.*, cap. 8, 2: ". . . Non licet sine episcopo neque baptizare neque agapen celebrare; sed quodcumque ille probaverit, hoc et Deo est beneplacitum, ut firmum et validum sit omne quod peragitur."—Funk, *loc. cit.*; *MPG*, V, *loc. cit.* *Ad Polyc.*, cap. 4; ". . . Nihil sine sententia tua fiat, neque tu sine Deo quid operare; quod autem operaris, sit bene stabile . . ."—Funk, *op. cit.*, I, 277; *MPG*, V, 721.

[6] Justin, *Apologia*, I, n. 67: "Praepositus preces et Eucharistiam facit . . ." —*MPG*, VI, 429; Tertullian, *De Baptismo*, cap. 17: "Superest de observatione quoque dandi et accipiendi baptismi commonefacere. Dandi quidem habet ius *summus sacerdos*, qui est *episcopus*; dehinc presbyteri et diaconi, non tamen sine episcopi auctoritate, propter ecclesiae honorem, quo salvo, salva est pax. . . ."—*CV*, XX, 214; *MPL*, I, 1217; Cyprian, *Epistolae*, 33: ". . . ut ecclesia super episcopos constituatur . . ., et omnis actus ecclesiae per eosdem prepositos gubernetur."—*CV*, III, 2, 566; Journel, *Enchiridion Patristicum*, n. 571; *MPL*, IV, 298 (ep. 27); Jerome, *Dialogus contra Luciferianos* (circa 382), cap. 9: ". . . Inde venit, ut sine chrismate et episcopi iussione neque presbyter neque diaconus ius habeant baptizandi. Quod frequenter, si tamen necessitas cogit, scimus etiam licere laicis."—Journel, *op. cit.*, n. 1359; *MPL*, XXIII, 164. Cf. footnote 2 above.

[7] "Solis dicta die omnium qui in urbibus vel in agris degunt in eumden locum conventus fit."—Journel, *op. cit.*, n. 129; *MPL*, VI, 429; Kirch, *Enchiridion Fontium Historiae Ecclesiasticae Antiquae*, n. 56.

writers of the time bear witness to the growth [8] and territorial extension into the rural districts of the new faith in their midst.[9] It was especially from the larger cities, in particular, from Rome, Antioch, Ephesus and Alexandria, that the Christian religion radiated into the surrounding villages and hamlets.[10]

§I. In the Orient

In his ecclesiastical history the learned Eusebius of Caesarea relates that Dionysius, bishop of Alexandria, when banished into the interior of Egypt, near a hamlet that bore the name of Arsinoë, was not deprived of the consolation of public church worship,[11] but found a number of priests in the countryside with whom he later held a conference for three days.[12]

It remains difficult to determine from the scant documents still extant and bearing upon the question, whether these primitive rural ecclesiastics exercised their spiritual ministry for the scattered rural population as the emissaries of the urban bishop or rather as an auxiliary clergy with a rural bishop in their midst. St. Justin the Martyr indicates in his *Apologia* (I. n. 67) after what manner the churches in his day consulted the religious needs of the rural population: *"Distributio fit cuique praesenti, absentibus per diaconos mittitur."* [13] The synodal letter which the bishops of the Council of Antioch in the year 269 directed against the recalcitrant Paul of Samosata is probably the oldest document that makes mention of "rural bish-

[8] Cf. Origen, *Contra Celsum,* III, 10—*MPG,* XI, 885.

[9] "Neque enim civitates tantum sed vicos etiam et agros superstitionis istius contagio pervagata est."—Pliny the Younger, *Epist.,* X, 97.

[10] "Nullum enim omnino genus est sive barbarorum, sive Graecorum, sive quodlibet nomine appellentur, vel hamaxobiorum qui in plaustris degunt, vel nomadum qui domibus carent, vel scenitarum qui pecora pascentes habitant in tentoriis, nullum, inquam, eiusmodi genus est, in quo non per nomen crucifixi Jesu preces et gratiarum actiones Patri et Creatori universorum fiant." —Justin Martyr, *Dialogus cum Tryphone Judaeo,* cap. 117, n. 9; cf. *MPG,* VI, 748; Kirch, *Enchiridion Fontium,* n. 59; Funk, *Manual of Church History,* I, §20.

[11] *Historia Ecclesiastica,* VII, 11—*MPG,* XX, 661-73.

[12] *Ibid.,* VII, 24—*MPG,* XX, 692-96.

[13] *MPG,* VI, 429; Journel, *Enchiridion Patristicum,* n. 129. Cf. also Gottlob, *Der abendländische Chorepiskopat,* pp. 1-5.

ops." [14] Zorell is of the opinion that in the Orient the institution of rural bishops was contemporaneous with the need of the rural pastoration of souls.[15]

The innate probability of this opinion gains strength from the consideration that the persecutions under the Emperors Maximinus, Decius, Gallus and Valerian manifested their fury principally in the western provinces of the Empire. The Church in the Orient was less hampered in its growth and expansion. Its membership overflowed into the country districts where their spiritual necessities were consulted by the appointment of a bishop in their midst so that they too, like their fellow Christians in the cities, could attend the sacred mysteries and receive the holy sacraments in a central place of worship where a bishop presided for them as the pastor of their souls.

In his informative article on the Church's development of the parochial idea during the early Christian centuries, Zorell draws the further conclusion that, in the extent of their episcopal functions and the scope of their authority over the rural clergy, these rural bishops are to be identified with the bishops of a later period known to us by the name of *chorepiscopi*.[16] For, whilst this latter class of bishops receives express mention for the first time in the Synod of Ancyra (314),[17] one of the synodal decrees inveighs against the abuses of their unauthorized assumption of certain episcopal faculties reserved to the bishops of the cities, which fact equally certifies that their institution must have been of a date early enough to allow for the

---

[14] Eusebius, *Hist. Eccles.*, VII, 30—*MPG*, XX, 709-20. Cf. also Hinschius, *System des katholischen Kirchenrechts*, II, 162; Funk, *Manual of Church History*, I, §20; Augustine, *Rights and Duties of Ordinaries* (Introduction), pp. vii-x.

[15] "Die Entwickelung des Parochialsystems bis zum Ende der Karolingerzeit," *AkKR*, LXXXII (1902), 74-98 and 258-89. Note especially p. 80 for the testimony cited.

[16] *Ibid.* Concerning the *chorepiscopi* of the Orient the reader will consult with profit Dr. Franz Gillmann, *Das Institut der Chorbischöfe im Orient;* for a richly documented study of their powers, Hinschius, *System des kath. KR.*, II, 161 ff.

[17] Cf. Thomassinus, *Vetus et Nova Ecclesiae Disciplina*, P. I, lib. I, cc. 27-28.

development of these usurpations of power.[18] It would seem that the passing of the rural bishops gave way immediately to the institution of the *chorepiscopi* who replaced them in the administration of the rural churches. That the *chorepiscopi* existed as a stabilized institution in the Church, at least with the advent of the fourth century, appears evident from canon 8 of the first Ecumenical Council at Nice in the year 325.[19]

Thus, the beginning of the third century saw the pastoration of rural churches in the Orient fully constituted under the superintendence of the rural bishops, and later the *chorepiscopi*, who in turn were subject to the authority of their urban bishops. Living with the *chorepiscopi* was the college of priests, deacons, and minor clerics, exercising the spiritual functions entrusted to them by their common pastor, the bishop. The auxiliary clergy at the rural cathedral could not undertake the celebration of mass nor the distribution of the consecrated Bread and Chalice in the presence of their bishop, but only when circumstances rendered it morally impossible to requisition his services.[20]

In view of the documents cited by Zorell,[21] it is beyond dispute that as early as the third century there existed, at least in scattered territories, Christian congregations whose spiritual needs were administered by priests of non-episcopal rank or consecration.[22] The sphere of their rights and offices cannot be de-

[18] Cf. Synod. Ancyran. (314), can. 13—Hardouin, II, 275-76, in which the *chorepiscopi* were put under restraint of not ordaining priests or deacons without leave from their urban bishops. Their fuller sphere of rights together with their restrictions may be learned from the canons of the synods indicated in footnote 20 below.

[19] Provision is made in this canon that the Novatian bishops who had returned to the profession of orthodoxy should be instituted as *chorepiscopi*. Cf. Kirch, *Enchiridion Fontium Historiae Ecclesiasticae Antiquae*, n. 494; Mansi, II, 671-72; Hardouin, I, 326; Hefele, *Conciliengeschichte*, I, 376 ss.

[20] Cf. Mansi, II, 541-42. Canon 13 of the Synod of Neocaesarea (314-25) reads as follows: "Vicani autem presbyteri non possunt in dominico offerre praesente episcopo, vel urbis presbyteris; neque panem dare precationis, neque calicem. Sin autem absint, et solus ad precationem vocatus fuerit, dat." —Hardouin (I, 286) gives the variant translations of this canon. Cf. also Synod. Gangren. (circa 330), cc. 6-8—Hardouin, I, 535 ss.; Synod. Antiochen. (341), c. 10—Hardouin, I, 591 ss.; Synod. Sardicen. (343-44), c. 6—Mansi, III, 10.

[21] Cf. *AkKR*, LXXXII (1902), 81 ff.

[22] Cf. footnotes 11 and 12 above; see also Walter, *Lehrbuch des Kirchenrechts*, p. 279.

termined with accuracy or certainty from the early sources at hand. Most probably their functions remained vaguely defined except in as far as they were specified by the urban or rural bishop through whose personal instruction and authorization they were undertaken. The rural priests whom Dionysius, bishop of Alexandria, discovered in the countryside of Arsinoë upon his banishment thither were most probably the emissaries of some African bishop of the interior who knew in this way to supply the services and the sacraments of the Church to a population too far removed from his cathedral to partake in the services there. As soon as their numbers had grown to sufficient proportions to demand the care that only a resident pastor in their midst could afford them, there could be detailed for them a rural bishop who with his auxiliary clergy would offer them the fuller ministrations of religion such as the Christians in the larger towns and cities enjoyed. In the Orient the seed of the parochial economy of souls was sown in the rural districts as early as the prior half of the third century, germinated under the institution of the first rural bishops in the latter half of the same century, developed with the appointment of *chorepiscopi* near the beginning of the fourth century, and reached its ultimate maturity in the century subsequent to the Council of Nice.[23]

§II. In the Occident

In the western provinces of the Roman Empire, where the Christian religion was made the object of more frequent and drastic persecutions than in the East, the territorial expansion of the Church suffered greater hindrances.[24] For the sake of their mutual strength and protection against the onslaughts of their enemies, the Christians banded together in the larger towns and cities. It may be presumed that at intervals when hostilities ceased and when, in consequence, the Christian population could with some degree of security venture to expand into the rural territories, their interests of religion were cared for by

[23] Cf. Hinschius, *System des kath. KR.*, II, 262 ff.; Zorell, "Die Entwickelung des Parochialsystems bis zum Ende der Karolingerzeit," *AkKR*, LXXXII (1902), 81 ff.

[24] Cf. Funk, *Manual of Church History*, I, §16.

the activity of missionary priests among them. In the absence of documents to the contrary, it seems allowable to draw the conclusion that the parochial discipline of the Church in the western parts of the Empire during the first three centuries never outgrew the Apostolic tradition, namely, to establish bishops with their assistant clergy in the larger urban centers, and to call upon all the Christian converts to satisfy their religious wants by attendance at the cathedral church in the city of the bishop's residence.

The discipline of the Church from the time of its foundation by Christ down to the time of the first Ecumenical Council clung tenaciously to the traditions of the Apostles which inculcated the establishment of religious centers and congregations in the towns and the cities wherever the word of faith was preached. The bishop of the city was the central head and exclusive pastor of his cathedral church and urban bishopric. Priests, deacons, even minor clerics were ordained to remain with their bishop. They formed his college of assistants in the multiplied cares of the growing cathedral church.

Priests were busied with the labors of catechizing the catechumens in preparation for baptism and of instructing the minor clerics for attaining to the higher orders;[25] deacons were occupied with the cares of collecting and distributing the public Christian charities;[26] minor clerics, besides being employed in the task of securing the good order of the House of God for the solemn celebration of the sacred mysteries, were simultaneously devoted to a life of study in pursuance of their ultimate aim, the diaconate or priesthood. All of these orders of the clergy together were intimately associated with the conduct of divine services and the preaching of the heavenly word by their bishop.[27] At

---

[25] Cf. *Pastor Hermae*, Visio III, 5: 1—Funk, *Patres Apostolici*, I, 440; *MPG*, II, 903; Journel, *Enchiridion Patristicum*, n. 84.

[26] Cf. Acts, VI, 1-7; *Pastor Hermae, loc. cit.*; Funk, *loc. cit.*

[27] Pope St. Evaristus (112-121) ordained that a band of seven deacons were to form a guard of honor for their bishop in his public preaching office. —*Roman Breviary*, Pars Autumnalis, October 26. Pope St. Zephyrinus (203-221) decreed that all the priests should be present with their bishop in his celebration of the Sacred Mystery.—*Roman Breviary*, Pars Aestiva, August 26. Pope St. Caius (283-296) singled out the various successive orders by the reception of which clerics were to approach to the priesthood.—*Roman Breviary*, Pars Verna, April 22.

such times when, through sickness or some other cause, some of the faithful could not attend the bishop's church for the reception of the Eucharist from his own hand, the sacred trust of bearing It to the absent ones devolved upon the deacons,[28] and on all the solemn days of liturgy, when the bishop pontificated, it was incumbent upon the priests to concelebrate with him.[29]

In the hindrance or during the absence of the bishop, priests were empowered; if priests were unavailable, even deacons were instructed to impose their hands on the sick and the dying who had received a *libellus* from the martyrs and thereupon wished to effect their reconciliation with the Church.[30]

Finally, according to the opinion proposed, the priests were requisitioned by their urban bishops to make excursions into the more remote territories where Christians were found, until their numbers had sufficiently increased to permit of an established and abiding service in their midst.

ART. III. POST-NICENE PERIOD

§I. PARISH ORGANIZATION IN THE EASTERN CHURCHES

In the East, the traditions which were current at the time of the first Ecumenical Council prevailed for some decades longer. In a synod held at the City of Gangra (probably the modern Kiangeri in Turkey) about the year 330, the acceptance of church dues by anyone other than the bishop or his appointee was anathematized.[31] The administration and the distribution of the public offerings were restricted within the same narrow limits.[32] The *chorepiscopi* still occupied their position of de-

[28] Cf. footnote 7 above. "Et eorum, in quibus gratiae actae sunt, distributio fit et communicatio unicuique praesentium, *et absentibus per diaconos mittitur*."—Justin Martyr, *Apologia* I, cap. 67, n. 6; Kirch, *Enchiridion Fontium*, n. 56.

[29] Cf. Mario Lupi, *De Paroeciis ante annum millesimum* (ed. Bergomi, 1788), p. 173, quoted by Bouix, *Tractatus de Parocho* (2. ed., 1867), p. 17. See also Walter, *Lehrbuch des Kirchenrechts*, p. 279.

[30] Cf. Cyprian, *Epistola* [Presbyteris et diaconis, a. 250] 18, 1—*CV*, III, 2, 523; *MPL* [ep. 12], IV, 259.

[31] C. 7—Hardouin, I, 535.

[32] C. 8.

pendency upon the urban bishop for the faculty of conferring the major orders,[33] whilst in parochial matters they were in full control of their churches. The clergy resident with them continued subject to their personal direction for the performance of all ecclesiastical functions,[34] and any priests or deacons who segregated themselves from their bishops for the sake of conducting public worship elsewhere were condemned for such unauthorized action by canon 5 of the same Council.[35]

The Church's strong adherence to the practice of centralizing her clerical forces around the court of the bishop is again given expression by a synod held at Sardica (343-344); yet, because of her desire to safeguard the honor and the dignity due to episcopal consecration, she interdicted the stationing of bishops in the smaller towns and villages where the services of missionary priests might suffice.[36]

The traditional ecclesiastical polity of multiplying the number of her bishops to attend to the needs of the increased and diffused Christian population suffered a definite innovation in the synod of Laodicea (circa 380) when the institution of the *Periodeutae* (visiting priests) was established. As a result, the authority of the *chorepiscopi* gradually lost its significance; eventually their office fell into desuetude.[37] The churches formerly governed by them were entrusted to priests appointed thereto by bishops who now ruled not only within their cathedral city, but over the surrounding country as well.[38] In view of this changed condition of parochial discipline the rural churches began to multiply, and, because of their distance from the cathedral church, to acquire certain parochial rights.[39]

Along the littoral of the Mediterranean Sea in northeastern Africa and in the territory adjacent to it one finds an even

[33] Synod. Antiochen. (341), c. 10—Mansi, II, 1311-12; Hardouin, I, 594; Kirch, *Enchiridion Fontium*, n. 494.

[34] C. 24—Hefele, *Conciliengeschichte*, I, 518.

[35] Mansi, II, 1310. See also Cappello, *De Visitatione SS. Liminum et Dioeceseon*, II, 10.

[36] C. 6—Mansi, III, 10.

[37] C. 57—Hardouin, I, 791-92. Cf. c. 5, D. 80, where this canon is reproduced by Gratian.

[38] Cf. Funk, *Manual of Church History*, I, §62.

[39] Cf. Zorell, "Die Entwickelung des Parochialsystems bis zum Ende der Karolingerzeit," *AkKR*, LXXXII (1902), 88.

earlier revelation of the same discipline. St. Athanasius relates that the district of Mareötes in the region of Alexandria possessed a number of churches which were subject to the bishop of Alexandria, and that, moreover, *all* the separate villages with churches were ruled by individual priests.[40] The existence of rural parochial churches had plainly become a permanent institution by the time of the third Ecumenical Council, celebrated at Ephesus in the year 431, since parish organization in the country districts had developed to a stage where even a village church might require the services of an auxiliary priest.[41]

The Council of Chalcedon (451) in canon 6 prescribes the ordination of priests for the various classes of churches. Furthermore, it regulates that no cleric is to be ordained except in view of a church that he is permanently to serve. A later canon (19) speaks of two kinds of churches: the larger ones of the separate villages which were the parish churches, and the smaller ones of the hamlets which were linked with the former as filial churches, or what, in our own day, might be designated as chapels of ease.[42] This latter class of churches did not enjoy

---

[40] *Apologia contra Arianos*—*MPG*, XXV, 385-400. Cf. Thomassinus, *Vetus et Nova Ecclesiae Disciplina*, P. I, lib. II, cap. 22, nn. 1-3. Maroto (*Institutiones Iuris Canonici*, II, n. 758, p. 71 ss.) lists an exhaustive enumeration of the duties and ministries assumed by the diocesan clergy upon the personal behest of their bishop. Sohm (*Kirchenrecht*, I, 240-47) cites copious documents in substantiation of the gradual disciplinary development in view of which priests and deacons began to exercise their ministrations in ever-decreasing dependency upon the personal authorization of their bishop for individual acts of the pastoration of souls.

The diocesan clergy, at first associated with their bishop in his pastoral and fiscal ministrations at the latter's personal option and discretion, later formed an integral part of his administrative council and eucharistic functions. This stage of discipline, in turn, yielded to the practice of a separately constituted exercise of merely pastoral functions by priests and deacons in the churches separated from the bishop's church. A common treasury for the common support of all the clerics was still maintained. The transformation became complete with the advent of the system of benefices. The parochial clergy thenceforth reaped their sustenance from the income derived from the landed properties and predial estates acquired by, or in behalf of, the individual parishes.

[41] Cf. Mansi, IV, 1357-58. Among the signatures of the priests present at the Council of Ephesus there is found the name of a certain Patricius, who is designated as the *second* priest of the village of Paradioxylon. The probability is not that he was the pastor of a *second church* in the village; he was the *second priest* at the same church.

[42] Cf. Hardouin, II, 603, 607. See also canon 17 of this Council.

the full rights of parish churches. Their lack in this regard may be ascertained from canon 31 of the Trullan Synod (692) which specified that clerics who baptized in these chapels were to be deposed in punishment of their disobedience.[43]

At the time of the seventh Ecumenical Council, celebrated at Nice in the year 787, the Church's general discipline on parish organization had taken very definite shape in her insistence on two paramount principles: 1) Clerics were not to leave the church for which they had been ordained; and 2) clerics were not to exercise the pastoral office in more than one church.[44]

It now remains to investigate the historical development of parochial discipline in the Western Churches in order to learn by what route they evolved the same canonical legislation.

§II. Parish Organization in the Western Churches

A. In Africa

The northern coast of Africa, and, in particular, the metropolitan see of Carthage with its suffragan dioceses, was the scene of intense missionary activity at the close of the fourth and the beginning of the fifth centuries. The Letters of St. Augustine [45] make mention of a number of churches and parishes in his own diocese of Hippo-Regius.[46] It is especially from the documents of the councils and the synods held at Carthage toward the close of the fourth century that the inquirer may learn, on the one hand, what powers and faculties the priests of rural parishes in this and the neighboring dioceses enjoyed, and, on the other, what functions remained reserved to the bishop.

In the second council of Carthage (390) the bishops stipulated that the confection of the holy oils and the consecration

[43] Cf. Mansi, XI, 955.

[44] Cc. 10, 15—Hardouin, IV, 769-70.

[45] *Epistolae:* 203, 212, 236, 240—*CV*, LVII, 315-17, 371-72, 523-25, 559-60; *MPL*, XXXIII, 938, 965, 1033-34, 1051.

[46] Cf. Browne, "The Coming Eucharistic Congress at Carthage," *AER*, LXXXII (1930), 253-63. The article contains very pertinent information on the early Christian history of Carthage. The ancient Hippo-Regius is now known by the name of Bona or Bone. The birthplace (Tagaste) of St. Augustine has become the modern Souk-Ahras or Sukarras. Cf. p. 258 of article.

of virgins were not to be undertaken by the priests. The faculty of reconciling public sinners at services over which the bishop presided was also withheld.[47] In the third council of Carthage (397) canon 15 prohibited priests from seeking a livelihood through the performance of menial and contemptible tasks and by mingling in the affairs of secular occupations. Canon 21 of the same council forbade them to accept or present for promotion any cleric not native to their churches, unless the latter had first obtained a concession from his own proper bishop.[48]

Still, the while their faculties were restricted and their activities confined within certain bounds, other canons of the same councils extended them definite rights and offices which they possessed as the pastors of their flocks. Thus, the prohibition regarding the consecration of virgins, still insisted on in the second council (390), was removed by the third council (397) in canon 36.[49] The *public* reconciliation of sinners and penitents indeed continued to be reserved to the bishop, yet, the priests of the various parishes enjoyed the faculty of reconciling them with the Church in case of serious illness and danger of death.[50] Furthermore, in a ruling which was once thought to be a canon of an African Synod celebrated in the year 398,[51] priests were accorded the power of initiating psalmists or chanters at their churches into the order of the inferior clergy, even without the previous knowledge or consent of their bishop.[52]

Whether all of these rights were enjoyed in virtue of a delegation from the diocesan bishop, or whether, even then, they were, at least in part, meant to form the content of the parish priests' ordinary and stable powers, remains a question which speculation seems unable to solve conclusively. Most probably the incumbents of the rural churches in those early times were

[47] Cf. cc. 3-4—Mansi, III, 693.

[48] Cf. Mansi, III, 883-84.

[49] Cf. Mansi, III, 885.

[50] Conc. Carthaginen. II (390), can. 4—Mansi, III, 693.

[51] Cf. Denzinger—Bannwart, *Enchiridion Symbolorum et Definitionum*, nn. 150-158. In a footnote, indicated at the head of this collection of canons, their date of origin is assigned to a period as late as the close of the fifth or the opening of the sixth century. See also Mansi, III, 952; Hardouin, I, 979, 981 (-c. 4, D. 95), 986-87 (-c. 33, D. 81).

[52] Cf. can. 10 of the collection—Mansi, *loc. cit.*

still regarded as the delegates of their bishop, and were given a claim to these functions in virtue of their parochial office only at a later period.[53]

B. In Spain

Christianity in Spain was of very early origin. Pope St. Clement I seems to indicate that the missionary labors of St. Paul carried the Apostle of the Gentiles to the western coasts of Europe, and if this be true, it is likely that by him the word of the Gospel was preached in Spain.[54] An extract from a letter of St. Cyprian of Carthage [55] also seems confirmatory of the early establishment of the Faith in Spain.

The early synod of Elvira (between 300 and 306) insinuates a parochial organization when it stipulates in canon 77 that the bishop himself must later perfect the ceremony of a baptism conferred by a deacon, when the latter has undertaken this sacred function without the superintendence of the bishop or of a *priest.*[56] From the manner in which the 24 priests who were present at this synod subscribed their names it is evident that they presided over rural congregations.[57] Canon 19 commands the clergy to reside continuously within the places of their ministry and canon 32 grants priests the faculty of receiving the sick and the dying back into communion with the Church.[58]

A century later, the first council of Toledo (400) instructed the rural priests throughout the diocese to obtain the holy oils from the bishop by despatching deacons or sub-deacons who

---

[53] Concerning this obscure question cf. Bouix, *Tractatus de Parocho*, p. 14; Funk, *Manual of Church History*, I, §62; Hinschius, *System des kath. KR*, II, 262 ff.; Scherer, *Handbuch des Kirchenrechtes*, I, 627; *AkKR.*, LXXXII (1902), 97-98.

[54] ". . . qui, postquam mundum universum iustitiam docuit, et *ad occidentis terminos* venit et coram praefectis testimonium perhibuit, . . ."—*Epistola ad Corinthios*, I, cap. 5, n. 7. Cf. Journel, *Enchiridion Patristicum*, n. 11. See also the testimony of St. Irenaeus, *De Praescriptione Haereticorum*, n. 20—Journel, *op. cit.*, n. 292.

[55] *Epistola 67—CV*, III, 2, 739; *MPL* [ep. 68], III, 1027; Journel, *op. cit.*, n. 588.

[56] Cf. Mansi. II, 18; Hardouin, I, 258.

[57] Maurus, presbyter de Illiturgi; Natalis, presbyter de Orsuna; Lamponius, presbyter de Carula; etc.—Mansi, II, 29. Cf. Thomassinus, *Vetus et Nova Ecclesiae Disciplina*, P. I, lib. II, cap. 22, n. 8.

[58] Mansi, II, 9, 11; Thomassinus, *loc. cit.*, n. 2.

would bring them from the cathedral to the parishes before the feast of Easter.[59]

In the beginning of the sixth century it was found necessary by the first council of Tarragona (516), under threat of canonical discipline, to constrain the rural clergy to reside at their parish churches in order that the daily services and ceremonies might not suffer interruption or neglect.[60]

Stability of assignment was still the title upon which any candidate depended in his ordination to the priestly office or even his promotion to the clerical rank. When promoted or ordained, he was to exercise his clerical functions at the church of his domicile or residence. So strictly was this principle inculcated that, when some of the bishops displayed arbitrary power rather than judicious discernment in the removal of priests from one parish to another, the second council of Seville (619) reserved this episcopal action to the ordinance of a council.[61] Another Spanish council of the same century[62] indicates the method invoked by the rural pastors for the perpetuation of priests, deacons, and minor clerics at their parishes. They associated unto themselves young men of blameless character and promising qualifications, whom they instructed in the Holy Scriptures, in the thorough acquaintance with the cycle of the Church feasts, in the chanting of the psalms, in the choir service, and in the various prayer formularies of the ecclesiastical ritual.[63] In recompense for the financial burdens thus assumed in the training of his clerics, the parish priest was permitted to appropriate for this laudable purpose one-third of all the general offerings of the faithful.[64]

Finally, whenever a sufficient number of auxiliary priests could be had in the diocese, each parish priest was to have a

---

59 Can. 20—Mansi, III, 1002; Hardouin, II, 1044.

60 Can. 7—Mansi, VIII, 542.

61 Can. 6: " . . . non . . . sine concilii examine . . ."—Mansi, X, 558-59.

62 Conc. Emeritense (666), can. 18—Mansi, XI, 85.

63 This method remained the general practice of the Church until after the Council of Trent. Cf. Lindner, *Die Anstellung der Hilfspriester*, p. 8, footnote 4.

64 Conc. Emeritense (666), can. 10—Mansi, XI, 84.

helper who could supply his place in case of sudden sickness or incapacity from other causes.[65]

C. In France

The existence of parish churches in France dates back to the early fourth century. The first council of Arles (314), by its prohibition to ecclesiastics of transferring from one church to another and by its insistence on permanency of residence in the *churches* where they were assigned, suggests that there existed a number of churches for public worship in the diocese distinct from the cathedral church.[66] The powers and the faculties of the priests resident at the churches were still rather limited and circumscribed,[67] but, that the incumbents of these churches exercised true parochial functions becomes evident from a statute in the first council of Vaison (442) which commanded them to obtain annually from their own bishop the consecrated oils which they needed in their ministrations of baptism and extreme unction.[68]

The first council of Orange (about 441) seems to have extended to parish priests even the faculty of conferring the sacrament of confirmation to repentant heretics at the point of death.[69] The assembled bishops in the second synod of Vaison (529) authorized the priests of all the parishes to address sermons and public instructions to their parishioners.[70]

As the rights and offices of parish priests became more and more defined, so also the parish discipline for the laity was invested with a more definite form. Just as they were obliged to

---

[65] Conc. Toletanum XI (675), can. 14—Mansi, XI, 145; Hardouin, III, 1029.

[66] Can. 2—Mansi, II, 470.

[67] Conc. Regiense (439), can. 5—Mansi, V, 1093.

[68] Can. 3—Mansi, VI, 453.

[69] Can. 1—Mansi, VI, 434; Hardouin, I, 1783. The canon uses the phrase *cum chrismate consignare* in a context where neither baptism nor extreme unction is under consideration.

[70] Can. 2: "Non solum in civitatibus, sed in omnibus parochiis verbum faciendi damus presbyteris potestatem."—Mansi, VIII, 726.

render the offerings and tithes to their respective parish church,[71] so also was it of obligation for them to attend thereat the solemnities of Christmas, Easter, and Pentecost.[72] Furthermore, the conferring of baptisms and the conducting of funeral rites were forbidden in the monastic chapels.[73] In all likelihood the reservation of these functions to the parish churches was conditioned upon the presumption of their strictly parochial nature.[74]

Since the priest appointed over the people [75] must devote his talents and his time to their well-being through his service at the altar, he is also to live by the offerings accruing to the altar. The law of tithes is strongly inculcated and the sanction of anathema is invoked against all who refuse, after a third admonition, to heed its injunction.[76]

There had to be certainty that all those who wished to be raised to holy orders were to be possessed of a benefice or some other mode of honorable livelihood. All the churches already served by priests and clerics should be endowed for the sustenance of the clergy that they might the more securely keep guard over their flocks and be solicitous for their welfare.[77]

The desire to see the parishes well administered and the clergy honorably supported led to the following legislation: " . . . *Unde interdicimus ut nullus praesumat Ecclesiam inter*

---

[71] Cf. Reiffenstuel, *Ius Canonicum Universum*, lib. III, tit. 30, §1, n. 23, in his commentary on c. 5, X, *de decimis, primitiis, et oblationibus*, III, 30, where he adduces the strong statements of Sts. Jerome and Augustine on the obligation of paying tithes. The sentiments of these two holy Fathers of the Church are reproduced by Gratian in cc. 65-68, C. 16, q. 1. See also canon 5 of the second council of Macon (585)—Mansi, IX, 951, and Doheny, *Church Property: Modes of Acquisition*, p. 46, footnotes 4 and 5 for a list of citations from the synods and councils.

[72] Cf. Conc. Agathense (506), can. 63—Mansi, VIII, 335; Hardouin, II, 1003.

[73] The 5th canon of a council whose exact date and locality are not known is quoted here; the approximate time of its celebration is fixed in the early part of the 7th century in France. Cf. Mansi, X, 546.

[74] Cf. Zorell, "Die Entwickelung des Parochialsystems bis zum Ende der Karolingerzeit," *AkKR*, LXXXII (1902), 265; Augustine, *Canonical and Civil Status of Catholic Parishes*, pp. 22-29.

[75] The word *plebs* is frequently used in this period to designate a congregation of the faithful who were attached to a given parish church.

[76] Conc. Rothomagense (saeculo septimo), can. 3—Mansi, X, 1200. See also the passages indicated in footnote 71 above.

[77] Statuta Synodal. Eccles. Rhemensis (627-630), cc. 12, 21—Mansi, X, 599-600.

duos, vel plures dividere, quia Ecclesia Christi uxor et sponsa esse debet, non scrotum, sicut Calixtus Papa testatur." [78] And again: *"Nullum absolute ordinari, neque presbyterum, nec diaconum, neque penitus quemquam eorum qui sunt in Ecclesiae ordine nisi specialiter ecclesiae civitatis, vel vici, vel martyrii, qui ordinandus est fuerit declaratus. Horum autem ordinationem huiusmodi, qui absolute ordinantur constituit sancta synodus* INEFFICACEM *esse, et nunquam posse ad ordinantis iniuriam praevalere."* [79]

From the foregoing citations of the various synods and councils of the churches and dioceses of France it must be acknowledged that by the end of the 8th century ecclesiastical legislation on parish discipline and organization had reached the same normation of principle as that expressed in the seventh Ecumenical Council of the Church at Nice in the year 787.[80]

D. In Italy

A word remains to be said about the development of rural parochial churches in Italy. Whilst its origin does not reach back as far as in Spain and in France, unmistakable traces appear as early as the fifth century. The Roman Synod of the year 402, celebrated under Pope St. Innocent I, accorded rural priests the right to baptize and to administer the sacrament of extreme unction, "because bishops, burdened with the care of many other occupations, could no longer visit all the sick." [81] Canon 26 of this synod commands priests not to leave the churches to which they are assigned, because in their ordinations they celebrated the nuptials of a spiritual union with them and pledged their abiding trust and ceaseless fidelity.[82]

The same pope, in a letter to Bishop Decentius of Gubbio, does not demand that the consecrated Bread be taken from the cathedral to the priests of the other churches which are rural

[78] Conc. Rhemense (630), c. 9—Mansi, X, 603.

[79] Capitulare Aquisgranense (789), c. 25—Hardouin, IV, 833. Cf. also cc. 1-2, D. 70, where the same ruling is mentioned by Gratian in his *Decretum*.

[80] Cf. footnote 44 above.

[81] Mansi, III, 1134-39. Cf. Thomassinus, *Vetus et Nova Ecclesiae Disciplina*, P. I, lib. II, cap. 23, n. 7.

[82] Mansi, *loc. cit.*

stations. Rather, in answer to a doubt submitted, he states that the rural priests of the diocese shall be empowered to celebrate the sacred mysteries for the convenience of the people who live a considerable distance from the cathedral church.[83]

In a letter to a certain Bishop Candidus, Pope Gregory the Great grants permission to supply the shortage of priests in his diocese by ordaining monks who are found worthy of the priestly dignity. Whilst no express mention is made that the newly ordained priests were to be stationed in vacant parishes, it may well be that they filled this particular need. In another epistle the Holy Pontiff allows the appointment of *presbyteri cardinales* at mere oratories and grants them permission to confer baptism there.[84] Although this grant was exceptional and went beyond the custom or usage of the time, it plainly shows the trend that in Italy, as elsewhere, the *parochial* economy of souls was becoming more and more a definite norm of organization to meet the needs of rural pastoration.[85]

ART. IV. RECAPITULATION

The early Christian tradition of concentrating all worship within the bishop's cathedral had yielded to the innovation of apportioning the churches for the people. The multiplication of priests and clerics at the city cathedral had given way to a distribution of their personnel in the rural districts. The functions which they erstwhile exercised under the direct superintendence of the bishop as their actual pastor were later discharged by them in virtue of his delegated powers to them at distant churches. In the course of time these delegated faculties came to be recognized as functions of an independent ordinary right. This was but a natural consequence elicited by the spread and diffusion of Christianity into the remoter districts of the converted countries. As the means of communication between distant places remained primitive and laborious, it was an auspicious alternative, readily and effectively sanctioned by usage until it obtained the force of law.

---

[83] Cf. Hardouin, II, 797-98; Thomassinus, *loc. cit.*, n. 9.

[84] Liber II, *Epistola XI—MPL*, LXXVII, 1225. See also Coady, *The Appointment of Pastors*, pp. 9-10.

[85] Cf. Hinschius, *System des kath. KR*, II, 265 ff.

Once the incumbents of the parish churches enjoyed their rights in virtue of their parochial office, they were enabled to associate with themselves the services of companion priests who would share with them the burdens and the functions of the parish ministry. Thus, just as formerly priests were linked with the bishop in the capacity of an auxiliary clergy, so now the junior members of the diocesan priesthood become the helpers of the rural priest throughout the diocese wherever the growing numbers of the faithful could no longer be effectually consulted by the unaided services of a single priest. Meanwhile, the bishop's cathedral continued for some centuries longer to remain the exclusive parish church in the city. It was only with the advent of the eleventh century that some of the monastic and collegiate churches, together with subsidiary chapels and oratories, began to acquire the legal standing of parishes.[86]

This preliminary study of the Church's fundamental regulations for giving expression to her development of parochial discipline heralds the historical beginnings of the institution of an assistant clergy in the strictly parochial pastoration of souls. The succeeding chapter will seek to trace this concept in its further historical progress and expression through the centuries up to the time when a new animation of Catholic thought and life during the pontificates of the Reform Popes called also for a new adaptation of canonical discipline in the parochial economy of souls.

---

[86] Cf. Bouix, *Tractatus de Parocho*, pp. 23-40, who cites the authority of many historians of ecclesiastical law in support of this contention which has now become the commonly accepted view. See also Hinschius, *System des kath. KR*, II, 277-82, and Scherer, *Handbuch des KR*, I, 629-30.

CHAPTER II

THE PAROCHIAL AUXILIARY CLERGY FROM THE TIME OF THEIR ORIGIN TO THE THIRTEENTH CENTURY

ART. I. EARLY ASSISTANT CLERGY

The priests stationed at the early rural parishes gathered about themselves clerics of the various lower orders for the ministrations of the ecclesiastical functions in which these latter could be of assistance in the churches. Many of the lesser functions connected with the public prayer and worship were exclusively entrusted to clerics who had been ordained by their bishops for this very purpose.[1] The deacons were authorized to baptize [2] and to reconcile penitents when so instructed by the priests,[3] each year before Easter to obtain the holy oils from the bishop,[4] to read the Sunday homily when sickness prevented the pastors from preaching,[5] and to share with them the weekly prayer and choir services.[6] Similarly, the subdeacons and the minor clerics were entrusted with specific ministrations in the churches of their residence.[7]

Another reason for the plurality of clerics associated with the priestly incumbents of the rural parishes may be deduced from the regulation of a Spanish council celebrated in the early seventh century.[8] It is to the effect that clerics should live in com-

---

[1] Cf. Lindner, *Die Anstellung der Hilfspriester*, p. 7.

[2] Conc. Eliberitanum (300-306), c. 77—Mansi, II, 18.

[3] *Ibid.*, c. 32—Mansi, II, 11.

[4] Synod. Toletana (400), c. 20—Mansi, III, 1002; conc. Vasense I (442), c. 3—Mansi, VI, 453.

[5] Conc. Vasense II (529), c. 2—Mansi, VIII, 737.

[6] Conc. Tarraconense (516), c. 7—Mansi, VIII, 542.

[7] Cf. Lindner, *Die Anstellung der Hilfspriester*, pp. 8-10.

[8] Conc. Toletanum IV (633), c. 24—Mansi, X, 626; see also conc. Emeritense (666), c. 18—Mansi, XI, 85.

munal residence near their parochial churches, where their training for the ultimate reception of sacred orders might be supervised by the priest in whose pastoral ministry they were given a share and to whose paternal vigilance they were committed. The existence of diocesan institutes of training for aspirants to clerical and priestly orders was unknown then. The universal method employed in the recruiting of candidates for the supply of the clerical ranks consisted in the course of training obtained at the parish churches under the guidance and direction of the parish priest. In the parish where the cleric had received his training, there also was he to exercise his future ministry. The Council of Chalcedon had established this norm for the Church at large,[9] and the usage continued that only such candidates should be raised to sacred orders whose pledge to abide permanently at the church for which they were to be ordained had been confirmed by the term of their willing service previously rendered there. According to the then current ecclesiastical discipline, ordination and assignment formed reciprocal elements of one indivisible canonical concept. The conferring of an order upon a cleric necessarily involved his simultaneous appointment. Since the church from which a cleric was ordained generally also became the parish at which he was to be appointed, it followed that every zealous rural pastor was desirous of establishing at his church a college of clerics whose number would prove sufficient for all the varied ministrations connected with the parish for the present and whose fuller training and consequent reception of higher orders would eventually lead them to a stage where the bishop could ordain them priests in the event of their pastor's sickness or demise.[10]

---

[9] Can. 6—Mansi, VII, 365; Hardouin, II, 603; Hefele, *Conciliengeschichte*, II, 504; cf. cc. 1-2, D. 70.

[10] Sohm, *Kirchenrecht*, II, §29 ("Der Titel"), 284-308, devotes a lengthy chapter to the discussion of the title for ordination. In his footnotes he adduces the previously cited canon of the Council of Chalcedon, the regulations of Pope St. Leo I (*MPL*, LIV, 596 ss., 666 ss., 709 ss.), the instructions of St. Isidore of Seville (*MPL*, LXXXIII, 779 ss.) and the ordinance of Pope Urban II (c. 2, D. 70) in the council of Piacenza (1095) as reflecting the discipline of the Church in her unequivocal stand against *absolute* ordination (i.e., one which was free from the inherent demand of simultaneous assignment) up to the twelfth century. His failure to distinguish between the *merely disciplinary* elements of *canonical integration* of the sacrament and the *essentially sacramental* elements in its *substantial*

§I. From the Sixth to the Ninth Century

A. Non-Sacerdotal Parochial Assistants

In the early sixth century the parish church of Laon comprised in its list of clerical assistants a full representation of all the degrees of minor and major orders preparatory to the priesthood.[11] There is scarcely any room for doubt that this same condition obtained at a considerable number of other parish churches, in particular, whenever the councils speak of a plurality of clergy.[12]

Clerics of non-sacerdotal rank formed for some time the parochial assistants of the rural pastors. In many, perhaps in most instances, there was no priest in their midst save their proper rural pastor. Indeed, the need for a second priest was not yet so imperative. But, when the churches began to grow in territorial extent, especially during the period that ushered in the existence of the "grand parishes" during the Merovingian reign, places of worship, shrines of prayer, and chapels of accommodation for the faithful were erected in the remoter districts.[13]

The parishes that gave origin to these multiplied chapels and shrines were for the greater part responsible also for supplying their spiritual needs. The priestly functions required at these subsidiary places of worship depended for their fulfillment upon

---

confection betrayed this author into the following untenable view: "Der Satz von der *Nichtigkeit* der absoluten Ordinationen, von einem streng kirchlich gesinnten Papst Ende des elften Yahrhunderts feierlich verkündet, ist allerdings wie ein Faustschlag in das Angesicht des heute geltenden neukatholischen Kirchenrechts, auch der heute geltenden neukatholischen Kirchenlehre." Unlike Catholic authors he concludes that all ordinations without a title to permanent appointment were without effect not only with regard to the *"executio officii et perceptio beneficii,"* but also in the *"veritas sacramenti."*

[11] Cf. Lindner, *Die Anstellung der Hilfspriester*, p. 7, footnote 1.

[12] Cf. conc. Tarraconense (516), c. 7—Mansi, VIII, 542; conc. Vasense (529), cc. 1-2—Mansi, VIII, 727-28, where reference is made to a similar practice of long standing in Italy; conc. Aurelianense (541), c. 33—Mansi, IX, 119; conc. Arelatense (554), c. 4—Mansi, IX, 702; conc. Turonense (567), c. 20—Mansi, IX, 797; conc. Parisiense (615), cc. 4, 6—Mansi, X, 541; conc. Toletanum (633), c. 39—Mansi, X, 629; conc. Emeritense (666), c. 18—Mansi, XI, 85.

[13] Cf. Hinschius, *System des kath. KR*, II, 262 ff.; Sägmüller, *Die Entwickelung des Archipresbyterats und Dekanats bis zum Ende des Karolingerreichs*, p. 48 ff.

the services provided by the parish priest of the parent church. When he was no longer personally able to attend to his multiplied cares, he associated with himself clerics endowed with priestly orders, who, as missionaries from the parochial centers, or as chaplains at the distant oratories, assisted him in the duties of preaching the word of God, of administering the sacraments, and of celebrating the sacred mysteries. In this new condition of parish life is found the origin of the institution of sacerdotal parochial vicars.

B. Sacerdotal Parochial Vicars

As far back as the sixth century the incumbents of rural parishes are designated by the II council of Tours (567) as *archipresbyteri*. This term obviously presupposes the subordination of other priests under them in the care of souls. In fact, the same canon (19) does speak of the *"reliqui presbyteri et diaconi et subdiaconi vicani."* [14] In other French councils the same nomenclature is observed.[15] The II council of Aix-la-Chapelle (836) [16] and a council celebrated at Nantes in the same century give further proof that a number of priests resided at one church and that one of their number was the *archipresbyter* whilst the others remained his helpers in the labors of the parish ministries.[17]

---

[14] Cf. Mansi, IX, 797.

[15] A council of unknown date and place, but celebrated shortly after the Council of Paris (615), uses the word *archipresbyteri* repeatedly in its eleventh canon.—Hardouin, III, 946. The council of Rheims (630) stipulates in its nineteenth canon: ". . . ut in parochiis nullus laicorum archipresbyter praeponatur; sed qui senior in ipsis esse debet, clericus ordinetur."—Mansi, X, 597.

[16] Cap. II, can. 16: ". . . ut presbyter per se eam [paroeciam] tenere possit aut etiam priori presbytero subjugatus ministerium sacerdotale perficere possit . . ."—Hardouin, IV, 1398-99; Mansi, XIV, 683.

[17] Can. 8: "Nullus presbyter plures praesumat habere Ecclesias, nisi forte alios presbyteros sub se in unaquaque habeat, qui nocturnum atque divinum officium solemniter adimpleant et Missarum celebrationes quotidianis expleant ceremoniis."—Mansi, XVIII, 168; Hardouin, III, 946.

In Spain there is found an unmistakable instance of a plurality of priests at parish churches as early as the year 675,[18] and in a Capitulary Decree drawn up by Louis the Pious for Italy in the middle of the ninth century, the method of selecting the rector of a parish—by vote of the resident parish clergy with subsequent presentation to the parishioners for approval—is referred to as an ecclesiastical prescription of long standing and traditional usage.[19]

These citations indicate a comparatively early origin of parochial vicars in the country parishes. Their services were required, in a great measure, for the chapels and oratories which had been erected to meet the need of distant parishioners as well as for the constantly growing rural parishes themselves. Many of the assistant clergy were detailed to take up their residence at these chapels or *tituli minores* [20] and to exercise there such pastoral functions as were not reserved to the mother parish. Thus, for example, preaching was reserved to the parish churches in the council of Pavia,[21] and the discipline of the "baptismal churches" was retained for a considerable time longer in Italy.[22]

The faithful were required to pay the tithes and the parochial fees to the churches where their children were to be baptized, that is, to the parent churches.[23] This usage continued up to the time when the chapels and oratories began to acquire their own proper parochial rights. Their autonomy and their independence from the parishes of their origin came into being in the ninth century.[24]

---

18 Conc. Toletanum, c. 14: ". . . Necessarium duximus instituere ut ubi temporis, vel loci, sive cleri copia suffragatur, habeat semper quisquis ille canens Deo vel sacrificans, post se vicini solaminis adjutorem: ut si aliquo casu ille qui officia impleturus accedit turbatus fuerit, vel ad terram elisus, a tergo semper habeat qui eius vicem exequatur intrepidus."—Mansi, XI, 145; Hardouin, III, 1029.

19 Cf. *Monumenta Germaniae Historica, Legum Sectio,* 2, *Capitularia Regum Francorum,* Tom. II, 84.

20 Conc. Parisiense (615), c. 8—Mansi, X, 82; *MGH, ibid.*, 515.

21 Conc. Ticinense (850-855), c. 4—Mansi, XIV, 932.

22 Cf. Sägmüller, *Die Entwickelung des Archipresbyterats und Dekanats bis zum Ende des Karolingerreichs,* p. 48.

23 Conc. Nannetense (saeculo nono), c. 2—Mansi, XVIII, 166; conc. Cabilonense (813), c. 19—Hardouin, IV, 1035.

24 Cf. Coady, *The Appointment of Pastors,* p. 12.

§II. From the Ninth to the Thirteenth Century

During the early ninth century, when such numerous dependent oratories and chapels had arisen in the remoter confines of their loosely defined territories, the extensive parochial communities or "grand parishes" of the Merovingian and incipient Carlovingian periods underwent a change of organization. More definite disciplinary measures and more exact territorial boundaries become the rule. Filial churches and chapels which the nobility and feudal lords had erstwhile erected for their own families and private accommodations were in great numbers formed into parish churches. Their parochial privileges, somewhat restricted in the beginning, eventually were recognized as rights equivalent to those of the parent church.[25]

It can readily be understood that the multiplication of parish churches with its consequent narrowing of the old territorial boundaries necessarily had to result in a decrease of their numerical size. Each additional chapel, each rural shrine, each private oratory that grew into the estate of parishhood served to lessen the numbers of the faithful who formerly were subjects to the larger regional parishes. In consequence of this change the need for priests additional to the pastor in his parish church became less and less a necessity. The almost common practice that each parochial church was served exclusively by an individual priest is attested by the nomenclature attached to parish priests at this time. They no longer were, as in the preceding centuries, called by the name of *archipresbyteri*. The simple title of *presbyter* or *sacerdos* was sufficient to designate and differentiate the parish priest from the remaining clerics resident with him.[26]

The first *definite* mention from any of the councils pointing again to a plurality of *priests* at a single parish in the rural districts is discernible in the council of Avranches which was celebrated in the year 1172.[27] But a letter of Pope Innocent II toward the close of the first half of this same century indirectly

---

[25] Cf. Lindner, *Die Anstellung der Hilfspriester*, p. 18.

[26] Cf. Sägmüller, *Die Entwickelung des Archipresbyterats und Dekanats bis zum Ende des Karolingerreichs*, p. 53.

[27] Can. 5 stipulates: "Item sacerdotes majorum ecclesiarum, quibus ad hoc suppetunt facultates, alium sub se presbyterum cogantur habere."—Hardouin, VIb, 1634.

offers evidence that the "*plebanus*" (a name current then to designate a parish priest) had in his service, for the suitable pastoration of his parish, auxiliary priests who were referred to as his chaplains.[28] Conclusive traces at a time earlier than this are not found. In view, then, of the fact that documents bearing upon parish organization do not reveal the presence of auxiliary or assistant priests, the conclusion appears justified that the parishes were commonly administered by an individual priest from the latter half of the ninth to the beginning of the twelfth century.[29]

The parishes of this period were of smaller size than the so-called "grand parishes" in the centuries preceding. Ordinarily, whatever ministrations the priest himself was unable to perform could be undertaken by the remaining non-sacerdotal clerics resident with him. Should there be a demand for the celebration of more than one mass on Sundays and Feast Days to accommodate the parishioners, the parish priest was fully competent to meet it, for at that time custom generally allowed a priest to celebrate two or three or even more masses on the same day. The measure of need within each parish was the sole determining factor in the repeated celebration of the Sacrifice.[30]

On the other hand, the letter of Pope Innocent III issued to the bishop of Worcester in the year 1206 [31] and the subsequent instruction of Pope Honorius III [32] to the Archbishop of Siponto in the early part of the thirteenth century clearly presupposes the reappearance and availability of an auxiliary priesthood in the organization of parochial administration; otherwise these decrees would have been futile and nugatory. These

---

[28] Cf. *MPL*, CLXXIX, 569. The *suffraganei* mentioned in canon 15 of the Council of Rouen, held in the year 1072, were most probably not assistant priests, but rather the *vicarii curati* who ruled over a parish in the name of the one who held it in title.—Hardouin, VIa, 1190. The *capellani* of canon 2 of the synod of Beneventum (1091) must be considered as belonging to the class of non-sacerdotal clerics who were employed in the choir- and prayer-services of beneficed chapels or oratories.—Mansi, XX, 739. See also Lindner, *Die Anstellung der Hilfspriester*, p. 45, footnote 7.

[29] Cf. Lindner, *op. cit.*, p. 22 ff., p. 35 ff.

[30] *Ibid.*

[31] C. 3, X, *de celebratione Missae, Sacramento Eucharistiae, et Divinis Officiis*, III, 41.

[32] *Ibid.*, c. 12: ". . . Quum . . . cuilibet sacerdoti, quacunque dignitate praefulgeat, unam in die celebrare missam sufficiat, ..."

ordinances were not technical speculations in search of a means whereby the abuse of "many masses" *might* be attacked; they were practicable laws, capable of observance, since the remedy against all simoniacal practices of this kind lay close at hand in the existence of a sufficiently large body of auxiliary priests whose employment in parish work would remove the slightest pretext for repeated celebration. The efficacy of these laws inhered in the unquestionable fact that an auxiliary priestly service was available wherever increased parochial duties required its aid.

ART. II. THE METHOD OF THEIR ASSIGNMENT TO PARISHES

The foregoing pages form a brief outline of the Church's history on parish assistants up to the thirteenth century. The following pages will investigate the mode of their appointment and the character of their priestly work within the parishes.

It will be remembered how, from the earliest times, the Church adhered unalterably to the principle of "relative ordination" and its inevitable corollary of "stability of appointment." [33] This discipline perdured from the time when parishes first began to exist as churches separate from the bishop's cathedral down to the period when the Church, after a long and courageous struggle, was eventually constrained to relinquish her traditional principles in face of the many inhibitions arising on every side.[34] As long as the actual practice cor-

---

[33] The word *relative* is here used in opposition to the term *absolute*. Absolute ordination was the granting of orders to an acephalous cleric, unamenable to any episcopal authority and unliable for any diocesan obligations. Relative ordination was the conferring of orders which of itself, without the intervention of a further collative act, attached the ecclesiastic to a certain office or incumbency. Stability of appointment implied perpetuity of service at the post or office assumed in view of the ordination. See footnote 10 of this chapter.

[34] Conc. Arelatense (314), c. 2—Mansi, II, 470; conc. Nicaenum I (325), cc. 15, 16—Mansi, II, 672; Hardouin, I, 327; synod. Romana (402), c. 13—Mansi, III, 1138; Leo I Papa, *Epistolae*, XII, c. 10—*MPL*, LIV, 654; *ibid.*, c. 17—Hefele, *Conciliengeschichte*, II, 505; conc. Chalcedonense (451), c. 6—Hardouin, II, 602 (reproduced in c. 1, D. 70); conc. Rhemense (630), c. 12—Mansi, X, 596; *Responsio Dialogi Ecgberti Archiepiscopi Eboracae* (734)—Wilkins, *Concilia Magnae Britanniae et Hiberniae*, I, 83; *Excerpta Ecgberti Archiepiscopi Eboracae* (750)—Wilkins, *op. cit.*, I, 102; conc. Nicaenum II (787), cc. 10, 15—Hardouin, IV, 769,

responded with the Church's ideal principles, the ordination of clerics and priests remained also the legal channel through which they were ushered into their permanent ecclesiastical services and priestly ministration at the various chapels, churches, and parishes.

The early method whereby bishop, clergy, and people together concurred in the approval of a cleric's fitness for ordination is still reflected in the synod of Eauze (a town in southern France), celebrated in the year 551.[35] At a later time, possibly even before the end of the sixth century, this usage gave way to the discipline of examination by the archdeacon at the bishop's court.[36] Since it was his office in the episcopal household to be the instructor of their training and the guardian of their clerical conduct, he had to present the candidates for ordination after a previous examination of their worthiness and fitness.[37]

For the clerics in service and training at the cathedral parish the archdeacon was well competent personally to exercise this office. But, when there was a question of promoting clerics of the rural churches to higher orders, he was aided by the archpriest who had superintended their education and preparation

---

770; capitulare Aquisgranense (798), c. 25—Hardouin, IV, 833; synod. Francofordensis (794), cc. 7, 28—Hardouin, IV, 905, 907; synod. Arelatensis (813), c. 24—Hardouin, IV, 1006; synod. Moguntiaca (813), c. 31—Hardouin, IV, 1014; synod. Parisiensis (829), c. 13—Hardouin, IV, 1356; synod. Meldensis (845), c. 52—Hardouin, IV, 1492; Ivo, Episcopus Carnotensis, *Panormia*, lib. III, c. 27—*MPL*, CLXI, 1136; conc. Placentinum (1095), c. 15—Mansi, XX, 806 (reproduced in c. 2, D. 70); conc. Londonense, seu Westmonasteriense (1125), c. 8: "Nullus in presbyterum, nullus in diaconum nisi ad certum titulum ordinetur. Qui vero absolute fuerit ordinatus, sumpta careat dignitate."—Mansi, XXI, 331. Coady (*The Appointment of Pastors*, p. 32, footnote 14) cites additional sources expressing the same law. It may be noted that the two canons cited by Gratian both had direct papal approval.

35 Can. 5: "De ordinatione vero clericorum id convenit observari ut, cum presbyter aut diaconus ab episcopo petitur ordinandus praecedentibus diebus VIII populus quemquam ordinandum esse cognoscat, et, si qua vitia in eum quis e populo forte esse cognoscit, ante ordinationem dicere non desistat."—Lindner, *op. cit.*, p. 16, footnote 1.

36 Cf. Lindner, *op. cit.*, p. 15.

37 C. 1, §11, D. 25. Cf. Hinschius, *System des kath. KR*, II, 184 ff.; Thomassinus, *Vetus et Nova Ecclesiae Disciplina*, P. I, lib. II, cc. 17-20 et P. III, lib. II, cc. 32-33. An accurate description of the same discipline in the ninth century is contained in canon 11 of a synod held at Nantes.—Mansi, XVIII, 169.

for their respective ordination. Since the archpriest occupied the same position for the rural ecclesiastics that the archdeacon enjoyed for the urban cathedral clergy, he was, like the archdeacon, given the right of presenting such candidates regarding whose fitness he could testify after previous surveillance and probation.[38] Upon his testimony, confirmed by the official sanction of the archdeacon, followed the bishop's act of ordination which established the clerics in the churches for which they were presented.[39]

This early provision was sanctioned by usage and tradition in the churches everywhere. It continued until the time when the "grand parishes" were supplanted by the many and smaller parishes in the rural neighborhoods. Of this latter class a considerable number had been the chapels and oratories of the feudal lords and nobles. Not infrequently these men of power and influence beguiled their hopes, or at least their fancies, with the proposition that, even after their altered condition, these chapels and oratories should still be recognized as *private-estate* churches, with the consequence that an unqualified right of administration in matters connected with the spiritual purposes, uses, and services of these sacred edifices should accrue to their owners.[40] This insistent determination on their part to supervise the appointment and dismissal of the priest and clerics resident at these churches, even after their quondam status had been elevated to the recognized rank of parish churches, offered the Church her first serious and never completely surmounted difficulty in the enforcement of the time-honored principles of relative ordination and stability of appointment in the plan of her parochial economy.

---

[38] According to canon 18 of the synod of Merida (666), the rural parish priest was to select his candidates for presentation from the subjects of his parish.—Mansi, XI, 85. In the Eastern Roman Empire since the time of Arcadius, and in the Western Roman Empire since the time of Justinian, it had been incorporated as a part of the civil law that the clerics of a church were to be recruited from its surrounding locality.—*Codex Theodosianus,* XVI, 2, 33; *Codex Justinianus,* I, 3, 11. See also Mansi, XVIII, 169.

[39] Cf. Sägmüller, *Die Entwickelung des Archipresbyterats und Dekanats bis zum Ende des Karolingerreichs,* p. 13.

[40] This vexing problem of lay-control in the intimate matters of the Church's administration of ecclesiastical properties and official appointments is given a most emphatic expression in its German equivalent of *Eigenkirchenwesen.*

The eighth century forms the beginning of the nobility's reign of self-assertion and insubordination. Whilst this abuse was not altogether general, yet, very many of the nobles appointed priests from other churches and dioceses for the service of their private chapels without first obtaining their own bishop's permission and approval. Some of them replenished the clerical ranks with candidates selected from the household of their serfs and villeins. They presented these men for ordination to a neighboring or a vagrant bishop who might accommodate their wish whenever their own diocesan ordinaries refused to yield to their imperious demands.

The Church's effort to abolish this abuse, which infringed so ruinously upon her long-established and jealously cherished traditions, met with neither immediate, nor ultimate, complete success. At most, she was able to check its morbid excrescences from assuming more baneful proportions. She had to rest content with remedial measures. By the weight of circumstances involved she was compelled to choose a policy of reluctant adaptation in the face of an unyielding march of events. Insistence upon her traditional claim and reaffirmation of her assailed right were no longer able to stem the tide. Indeed, she never openly disclaimed her former policy; yet, she tacitly tolerated the development of a discipline elaborated by the spirit of the age.[41]

The compromise that resulted from this long struggle between the bishops and the nobles can be summed up in one word: Lay Patronage. The nobles acquired the right of presentation for their churches and their presentees became the new incumbents in the parochial vacancies as soon as their bishop's formal authorization and approval confirmed their acts. Nor was their bishop's action dowered with the range of arbitrary freedom in confirming or rejecting the candidate submitted for his approval.[42] In a Capitulary decree of the year 819, chapter 9 enacts the following:

> Statutum est, ut sine auctoritate vel consensu episcoporum presbyteri in *quibuslibet* ecclesiis nec constituantur nec expellantur, et si laici clericos probabilis vitae et doctrinae

[41] Cf. Lindner, *Die Anstellung der Hilfspriester*, p. 23 ff.

[42] Cf. *MGH, Legum Sectio, 2, Capitularia Regum Francorum*, Tom. II, 110, 173, 178, 182.

episcopis consecrandos suisque in ecclesiis constituendos obtulerint, *nulla qualibet occasione eos reiiciant.*[43]

Another element that thwarted the Church's best efforts in upholding her time-honored principles regarding the practice of relative ordination was the low ebb to which clerical discipline had sunk in consequence of the dissolution of the civic together with the upheaval of the social order that had become quite general throughout the continent.[44] The desire for personal liberation from authority, the craving for reckless unrestraint and the thirst for lawless independence wielded a power of attraction for the clergy no less than for the laity.

The Church made ceaseless efforts to arrest the impulse of clerical insubordination, but her success was faint if it is measured by the Church's inability to restore her traditional discipline.[45] One of the underlying reasons why she revolted at the idea of the absolute ordination of her clergy is found in the precarious uncertainty necessarily connected with their congruous sustenance. As long as the relative system of ordination was observed, all clerics were assured of a station, an office, or a benefice whose revenues could be requisitioned for their honorable support. With the advent of the absolute system of ordination, however, the number of clergymen left without a suitable means of support was not insignificant. The current clerical pursuit after ecclesiastical offices and emoluments, which but too often were surrendered only after their seekers had assumed previous personal liabilities with a view to obtaining them, was too exacting to prove profitable for all who essayed to engage themselves in it.

In the very midst of this seething order of wanton liberty and lawless unrestraint the Church never forgot to raise her

---

[43] *Ibid.*, II, 277; cf. also Funk, *Manual of Church History*, I, §97. Italics by the present writer.

[44] Cf. conc. Parisiense VI (829), lib. I, cap. 47—Hardouin, IV, 1324; Walter, *Lehrbuch des KR*, p. 283, footnote 3, where the author adduces the incisive words of Agobard, the then archbishop of Lyons, aptly describing how the secular spirit had entered into the clerical ranks in his own day.

[45] Cf. Lindner, *Die Anstellung der Hilfspriester*, p. 28, footnote 1. A long list of general admonitions, capitulary decrees, synods and councils whose reform measures remained fruitless of their desired result will be found recounted there. The very fact of their unwonted frequency suggests evidence that the Church's efforts terminated in futility. See also footnote 34 above.

authoritative voice, "instant in season, out of season, reproving, entreating, rebuking in all patience and doctrine." [46] The wording of a council in northern France typically illustrates the Church's solicitude for seeing every priest suitably provided with an honorable income for his sustenance. The quotation runs as follows: " . . . *ita unusquisque presbyter in sua ordinatione ac dispensatione, cura habeat parochiam suam cum dote et decimis ecclesiae.*" [47] But, a fuller compliance with this and similar decrees was achieved only then when the spirit of the age had reconstructed itself into a better estate.

History did, indeed, assert its better self again. Its lights began to penetrate where its shadows had fallen. Under the leadership of the saintly Reform Pope, Gregory VII, the Church in her members revived to a loftier discipline. Her influence once more touched all the laudable interests of life and the era was dawning when she was to offer the world "the greatest of her centuries." Vocations increased, churches multiplied, conversions grew apace. So astounding was the Church's external growth as a result of her internal renewal that many of the churches erected could be only partially endowed or not at all, and, for this reason, the last vestige of her hope in quickening the old principles back to life in a new and different order of things must have definitely fled. Things became reversed. In the eighth, ninth, tenth and eleventh centuries she feign would have reinstated her early traditions, but could not. Thereafter, even if she could, she would not. She rested content to let the new order develop its own expression in the law. In the end, the bishop's provision for his clerics assumed an administrative rather than an executive rôle in his determination: "*Capellanos, qui contra statutum numerum sine consensu sui episcopi militaverint . . . ab officio et beneficio interdicimus.*" [48]

Finally, the words of Rufinus, one of the earliest commentators on the *Decretum Gratiani*: "*In tota pene Romana provincia hodie clerici, maxime a subdiacono infra, ex longaeva consuetu-*

[46] II Timothy, IV, 2.

[47] Conc. Troslejanum (909), c. 6—Hardouin, VIa, 520.

[48] Synod. Beneventana (1091), c. 2—Mansi, XX, 739. See footnote 28 of this chapter.

dine absque titulo ordinantur," [49] together with the teaching of other canonists,[50] as well as the decrees of Alexander III [51] and of Innocent III [52] definitely parted with the principle that even the lesser or minor clerics must be provided with a title to an income from a benefice as the earlier synods and councils had stipulated. When changed conditions made advisable a new adaptation of discipline, the Church was ready to acknowledge and sanction the innovation.

Toward the close of the twelfth century the history of the Church lingered at the threshold of a new period. Customs and usages were working out a new order. In the chapter following, these will be considered in as far as they bear relation to the mode of appointment, the sphere of rights and duties, and the removal from their station relative to parish assistant vicars.

---

[49] Cf. Lindner, *Die Anstellung der Hilfspriester*, p. 31, footnotes 1 and 2. See also Sägmüller, *Lehrbuch des kath. KR*, §64, p. 330, footnote 6.

[50] E.g., Huguccio: "Huic constitutioni (sc. quod nullus clericus est ordinandus absolute) in multis provinciis et praesertim in Italia derogatur contraria consuetudine, quam papa scit et non improbat, immo, talem ordinationem fieri patitur et approbat."—Lindner, *op. cit.*, p. 31, footnote 3.

[51] C. 4, X, *de praebendis et dignitatibus*, III, 5. This ordinance was formulated in the Third Lateran Council (1179).

[52] C. 16, *eiusdem tituli.*

CHAPTER III

PAROCHIAL ASSISTANT VICARS FROM THE THIRTEENTH CENTURY TO MODERN TIMES

ART. I. DISCIPLINARY READJUSTMENT

The latter ninth, the tenth, and the early eleventh centuries are not infrequently called the Dark Ages of the Church. To show that this sweeping statement, as affecting the entire life of the Church, is not consonant with historical accuracy, remains outside of the point here in question. The Church's discipline of parochial economy is the sole magnet of interest in this work. Whilst her legal institutions and regulations during these centuries had followed the currents of her traditional laws, her actual practice and observance of them drifted into devious courses. Concerning her parish life and discipline no historical doubt remains that "the gold had become dim and the finest color had been changed." [1]

The energetic reform instituted by St. Gregory VII and continued by his successors, in the attempt of abolishing lay investiture and lay appointment to ecclesiastical offices and benefices, was crowned with ultimate triumph only after it had broken the fury of multiplied, spirited, and stubborn opposition furnished by Emperor and nobility alike. The interior reform of the Church in clerical life and discipline had preceded it, and when, at the end of the twelfth century, Cardinal Lothaire of Segni ascended the papal throne under the name of Innocent III, the Church had once more risen to a sovereign position amid the political, social, and religious world round about her. Of the reign of Innocent III Funk declares: "If we consider the

---

[1] Lamentations, IV, 1.

consequences, we may give his pontificate the first place in the history of the Papacy." [2]

One of the manifestations of the interior revival of the Church's discipline at this period is offered by the increased number of clerical vocations. The multiplication of her schools, the extension of her universities, the elevated standards of clerical learning, the Church's high repute among the nations of the world,—all these forces lent added attraction to a state of life which was closely identified with her glorious organization. Hand in hand with the deep religious spirit that served to augment the clerical ranks there were operative also the spiritual forces of conversion among the lay people. Not only did the old established parishes enlarge the lists of their memberships, but new parishes sprang up for the constantly growing numbers of the faithful. It became inevitable that the churches should require the services of additional priests, and it is precisely in this period that assistant priests at parishes make their appearance.[3]

Another manifestation that confronts us generally in this period, and in some countries at an even earlier time, is the flowering of monasticism. Partly the eleventh together with the twelfth century marked the heyday of the monks, as the thirteenth connoted that of the friars. It is principally only in the fourteenth and fifteenth centuries that the secular clergy could

---

[2] *Manual of Church History,* I, §112. Cf. Artaud de Montor, *Lives and Times of the Popes,* III, 99-124, for a comprehensive summary of Innocent's pontificate.

[3] Authors, irrespective of their religious prepossessions, render testimony to the renewed vitality of the Church's life during this century. Cf. Taylor, *The Mediæval Mind,* I, 257-66; Smith, *Church and State in the Middle Ages,* pp. 1-56, whose statements, however, cannot be universally subscribed; Munro-Sontag, *The Middle Ages* (The Century Historical Series), pp. 366-401; of especial interest is their quotation on p. 385 from Henry Adams: "According to history, in a single century between 1170 and 1270 the French built 80 cathedrals and nearly 500 churches of the cathedral class, which would have cost, according to an estimate made in 1840, more than five thousand millions to replace. Five thousand million francs is a thousand million dollars, and this covered only the great churches of a single country." See also Shahan, *The Middle Ages,* pp. 163-88, 196-211, where the personal, civic, social, educational, moral, and religious life of the people of the thirteenth century is ably sketched; Walsh, *The Thirteenth, Greatest of Centuries,* pp. 18-95, 337-49, 375-92, and Appendix XII ("The Pope of the Century"), pp. 445-46.

reassert their former standing, as it were, when the foundations of collegiate and canonical chapters composed of the diocesan clergy began to flourish again.[4]

The preponderant number of the regular over that of the diocesan clergy appears very evident in France.[5] The *regular* clergy were in great favor with the populace of the time. Under the weight and the pressure of popular esteem many of the parishes were committed to the care of their monasteries and convents through the medium of incorporation with their institutions. If the incorporation embraced both the spiritualities and the temporalities of the parishes it was called a *plena incorporatio vel unio* and left such churches practically under the immediate exclusive administration of the abbots or priors who presided in the respective monasteries and convents. They were to nominate their vicars who ruled over these parishes as their actual incumbents in the care of souls whilst the title to the parishes attached to the monastery or the convent itself.[6]

If the incorporation was *quoad temporalia tantum*, it was called *minus plena*. In this case the superiors of religious institutes enjoyed the right of presenting a *vicarius curatus*, selected from the diocesan clergy, to the bishop from whom the appointment followed.[7] In the twelfth and thirteenth centuries, moreover, such parish churches as were committed to the care of the secular clergy were often conferred *in titulum* to ecclesiastics who

---

[4] Cf. Davis, *Mediæval England*, p. 408.

[5] Cf. conc. Arelatense (1260), c. 5: "Quia maior pars Ecclesiarum Parochialium huius Pronvinciae ad Monachorum vel Conventuum Regularium pertinet Prioratus . . ."—Hardouin, VII, 512.

[6] Cf. Lindner, *Die Anstellung der Hilfspriester*, p. 35; Reiffenstuel, *Jus Canonicum Universum*, in his commentary on the following titles of the Decretals: "*De officio vicarii*, I, 28; *de clericis non residentibus in Ecclesia vel praebenda*, III, 4; *de praebendis et dignitatibus*, III, 5;" and especially, "*de Capellis Monachorum et aliorum Religiosorum*, III, 37," together with "*ut Ecclesiastica beneficia sine diminutione conferantur*, III, 12."

[7] C. 31, X, *de praebendis et dignitatibus*, III, 5, had established the following law: "In Ecclesiis quae ad eos pleno iure non pertinent, instituendos presbyteros Episcopis praesentent, ut eis de plebis cura respondeant. Ipsis vero [Religiosis] pro rebus temporalibus rationem exhibeant competentem. Institutos autem, inconsultis Episcopis, non audeant removere." Other instances of common law are c. 1, *eiusdem tituli*; c. 6, C. 16, q. 2; cap. unic., *de praebendis et dignitatibus*, III, 4, in VI°; c. 13, *eiusdem tituli*, III, 2, in Clem. Cf. Scherer, "Incorporatio plena oder minus plena," *AkKR*, LIII (1885), 105-25.

had not yet received priestly ordination. These rectors, or *plebani,* as they were also called,[8] in many instances availed themselves of the law which allowed them to be absent from their parishes over a period of years for the sake of study, if during the term of their non-residence they provided for their churches through the assignment of vicars.[9]

To establish norms and standards which would regulate the appointment of vicars for the incorporated churches attached to the religious institutes as well as for the parishes committed to the *plebani;* to differentiate the mutual obligations of the *rectores habituales* and their *vicarii actuales;* to designate the latters' sphere of pastoral rights and privileges; to secure a proper method of support for the vicar in pursuance of his claim upon a *congrua sustentatio* from the revenues of the churches against the possible encroachments of the titulars; to define the grant of freedom from residence and the limits within which it was allowable for the one, and to determine the obligation of residence and the scope within which it was binding upon the other;—these were the manifold questions whose adjustment, through the sanction of a common law, primarily occupied the Church's legislative vigilance in parochial matters. The institution of vicarial pastoration, enjoying priority both of time and of importance over the institution of auxiliary pastoration in this age of the Church, engrossed her attention for the former to the practically complete silence regarding the latter. Even the contemporaneous commentators on the Decretals are most sparing in their treatment of the question that relates to assistant priests in parishes. As an example of this one may cite the otherwise searching writings of Cardinal Henry of Susa (1253).[10]

For the period reaching from the thirteenth century down to the time of the Council of Trent one must consult the sources of particular legislation as exhibited by the local synods and provincial councils of the time. Some isolated references have

[8] Cf. letter of Pope Innocent II to a *plebanus* of the diocese of Lucca.—*MPL,* CLXXIX, 569-70. See title of letter in footnote 15 below.

[9] Cf. c. 4, X, *de clericis non residentibus in Ecclesia vel praebenda,* III, 4; c. 34, *de electione et electi potestate,* I, 6, in VI°, in which decretal Boniface VIII extended the five years' privilege to seven years.

[10] Hostiensis, *Summa Aurea,* lib. I, tit. 28, n. 5.

been adduced in the preceding chapter in confirmation of the statement that parish assistants made their reappearance in the economy of parochial administration as early as the twelfth century. The task of this treatise will now be summarily to turn the pages of history in order to discover by what canons of law and tenets of practice these parish assistants reached their present status in the Church.

§I. NOMENCLATURE

Similarly as the term *parochus* [11] did not reach the status of a uniform and common usage until its nomenclature [12] was sanctioned by the Council of Trent,[13] so also the term *vicarius cooperator* did not acquire stability of appellation until it was canonized in the recent codification of Church Law.[14]

---

[11] Ayrinhac, *Constitution of the Church in the New Code of Canon Law*, p. 301, translates canon 451, §1, as follows: "A parish priest or pastor is a priest or moral person upon whom a parish has been conferred in title, with the care of souls to be exercised under the authority of the local ordinary."

[12] Concerning the names formerly used to designate the parish priest and regarding the time when the present terminology first came into use, cf. Cappello, *De Visitatione SS. Liminum et Dioeceseon*, II, 5 ss.; Wernz, *Ius Decretalium*, II, n. 821; Leurenius, *Forum Beneficiale*, Tom. I, Q. 142; Bouix, *Tractatus de Parocho*, p. 7; Schoepf, *Handbuch des Kirchenrechts*, III, 421-22; *Tübinger Quartal-Schrift*, LXIV (1882), 3 ff.; LXXII (1890), 57-90; LXXXIX (1907), 424-48; VC (1913), 193-203; CVIII (1926), 1-8; *AkKR*, LXXXIX (1909), 38 ff. The origin of the word *parochus* falls within the fifteenth century when it was first appropriated in Spain. The synods of Cologne (1536), of Strassburg (1549), and of Mainz (1549)—Hartzheim, *Concilia Germaniae*, VI, 266, 450, 577—had also used it before the Council of Trent assumed it, and its usage was perhaps all but universal by the year 1563 when the Council incorporated its use in the decree "*Tametsi*." Cf. Hinschius, *System des kath. KR*, II, 291-92.

[13] Cf. Sessio XXIV, *de ref. matr.*, cc. 1, 2, 7—*Canones et Decreta*, pp. 181, 182, 187.

[14] Cans. 472 2°, 476 §§1-5, §8, 477 §2, 478 §2. Cans. 420 §1 4° and 1433 still retain the term *coadiutor*, which bears equal reference to the *adiutor* of cans. 475 §§1-4, 478 §1, 2147 §2 1°. The superscription of Liber II, Pars I, Sectio II, Titulus VIII, Caput X of the Code together with cans. 477 §1, 478 §1, 631 §3, 1429 §2 uses a still more generic term by including the *vicarius cooperator* under the class of *vicarii paroeciales*. At least one of the first editions of the Code (Romae, 1918) uses the phrase *de vicariis paroecialibus* in its index, but resorts to *de vicariis parochialibus* in the actual superscription to the text of canons 471-478.

The succession of the centuries furnishes a rich and varied nomenclature for the auxiliary priests engaged in parish work whom we now designate as *curates* or *assistants*. Pope Innocent II used the word *capellanus*.[15] The council of Avranches (1172), when instructing pastors to receive auxiliary priests for their parishes, employs the indeterminate form of "*alium sub se presbyterum cogantur habere*." [16] The council of Poitiers (1280) designates him with the word *sub-capellanus*.[17] In the central states of Europe the appellation of *socius* seems to be the more common usage.[18]

At times when ecclesiastical functions were performed by them also in the chapels and oratories connected with the parish churches, they were referred to as *altaristae, primissarii, sacellani, capellani, applicati, expositi, localistae, praebendarii, commendarii* and *filialistae*.[19]

As long as the incumbents of parish churches bore the name *plebani*, their parochial assistants were called by the corresponding name of *vice-plebani* or *sub-plebani*.[20] The word *cooperator* was used in a synod at Eichstaett, and repeatedly by later synods and councils.[21] The council of Trent employed the phrase *sacerdos ad hoc* [parochiale] *munus* for assistant priests

---

[15] *Epistola 505* (1139-1142), "Ad D. plebanum de Massa et universos Capellanos eiusdem plebis."—*MPL*, CLXXIX, 569-70. See also *Communia Praecepta Synodalia Odonis* [Eudes de Sully] *Episcopi Parisiensis* (circa 1197), cc. 34, 54—Mansi, XXII, 683-84; Hardouin, VIb, 1944-46. Cf. footnote 8 preceding.

[16] Cf. c. 5—Mansi, XXII, 1157.

[17] Cf. c. 3—Mansi, XXIV, 382; Hardouin, VII, 850; synod. Santonensis (1282), c. 5—Mansi, XXIV, 467.

[18] Hostiensis, *Summa Aurea*, lib. I, tit. 28, n. 5; Glossa of c. 15, C. 7, q. 1, sub v. *adjutorem;* Glossa of c. 21, C. 7, q. 2: "Sed dicas talem *coadjutorem vel socium;* synod. St. Poelten. (1284), c. 8—Hartzheim, III, 674. The word *socius* is also found in combined forms such as *socii in ecclesiis, socii in divinis, socii plebanorum.*

[19] These terms occur chiefly from the 14th to the 16th century. Cf. Permaneder, "Frühmesser," *Herders Kirchenlexicon*, IV, 2029.

[20] Cf. Van Espen, *Jus Ecclesiasticum Universum*, P. I, tit. III, c. 2, *De Vice-pastoribus.*

[21] The two synods of Eichstaett were held in the years 1465 and 1484. Cf. Hartzheim, V, 473, 569, 571. Other synods in which the name occurs were held in the early half of the 17th century. Cf. synod. Constant. (1609), P. II, tit. V, c. 2; synod. Augustan. (1610); synod. Salisburg. (1616)—Hartzheim, VIII, 897; IX, 70; 266.

properly so called,[22] whilst it reserves the term *coadjutor* for him who was assigned to a pastor whose personal impediments, whether of mind or body, demanded the help of an additional priest.[23] But this latter term was also used both prior and subsequent to the great Council to designate him whose services in a parish were required because of local conditions and objective reasons rather than the personal and subjective causes engendered by a physically or mentally incapacitated parish priest.[24]

Because of the reason that the curate's work was regarded as a kind of secondary pastorate, he was called *secundarius*.[25] Illustrative of his priestly as well as his auxiliary capacity were the terms *sacerdos adminicularis* and *sacerdos* or *presbyter auxiliaris*,[26] or again, as more expressive of his merely auxiliary status in parish work, *minister auxiliaris*.[27]

Terms such as *provisor*,[28] *vicarius*,[29] *provicarius*,[30] *pro-parochus* and *vice-parochus*,[31] *adjutor*, or *adjutor in Divinis*, or, again, *adjutor Divinorum* [32] are demonstrative of his substitutive relationship to the pastor.

At the time when the relationship between pastor and assistant was conceived on a rather uninspiring plane, such words as *conductitius* and *mercenarius* were not uncommon.[33] The terms which appear more frequently in the councils of the nineteenth century are *vicarii*, *cooperatores*, and *adjutores*.[34]

---

22 Sessio XXI, *de ref.*, c. 4—*Canones et Decreta*, p. 128.

23 Sessio XXI, *de ref.*, c. 6—*op. cit.*, p. 129.

24 Conc. Coloniense (1300), c. 3; conc. Basiliense (1603), tit. 4; synod. Firman. (1726), tit. XX; decreta conc. prov. Bituricen. (1850)—Hartzheim, IV, 38; VI, 7; *Collectio Lacensis*, I, 606; IV, 1098.

25 Synod. Avenion. (1725), tit. XXI, c. 7—*Coll. Lac.*, I, 517.

26 Conc. Cameracen. (1565), tit. 7, c. 7—Hardouin, X, 587; Clemens XIV, ep. encycl. "*Inter Multiplices*," die 21 Sept. 1769, §§10-11—*Fontes*, n. 466.

27 *Ibid.*, §11.

28 Cf. Lindner, *Die Anstellung der Hilfspriester*, p. 39, footnote11.

29 Synod. Salisburgen. (1616); cf. footnote 21 above.

30 Pallottini, *Collectio omnium Conclusionum et Resolutionum . . . S. Cong. Cardinalium S. Conc. Trid. interpretum ab anno 1564 ad annum 1860*, I, p. 24, §2, n. 6.

31 Cf. footnote 26 above; *Fontes*, n. 466, §§7-9.

32 Cf. Lindner, *op. cit.*, p. 39, footnote 6.

33 *Ibid.*, footnotes 7 and 8; Augustine, *The Canonical and Civil Status of Catholic Parishes*, p. 238.

34 Cf. *Coll. Lac.*, Vols. IV, V, VI *passim*; Hinschius, *System des kath. KR*, II, 318; Lindner, *op. cit.*, *loc. cit.*, for fuller information.

The Code has now stabilized the canonical appellation of assistant priests by giving them a name which embraces the concept of assistance rendered through the double medium of substitution and co-operation.[35]

This enumeration, lengthy as it may appear, bespeaks no claim to exhaustiveness. Nevertheless, it will prove sufficiently representative to furnish a proper conception of the station which the assistant priest occupied in his past history of parochial ministrations. He was ever considered a helper, dependent upon the instruction of the one who engaged his services. The points that will naturally suggest themselves for immediate consideration are: How did the assistant priest receive his appointment, and who claimed the ultimate right over his assignment to a parish?

§II. Mode of Appointment

When the traditional principles of relative ordination and stability of service had succumbed to a newer discipline under the influence of the various causes previously delineated, there was also developed a new tradition with regard to the right of appointment for the auxiliary clergy. The older system by which the bishop's ordination and appointment of a cleric constituted an indivisible act was relegated to the realm of abolished law. New usage demanded that these acts need no longer be considered in the light of a legal unity. Factually they were separable acts. The act of ordination did not preclude the possibility of the act of appointment falling within the province of non-episcopal authority. It required no long time for the legal concept to shape itself into actual practice.

---

[35] Cf. footnote 14 above. In Italy the terms *pro-parroco, sotto-curato,* and *vice-curato* obtain: in France the word *vicaire* is in use: in Germany and Austria the expressions *Kaplan* and *Hilfspriester* seem the most common; in the British Isles the term *curate* is universal; in the United States *curate* and *assistant* are both current. The former seems more prevalent in the extreme eastern section, while the latter is of more general usage in the southern, midwest, and western sections of the country. Cf. Scherer, *Handbuch des KR,* I, 649, footnote 24; *Cath. Ency.,* under article "Curate;" Hilling, "Cooperator: Eine einheitliche Amtsbezeichnung," *AkKR,* IC (1919), 146-47; *Personenrecht,* p. 228.

From the thirteenth century onward, down through the entire Middle Ages, the appointment of his sacerdotal assistants rested, by common law, in the hands of the parish priest. Not a single author is found who does not admit that this was the universal law throughout the Christian world. It is only in the century succeeding that of the council of Trent that one begins to find indications of a change. The further discussion on this reversion of discipline must, however, be reserved to a later section in this chapter.

The first public expression that accords the right of appointment to parish priests seems offered by the council of Avranches (1172): *"Item sacerdotes, alium sub se presbyterum cogantur habere."* [36] Whilst the wording of this canon might possibly be interpreted in the light of episcopal appointment, its more natural and evident meaning seems rather to imply the constraint that was placed upon pastors to assume into their service some other priest subject to them in the performance of parochial functions. The synodal statutes of Bishop Odo of Paris at the turning point of the twelfth century are more explicit: *"Item praecipitur presbyteris, ne recipiant capellanos sine conscientia episcopi vel archidiaconi."* [37] In the thirteenth century similar testimony becomes quite abundant.[38] Parish priests could select their own assistants not only for their own parish churches but also for the chapels and filial churches in the more distant parts of the parochial territory subject to them.[39]

Although parish priests were given a free hand in the selection of their assistants, yet, whenever they were found negligent in their duty of assuming a sacerdotal helper, the bishop bespoke the right, either personally or through his archdeacon, to intervene by executing the right which the pastors had defaulted.[40] Similar restrictions were set up by other synods and councils, at least to the extent of requiring certainty of the fitness of the candidates in a previous examination, either at the

---

[36] Can. 5—Mansi, XXII, 1157.

[37] *Praecepta Communia*, cap. 54—Hardouin, VIb, 1946.

[38] Cf. Lindner, *Die Anstellung der Hilfspriester*, p. 44, for numerous examples.

[39] Synod. St. Poelten. (1284), c. 7—Hartzheim, III, 674; conc. nationale Herbipolense (1387), c. 16—Hardouin, VII, 1136.

[40] Synod. Worcestrensis (1240), c. 26—Mansi, XXIII, 535.

time of their ordination or on the occasion of their appointment.[41] The councils of Salzburg (1420) and of Lyons (1449) passed still stricter regulations by the observance of which every safeguard was prescribed against unordained, unfit, excommunicated, or vagrant clergymen seeking and obtaining admission to parish assistancies.[42]

But, the pastor's strict right of appointment was never called in question by any of these councils. For, since his assistant received a salary from the church revenues which yielded properly to the pastor, and since, in consequence, the latter became responsible for his honorable sustenance, it would have been considered a breach of equity, if not an infringement on justice, to gainsay the right that every man possesses of selecting whomsoever he associates with himself in his personal labors. In the light of this conception the pastor's right of appointment was sealed.

The relationship of pastor and assistant was regarded as analogous to that of master and apprentice. This becomes apparent from the names which were then current for parochial assistant priests. It has been stated in an earlier part of this chapter,[43] that the terms *socii, mercenarii,* and *conducitii* were rather generally employed in designation of parochial sacerdotal assistants. The time-period of assistancy at a parish depended upon the specifications that was stipulated in the contract. While in some cases the pastor reserved for himself the arbitrary freedom of dismissing his priestly associate at whatever time he might choose, this indeterminate arrangement was grimly counterbalanced by the assistant's equally peremptory faculty of abandoning his post whenever he liked. But this proved to be a rather noxious system of equalization. Only too often it created serious embarrassment for priests and people alike. In view of these vexatious possibilities, the contracts between pastors and their assistants were subjected to a more definite and binding form. Lindner adduces a noteworthy example.

---

[41] Conc. apud Castrum Ganterii (1231), c. 18—Hardouin, VII, 194; conc. Pont-Audomarense (1279), c. 19—Hardouin, VII, 796; synod. Pictaviensis (1280), c. 3—Mansi, XXIV, 382; synod. Coloniensis (1423), c. 7—Hardouin, VIII, 978-79.

[42] Cf. Mansi, XXVIII, 1010; XXXII, 94-97.

[42] Cf. Mansi, XXXII, 94-97; Hardouin, VIII, 978-79.

[43] Cf. footnotes 18 and 33.

At the parish of Ingolstadt the famous Dr. Eck had in his service three assistant priests. Their term of service continued for one year, beginning and ending on February 2nd. They were required to give notification not later than September 1st as to whether they wished to continue in or desist from their service in the next following term. In like manner the pastor was to certify his mind to them. Apparently, some of the curates made light of the binding force of the articles of their contracts under given conditions and in particular eventualities. For this reason Dr. Eck instructed his successors to request from their curates an unconditional promise that they would not depart from the church during the year. Furthermore, the days on which the pastor was officially to serve notice of his intention to re-engage or dismiss them, and similarly, the days on which the curates were to make known their desire to re-enlist in or depart from their services for the pastor should be increased to correspond with quarterly periods.[44]

Whilst the pastor's right to select his assistant was not questioned by episcopal authority, he was sometimes constrained to let his parishioners have a share in the assignment made for their churches. The various restrictions and safeguards which diocesan decrees and synods, or even provincial councils had stipulated,[45] were not an encroachment upon his rights; they were rather the enactment of the proper legal sanction against abuses of that right. On the other hand, it was not uncommon for parishioners to bespeak a claim upon their pastor to be consulted in the appointment of a new assistant priest at their parishes. The reason underlying this action may be properly sought in their conviction that the curate was as much the servant of *their* needs as those of the *pastor*, as also in their consciousness that the assistant was dependent on them for his financial support, and hence, should be enlisted in their service only after their voice and approval. But the most weighty reason seems to have been their desire to obtain the ministra-

---

[44] Lindner, *Die Anstellung der Hilfspriester*, pp. 47-48.

[45] Cf. footnotes 40-42 of this chapter.

tions of a fit and competent priest.[46] In certain places even local traditions played an important rôle in determining the specified limits within which the pastor could exercise his right of appointment.[47]

But neither the people's demand to be consulted nor the bishop's regulations concerning previous examination and approval, especially when an extra-diocesan ecclesiastic was assumed in the service, ever detracted from the parish priest's *essential right* or appropriated his *acknowledged faculty* of selecting his own assistant priest.[48] It is true that cases in which the bishop denied the pastor ratification of his appointment because of the actual unfitness, at least seriously questionable fitness, of the candi-

---

[46] ". . . Es soll kain pfarrer kain unterherrn dingen . . . ohne des richters, kirchprobst und der nachbern wissen und willen, und kainen minich (Mönch) oder welschen priester aufnemben, sondern nur teitsche priester."—Lindner, *Die Anstellung der Hilfspriester*, p. 56, footnote 3. Another document insists that ". . . ain iglicher pfarrer gute gewissne priester hält die den gotsdienst mit singen, predigen, und ain gemainschaft versorgen kunnen und mügen."—*Op. cit.*, p. 57, footnote 1.

[47] Cf. Sägmüller, in a review of Lindner, *Die Anstellung der Hilfspriester*—*Theologische Revue*, XXIV (1925), 164-65—cites the following passage from J. Krieg (*Die Landkapitel im Bistum Würzburg von der 2ten Hälfte des 14ten zur 2ten Hälfte des 16ten Yahrhunderds*, p. 55, footnote 1): "Es setzte unser Kapitel fest, dass die Pastoren oder Rectoren der Pfarrkirchen, wenn es die Seelsorge verlangt, als Kapläne oder Gehilfen im Gottesdienst keine Mönche anstellen, ausser sie hatten ein besonderes Privileg. Andernfalls sind letztere vom Kapitel gänzlich ausgeschlossen; denn wie der Fisch ausserhalb des Wassers stirbt, geht der Mönch ausserhalb des Klosters zugrunde . . . —Statuten des Landkapitels Buchen vom 14 April, 1561, nr. 10."

In interpreting this passage the reader will not be unaware of the fact that this ordinance perhaps fell within the critical period of the purposive restoration of the diocesan clergy to their lost prestige. The trend of this era strongly suggests a consideration in this modified light. Cf. also conc. Coloniense (1423), c. 7—Hardouin, VIII, 1011.

[48] Cf. synod. Pictaviensis (1280), c. 3: ". . . monemus, ne rectores ecclesiarum parochialium saeculares vel religiosi, sub-capellanos vel presbyteros ad executionem huiusmodi potestatis in suis ecclesiis vel parochiis, admittant . . . sine nostra licentia speciali."—Hardouin, VII, 850; synod. St. Poeltensis (1284), c. 5—Hartzheim, III, 674; synod. Coloniensis (1300), c. 3—Hartzheim, IV, 38; conc. Salisburgense (1420), c. 5—Hardouin, VIII, 978; synod. Avenionensis (1509), c. 17—Mansi, XXXII, 543; and especially the words of the archbishop of Cologne in the year 1549: ". . . Inhibentes . . . Parochialium ecclesiarum rectoribus sub excommunicationis poena . . ., ne deinceps ullum vice-curatum, adjutorem vel socium ad regimen et curam animarum absque litteris testimonialibus proprii episcopi et nostra seu archidiaconorum nostrorum praecedente examinatione et permissu assumant."—Hartzheim, VI, 701; Mansi, XXXII, 1370.

dates presented for examination and approval could be multiplied upon a more minute research in the historical sources of these centuries. But, on the other hand, not a single instance seems to be on record in which any bishop overruled the appointment made by the pastor once the candidate had given proof of his fitness in a previous examination.

The expressions used in canon 5 of the council of Avranches in 1172 as also in canon 26 of the synod of Worcester in 1240, wherein the archdeacon is authorized to supply the pastor's negligence in the appointment of assistant priests at the parishes where they were needed, do indeed reserve the appointment in given cases to the bishop's authority.[49] But, if rightly understood, it will be seen that this reservation devolved upon the bishop only then when the pastor had forfeited his right by a criminal neglect and ignominious betrayal of the spiritual interests of his parish through his lack of engaging the required priestly aid.

The foregoing representative excerpts of the synods and the councils held prior to the celebration of the Ecumenical Council of Trent, led to the certain conclusion that the right of appointing assistant priests remained within the province of the parish priest. This General Council made no innovation, but rather dignified the generally existing legal traditions in this regard with the sanction of its universal law when it decreed:

> Episcopi, etiam tamquam Apostolicae Sedis delegati, in omnibus ecclesiis parochialibus vel baptismalibus, in quibus populus ita numerosus sit, ut unus rector non possit sufficere ecclesiasticis sacramentis ministrandis et cultui divino peragendo, cogent rectores, vel alios, ad quos pertinet, sibi tot sacerdotes ad hoc munus adiungere, quot sufficiant ad Sacramenta exhibenda et cultum divinum celebrandum.[50]

---

[49] Cf. Mansi, XXII, 1157; XXIII, 535.

[50] Sessio XXI, *de ref.*, c. 4—*Canones et Decreta*, pp. 127-28. The parish priest's personal right to select his assistant is repeatedly confirmed by official responses from the Sacred Congregation of the Council. Cf. S. C. C. *in Civitatis Castellanae*, die 26 Aug. 1628; S. C. C. *in Grossetana*, die 16 Sept. 1645; S. C. C. *in Lauden. Jurisdictionis*, die 30 Julii 1678, where this right is declared to belong not to the *habitual*, but to the *actual* parish priest; S. C. C. *in Tridentina Deputationis Coadiutoris*, die 11 Jan. 1716, where

The discipline of the past was left unchanged except in this that such dioceses which had not yet established regulations for the necessity of episcopal approbation prior to a curate's appointment were now made subject to the law:

> Decernit tamen sancta synodus, nullum, etiam Regularem, posse confessiones saecularium, etiam sacerdotum, audire, nec ad id idoneum reputari, nisi . . . aut parochiale beneficium, aut ab episcopo per examen, *si illis videbitur necessarium,* aut alias idoneus judicetur, et approbationem, quae gratis detur, obtineat, privilegiis et consuetudine quacumque, etiam immemorabili, non obstantibus.[51]

Although a liberal degree of latitude was still extended to the bishops by the phrase "*si illis videbitur necessarium,*" nevertheless many of the dioceses which had not insisted on previous examination and approval for the candidate who was to be assumed by the pastor as an assistant did require this additional safeguard soon after the Council. Thus, in a provincial council celebrated at Salzburg in 1569 and in subsequent General-Visitation Statutes of the year 1616, it was stipulated that no priest could be assumed as a curate who had not been declared as fitted for exercising the care of souls by either the bishop, the vicar general, or the diocesan official.[52] Other dioceses also adopted the same regulations,[53] and while in certain dioceses the examination and approval of the bishop made the services of the candidate available for only that parish to which he was to be assigned, in other territories they qualified him for service throughout the entire diocese. Sometimes the approval was ac-

---

a bishop's action in allowing a pastor merely four days for presenting an assistant for approval is not sustained; S. C. C. *in Mediolanen.*, die 26 April. 1732, where the bishop's interference with the right of the pastor is acknowledged only then when there is *special* need of authoritative provision; S. C. C. *in Terracinen.*, die 2 Maii et 6 Junii 1739—Pallottini, *Collectio omnium Conclusionum et Resolutionum,* XIV, 519, n. 35; 513, n. 3; 520, n. 40; 517, n. 19; 519, n. 33; 514, n. 4.

[51] Sessio XXIII, *de ref.*, c. 15—*Canones et Decreta,* pp. 162-63.

[52] Cf. Dalham, *Concilia Salisburgensia Provincialia et Dioecesana,* pp. 436, 602.

[53] E.g., synod. Cameracensis (1565); synod. prov. Aquileiensis (1596); synod. Namurcensis (1625)—Mansi, XXXIII, 1407; XXXIV, 1419; Hardouin, IX, 340.

corded for a continued period of time so that the young priest would not be subjected to a repeated examination should a change of appointment intervene. In these latter circumstances, however, there was commonly added a provision that, whenever an assistant assumed a new parochial assignment, he was to present his standing credentials to the archdeacon, the rural dean, or the rural chapter at their next meeting.[54]

In Spain alone there seems to have continued a general discipline which did not strictly require previous certification of fitness through an official examination and ultimate episcopal approval. It correspondingly occasioned more ready access for the development of abuses. That abuses must actually have arisen is evident from the papal legislation enacted against them by Pope Innocent XIII in his Constitution, "*Apostolici Ministerii,*" of May 23, 1723.[55] Nor is it to be doubted that a relaxation of the Tridentine law was noticeable in other countries also. For this reason Pope Benedict XIII raised his predecessor's Constitution into the estate of a universal law when he promulgated his own Constitution, "*In Supremo,*" of September 23, 1724, for the entire Church.[56]

ART. II. CHANGE OF DISCIPLINE

§I. IN AUSTRIA

In the preceding century circumstances had arisen in certain sections of the Christian world which more and more favored the introduction of a practice by which the appointment of curates became alienated from the province of the parish priest to be placed in the hands of episcopal authority.[57] The Thirty Years' War in the first half of the seventeenth century had left great desolation in its wake. It was inevitable that parish organizations in the devastated districts should suffer in consequence. A canvass of the diocese of Freising in the year 1665 revealed at least 24 vacancies in which assistant priests had for-

---

[54] E.g., synod. Trevirensis (1622)—Hartzheim, IX, 330.

[55] Cf. §13—*Fontes,* n. 280.

[56] Cf. §10—*Fontes,* n. 283.

[57] Many pertinent ecclesiastical documents on this point may be found cited by Kohn, "De cooperatoribus," *AkKR,* XXXIX (1878), 3-18.

merly served. An effort was made by the bishop to have these vacancies filled when he bade the pastors to assume the needed assistants. The pastors pointed out the decrease of membership and the consequent meagerness of income in their parishes as reasons for delaying their appointment. Apparently their plea was heeded at the time; but, there is evidence also that it lost its compelling force before the lapse of many decades, for, the sources recount instances in which the appointment and transfer of curates was promptly undertaken by the bishop when the pastor was slow to use a right which in the mind of episcopal authority had simultaneously become a duty.[58]

In the year 1677 an ordinance was issued by the episcopal curia of Freising in which both the appointment and the transfer of assistant priests is characterized as its own proper right.[59] The old discipline was fast giving way to a new order. It is not surprising, then, that a later instruction issued on March 22, 1691, demanded that the matter of assuming and dismissing curates had to be referred to the diocesan court of the bishop for final adjudication and ultimate execution.

On the other hand, even a few decades later the binding power of this instruction was still seriously questioned. One of the deans of the diocese, more jealous than his companions of the old traditional right of assuming his own assistants, had recourse to Rome for a final settlement of his disputed claim. He was abetted in his action by the Bavarian Elector, Karl Albrecht, who was a generous patron of the parish. An answer was received from the Sacred Congregation of the Council under date of March 24, 1729, which invalidated the bishop's hasty act and accorded the dean his traditional legal right.[60]

---

[58] For the history of the Freising and the Salzburg dioceses consult Lindner, *Die Anstellung der Hilfspriester*, pp. 76-107. The majority of the sources cited by him consist of unpublished documents which are available only in the dioceses where they are preserved.

[59] In the year 1684 another instruction uses the following words: ". . . der dem Pfarrer 'in partem curae' von Uns assignierte Priester . . ." See also footnote 99 of this chapter and footnote 28 of Chapter V.

[60] This response is not to be found in the *Thesaurus Resolutionum* (Tom. IV for the year 1729). The omission may be due to the semi-private nature of the response or, possibly, to the fact that an element of judiciary action was involved in it. Cf. Lindner, *op. cit.*, pp. 86-87, for a short summary of the reasons assigned by the Congregation in its confirmation of the pastor's rights.

Whilst the diocesan ordinary submitted to his superior authority in this individual case and within the same year even accorded the dean and his successors the perpetual right of free and unhindered assignment of their curates upon previous examination and approval, still, the particular diocesan practice which had come into vogue was elsewhere maintained throughout the diocese and the authority of the ordinary was recognized in his acts of appointment to parochial assistancies.

In the archdiocese of Salzburg there appear even earlier traces of an attempt on the part of episcopal authority to appropriate the administration, or at least the intimate superintendence, of this same right of appointing parochial assistants. In 1623 the archdiocesan curia freely interpreted the appeal of a pastor, whose curate had arbitrarily left him, by sending him another priest to be his helper in the administration of his parochial labors. Instances similar to this are not wanting in the decades following.[61] As early as 1675 the archbishop's court determined by a public decree that the assignment of curates to the parishes was not within the sphere of pastoral rights, but belonged to the authority of the local ordinary.

Yet, here as in the diocese of Freising, the decree did not meet with immediate universal acceptance. The archdeacons who were placed over the three archdeaneries of Baumburg, Chiemsee, and Gars, which territorially constituted the electorate of Bavaria, were ready and gallant defenders of their institutional rights. The struggle between them and the archiepiscopal curia continued for over a century. Ultimate defeat was acknowledged by them only after a royal rescript of February 28, 1809, had converted their jurisdictional territories into rural deaneries and left both their name and their office a memory of history.[62]

It was because these two ecclesiastical territories, earlier than any others, revealed a change of discipline, that they were treated in some detail. It may be surmised that the practice which was established in these two important dioceses exercised its influence on the surrounding territory.

From the documents cited by Lindner [63] it appears that the

---

[61] Cf. Lindner, *op. cit.*, p. 89 ff., where repeated cases are cited from the archdiocesan curial documents.

[62] Cf. Lindner, *op. cit.*, p. 107.

[63] *Op. cit.*, pp. 108, 111, 112, 114.

newer discipline had taken root in the dioceses of Regensburg, Brixen, Bamberg, and Eichstaett possibly before the end of the eighteenth century. The dioceses of Passau, Gurk, Lavant, Seckau, Augsburg, Mainz, Speyer, and Constance, seemed to retain the old tradition until after the beginning of the nineteenth century, as did also the dioceses of northern Germany.[64]

In Austria, the nomination and transfer of parochial assistants were entrusted to episcopal authority by Emperor Leopold II in 1791 for all such curates whose salaries were either totally or partially paid by the state's "Religion Fund." [65] The extension of this episcopal prerogative so as to embrace control of appointment for all curates alike was but a question of time. The expression *"tot sacerdotes ei* [parocho] *adiungantur,"* used by the council of Vienna in 1858, points to a well-established usage throughout that country.[66]

§II. In France

In France the assignment of assistants to the parishes by the bishops was occasioned by the Revolution towards the end of the eighteenth century. Authors are not agreed as to what furnished the basic cause for the change of discipline. Chaillot [67] ventures the explanation that, since many of the pastors had taken the oath of the Civil Constitution, the right of appointing their *vicaires* had necessarily to be denied to them. The prohibition was at first considered a transient measure, but in the course of the years became the acknowledged usage.

Bouix [68] believes that the ordinations to higher orders without a canonical title to sustenance began with, or immediately subsequent to, the French Revolution. In order to lend some

[64] Cf. *TQS*, X (1828), 36 ff.; *AkKR*, XXXIX (1878), 3-18; XLII (1879), 410-22. In these articles the references are principally to the dioceses of Württemberg, Mainz and Olomouc (Olmütz).

[65] Cf. Lindner, *op. cit.*, p. 113.

[66] Cf. *Coll. Lac.*, V, 157a.

[67] "Traité des Vicaires paroissiaux," *Analecta Juris Pontificii*, V (1861), 838-902; 970-1015. The question of nomination is discussed on pp. 855-99; that of removal on pp. 1004-14. After discussing the teaching of the canonists (pp. 884-97), the author intimates his own opinion on p. 898.

[68] *Tractatus de Parocho*, pp. 643-44.

assurance of income to the non-beneficed clergy, their appointment and removal was placed in the hands of the bishop, who was better qualified to maintain them in constant service, because he could thus the more securely guard them against unforeseen dismissal from the parishes. This conception would seem to do fuller justice in its explanation than the former, provided, of course, the premise be true that ordination without a title came only with, and not prior to, the time of the Revolution. Recalling, however, that the preamble to the "Organic Articles" designated the *"ordinations vagues et sans titre"* [69] as the mainspring of widespread clerical undiscipline in the country, one might wish to disincline from this view and look for one that harmonizes better with historical facts.

Lindner [70] offers the following elucidation. Since the Revolution succeeded most ruthlessly in its decimation of the clerical ranks, France suffered from a dearth of priests, especially the junior clergy. Their preparation and training for ordination were attended by immense difficulties and dangers in the turmoil of that age. The right which the *curé* enjoyed of selecting his own *vicaire* was scarcely short of meaningless under such conditions. Pressed by necessity, he considered it an advantage to be able to appeal to his bishop for the privilege of obtaining parochial assistants through the latter's appointment when his own restricted search for the necessary help could remain but fruitless. The measure thus conceived in the stress of dire necessity continued serviceably through the decades that followed, even after the primal need had been relieved. So general and continuous had the practice become that when Bishop Epivent of Aire in France addressed a query to the Sacred Congregation of the Council to receive a definitive decision regarding the right of appointing *vicaires*, the Congregation bade him follow the custom prevalent in the other dioceses of France.[71]

---

[69] Mansi, XLI, 507 ss.

[70] *Die Anstellung der Hilfspriester*, pp. 116-18.

[71] Cf. *Revue des Sciences Ecclésiastiques*, XI (1865), 274; *Nouvelle Revue Théologique*, XXIV (1892), pp. 603, 607. The decision was not published by the bishop until February 22, 1865. Following is the text of the query and its response:

> Ad V: An nominatio vicariorum, a fortiori capellanorum, prout res nunc se habent in Gallia, et eorum stipendia componuntur, exclusive pertineat ad parochum.

§III. In Other Countries

In other countries the practice of appointment by the bishop also obtained the force of law. It was recognized in Belgium,[72] Holland,[73] Hungary,[74] Spain,[75] Ireland,[76] England,[77] Canada,[78] Haiti,[79] and Venezuela,[80] in the early half of the last century.

Other countries in South America, however, did not all recognize the same discipline. Thus, for instance, in the Republic of Colombia there was celebrated a provincial council in the year 1868 which leaves the right to the appointment of assistants vested in the parish priest under the strict surveillance of the bishop.[81]

R. De jure spectare ad parochum cum approbatione Episcopi; attentis vero peculiaribus circumstantiis, servandum esse usum in ceteris Galliarum dioecesibus obtinentem, usque dum aliter a S. Sede declaratum.

This query, along with 30 others, was occasioned by the refractory behavior of a certain M. Molet, curé in the town of Mont-de-Marson, who first wrote a pamphlet, and later a book in which he circulated untenable opinions concerning his rights in the capacity of a parish priest. The condemnation of these writings ultimately effected the submission of the curé to his bishop. The delayed publication of the Congregation's responses may have been actuated by the bishop's deep Christian sense of judicial forbearance. Cf. *NRT*, XXIV (1892), 600 ss.

[72] Cf. *Anal. Jur. Pont.*, V (1861), 898; Deneubourg, *Étude canonique sur les vicaires paroissiaux*, p. 102; Van den Berghe, *Institutiones Canonicae* (Tractatus de vicariis paroecialibus), pp. 8-9.

[73] Conc. Prov. Ultrajectense (1865)—*Coll. Lac.*, V, 795c.

[74] Decreta Conc. Provinciae Strigoniensis (1859)—*Coll. Lac.*, V, 50d. This council was celebrated in the City of Gran (the modern Esztergom).

[75] Cf. Mercati, *Raccolta di concordati su materie ecclesiastiche fra la Santa Sede et le autorità civili*, p. 785; Nussi, *Conventiones de rebus ecclesiasticis inter S. Sedem et civilem potestatem*, p. 290c—concordat between Pope Pius IX and Queen Isabella II of Spain in 1867.

[76] Conc. Plen. Hiberniae (1850)—*Coll. Lac.*, III, 789d and f. This council was celebrated at Thurles.

[77] Conc. Prov. Westmonasteriense (1852)—*Coll. Lac.*, III, 942.

[78] Conc. Prov. Quebecense II (1854)—*Coll. Lac.*, III, 657.

[79] Mercati, *op. cit.*, p. 932; Nussi, *op. cit.*, p. 347d, n. 9—concordat between Pope Pius IX and the president of the Republic in 1860.

[80] Mercati, *op. cit.*, p. 976; Nussi, *op. cit.*, 359a, art. 16—convention between the Holy See and the Republic of Venezuela in 1862.

[81] Cf. *Coll. Lac.*, VI, 483. It is stated there that, if the parish priest does not comply with the bishop's instruction to engage a curate in his service within a term of three months, the right of appointing one will cede to the bishop. A curate appointed by the latter becomes "*amovibilis ad nutum episcopi.*"

The Central American countries also retained the old discipline. In a plenary council celebrated by them in Rome during the year 1899, the clause, "*vicarii, vice-parochi qui ad adiuvandum parochum assumuntur,*" [82] furnishes rather reassuring evidence that the assignment of parochial assistants remained within the sphere of the pastor's prerogatives. If, within the same chapter of the council the regulation is laid down that whenever a parish priest is not able singly to administer to the needs of his parish, then as many priests are associated with him *(ei adiunguntur)* as the number of souls, the extent of the territory, or other similar causes may require, the meaning of the council simply is that the existing needs are to be supplied. The construction does not indicate the method by which, but the circumstances under which, assistants are to receive their assignment to parishes. It remained the parish priest's primary duty and prerogative to supply the particular need of assistants when it arose. Only indirectly, that is, in case of the pastor's neglect, did the bishop gain competency in the matter of appointing assistants.

Again, in the canton of Lucerne in Switzerland, the pastor's right to nominate his assistants continued down to our own times, whilst in the surrounding cantons the practice of assignment by the bishop was the generally recognized usage of law.[83] And finally, in Italy and Sardinia, parish priests enjoyed their traditional rights not only toward the close of the last century,[84] but even in our own.[85]

The practice of Italy and Sardinia, of the canton of Lucerne in Switzerland, of the entire group of the Central American countries, as well as that of one or the other South American Republics, was never at any time prevalent in our own country. It is well known that the appointment of assistant priests in this country has *always* rested in the hands of the bishops.

---

[82] Cf. *Acta et Decreta Concilii Plenarii Americae Latinae in Urbe celebrati, anno 1899*, p. 127.

[83] Cf. Lindner, *Die Anstellung der Hilfspriester*, p. 129, footnote 2.

[84] Synod. Prov. Ravennensis (1855)—*Coll. Lac.*, VI, 196; *Anal. Jur. Pont.*, *V* (1861), 877; synod. Neopolitana (1882)—*AkKR*, LI (1884), 84; Berardi, *De Parocho Compendium*, n. 884, III: "Talis enim videtur esse consuetudo (saltem apud nos)."

[85] Cf. Sorrentino, *I vicarii parrochiali nel dritto canonico e nelle legge italiane ecclesiastiche*, pp. 14, 15, 31 ss.; *AAS*, XIII (1921), 45.

This is plainly evident from nn. 111 and 112 of the Acts and Decrees of the II Plenary Council of Baltimore. The norm there indicated was borrowed from the I Plenary Council of Baltimore (c. 3), which in turn appropriated the ruling from the I Provincial Council of Baltimore celebrated in the year 1829.[86]

A discussion of the less usual methods by which the appointment of parochial curates reached its ultimate sanction through the mediation of consecutively correlated acts between bishop and parish priest would take this treatise too far afield in its limited scope. A deeper study of this question would indeed permit one to catch glimpses of the minutest ramifications of discipline in the different countries throughout the successive stages of the Church's history.[87] But the usefulness of a knowledge so studiously acquired would, after all, remain more academic than practical. For this reason its consideration may be waived here.

It may be of service, however, to point to a few pertinent decisions rendered by the Sacred Congregation of the Council during the past centuries. It is not always easy to determine to what degree they may establish a norm for universal observance. Many of its decisions bear exclusively upon local needs, conditions, and circumstances. Still, there are a number of them wherein the common law received authentic interpretation.

A bishop, when informed that grave suspicions of negligence attached to the parochial ministrations of a certain parish priest within his diocese, forthwith sought to consult the spiritual welfare of the parish in question by the appointment of a curate. No previous official investigation had been made concerning the truthfulness of the allegations lodged against the pastor. The latter appealed against the bishop's action of appointment and

---

[86] Cf. *Coll. Lac.*, III, 144-45 and III, 25.

[87] Cf. Hergenroether, "Ueber den kirchenrechtlichen Begriff der Nomination," *AkKR*, XXXIX (1878), 193-214. The words *commendare, insinuare, proponere, praesentare, nominare, designare, seligere, eligere, committere, conferre, sufficere, praeficere, destinare, deputare, creare, approbare, confirmare*, etc., were the words generally used to give expression to the manifold methods involved by the rights of lay or clerical patronage, of presentation, of nomination, of election, of confirmation, of admission, of institution, and of free collation.

his claim was sustained by a decision of the Sacred Congregation.[88]

In another case the query was whether priests who are members of a religious order can be assigned as assistants by their superiors without the express permission of the bishop, or whether it remains within the scope of the latter's competence to restrict the faculties of Regular confessors, not only with regard to time, but also with regard to persons as well as the places in which they are to hear confessions. The reply was negative for the first, and affirmative for the second part of the question.[89]

When a pastor refused to assume an assistant upon the bishop's command, the latter became qualified to assign one in accord with the ruling of Pope Benedict XIII in his Constitution *"In Supremo"* of September 23, 1724.[90] There could be no appeal which would suspend the execution of the bishop's act of intervention.[91] It remained for the bishop to determine when assistants were to be appointed.[92]

The Constitutions of the popes touching on the question of parish assistants were principally occupied with enforcing the decree of the council of Trent.[93] But, since the Tridentine legislation was somewhat undetermined in its specification of the sanction whereby the bishop became qualified by an alternate

---

[88] S. C. C. *in Ferentina Coadjutoriae*, die 29 Feb. 1744—Pallottini, *Collectio omnium Conclusionum et Resolutionum*, XIV, 517, n. 23.

[89] "Ad dubium: An regulares dari in coadjutores . . . possint a Superioribus Regularibus, sine expressa licentia Episcopi, sive potius sit in potestate Episcopi in approbatione Confessariorum Regularium limitare eorumden facultates, non solum quoad tempus, sed etiam quoad personas et loca, in quibus debent Confessiones audire.

"Resp.: Negative ad I, affirmative ad II partem."—S. C. C. *in Olomucen. Jurisdictionis*, die 7 Junii 1755, ad IV—Pallottini, *op. cit.*, XIV, 519-20, n. 38.

[90] Cf. *Fontes*, II, n. 283, §10, pp. 603-04; S. C. C. *in Novarien.*, die 6 Maii 1647; S. C. C. *in Forosempronien. Jurium Parochialium*, die 11 April. 1761; S. C. C. *in Balneoregien. Visitationis SS. Liminum*, die 24 Mart. et die 14 April. 1821—Pallottini, *op. cit.*, XIV, 519, n. 30; 522, nn. 1, 3, 5; 627, n. 12. See also *ASS*, VIII (1875), 694-700 for a comprehensive case decided by the Congregation on July 24, 1875.

[91] S. C. C. *in Ausculana*, die 22 Jan. 1763—Pallottini, *op. cit.*, XIV, 517, n. 21.

[92] S. C. C. *in Romana*, die 3 Julii 1819—Pallottini, *op. cit.*, XIV, 515, n. 18.

[93] Sessio XXI, *de ref.*, c. 4—*Canones et Decreta*, pp. 127-28.

competence to undertake personally the appointment of assistants, the bishop was empowered to constrain the rectors of parishes, *within a certain time-limit,* to assume a curate or forfeit his right of appointing him. This is the import of a number of papal documents.[94]

To the same degree that the Church began to consider parish assistants as the ministers of her public service rather than the servants of the pastor's personal accommodation, in the same measure was it a natural consequence that the disposition of their services should fall under the direction of the bishop's public authority rather than under the behest of a pastor's private precepts.

Indeed, this concept, more than any other single motivating cause, provides the basis for the legal structure of the present discipline. Canon 476, in §§3-4, indicates unequivocally that henceforth the public service of parish assistants is no longer confined within the narrow bounds of a personal contract between them and their pastors. The trust of their official service of the Church is embodied in the public personalities of their respective ordinaries.[95]

ART. III. SPHERE OF RIGHTS AND DUTIES

As long as it was within the province of the parish priest to select and assume his parochial assistant, so long also did it generally remain within his own discretion and will to determine the sphere of rights and duties within which his curate was to exercise his priestly assistance.[96] The parish priest was to recall,

---

[94] Cf. Innocentius XIII, const. "*Apostolici Ministerii,*" die 23 Maii 1723, §§11-13; Benedictus XIII, const. "*In Supremo,*" die 23 Sept. 1723, §§8-10; const. "*Pastoralis Officii,*" die 27 Martii 1726, §3; Benedictus XIV, ep. encycl. "*Etsi Minime,*" die 7 Feb. 1742, §14; const. "*Ad Militantis,*" die 30 Martii 1742, §12; const. "*Etsi Pastoralis,*" die 26 Maii 1742, c. 5, §9; Clemens XIV, ep. encycl. "*Inter Multiplices,*" die 21 Sept. 1769, §7—*Fontes,* I, n. 280; n. 283; n. 292; n. 324; n. 326; n. 328; *Fontes,* II, n. 466.

[95] Cf. S. C. C. *in Zagabrien. Nominationis vicariorum cooperatorum,* die 13 Nov. 1920—*AAS,* XIII (1921), 43-46.

[96] Cf. Zimmermann, "Die amtliche und rechtliche Stellung der Pfarrkapläne," *AkKR,* XLII (1879), 410-22 especially p. 416; Suarez, *Opera Omnia,* XXII, Disp. XXVI, Sectio I.

however, that the parochial ministrations remained his own personal labors and that the assistant's service should be merely one of supplementation.[97] The pastor was to assist personally at all marriages within his parish unless he was hindered by a legitimate and pressing reason.[98] He was to remember that he had assumed his curate *"in adjutorium ministerii"* and not *"in partem curae."* [99] He was not to leave all the arduous tasks to the assistant's performance and thus make himself the idle spectator of the labors of another in the fulfillment of duties that remained his own.[100]

In cases where the curate assisted not only at the parish church, but ministered also to the needs of a filial church or chapel, his faculties and powers at the latter were frequently determined by the specifications contained in the documents of erection or foundation.[101] When his assignment was made by the bishop, he was to learn the scope of his faculties from the document of his appointment, from the statutes of the diocese, or, if no other norm was available, from the charges committed to him by the

[97] "Quando ampla est animarum cura, Parochum posse adhibere Coadjutorem, ita tamen, ut ea quae potest per seipsum circa Sacramentorum administrationem facere non omittat."—S. C. C. *in Grossetana,* die 16 Sept. 1645. Cf. Pallottini, *Collectio omnium Conclusionum et Resolutionum,* XIV, 513, n. 3.

[98] Benedictus XIV, ep. encycl. *"Nimiam Licentiam,"* die 18 Maii 1743, c. 9; ". . . nisi legitima gravissimaque causa impeditus."—*Fontes,* I, n. 337. Berardi, however, writing in the last century, could say: ". . . Sed apud nos consuetudo est contraria, quae tolerabilis videtur."—*De Parocho Compendium,* n. 478. The custom mentioned by Berardi was not indigenous to Italy alone; it was current and recognized throughout the Christian world.

[99] Cf. *Coll. Lac.,* IV, 140a, 266d, 416d, 417a, 587b, 883d, 984c, 1098b, 1180b and c, for these and similar expressions. The councils in which these expressions were used belong to the middle of the 19th century. See also footnote 59 of this chapter and footnote 28 of Chapter V.

[100] Decreta conc. prov. Ravennatis (1855)—*Coll. Lac.,* VI, 196. The words used by the council are: ". . . alieni laboris spectatores magis quam ecclesiae suae rectores existunt." This instruction was directly based on the Council of Trent, Sessio XXIII, *de ref.,* c. 1—*Canones et Decreta,* pp. 153-56.

[101] S. C. C. *in Mediolanen.,* die 16 Feb. 1867—*ASS,* III (1867-1868), 92-96. In connection with this question see also *ASS,* II (1866-1867), 327; *ASS,* VIII (1875), 694-700.

pastor.[102] He could never subdelegate *"ad audiendas confessiones,"* [103] and possessed only strictly limited powers *"ad assistendum matrimonio."*[104] In consequence of his restricted powers as a delegate, his ability to subdelegate to another the right of assisting at marriages was almost totally inoperative.[105]

In the absence of a certified authorization, a general misapprehension or common error on the part of the faithful could alone supply the lack of authorization through the medium of a supplied jurisdiction. This is deducible from the following case: An assistant priest continued his ministrations in a parish during its vacancy without receiving authorization therefor. He assisted at a marriage attended by thirty or more of the parishioners who thought him to be their parish priest. Some time later misgivings arose concerning the valid form of the marriage. The solution of the doubt was ultimately submitted to the

---

[102] S. C. C. *in Toletana,* die 2 Julii 1729—Richter, *Canones et Decreta Concilii Tridentini,* p. 117, n. 4; S. C. C. *in Romana Jurium Parochialium,* die 29 Aug. 1744; S. C. C. *in Andrien.,* die 20 Dec. 1766; S. C. C. *in Melevitana Nullitatis Matrimonii,* die 22 Junii 1839—Pallottini, *op. cit.,* XIV, 521, n. 48; 519, n. 31; XIII, 277-78, nn. 103-04. Cf. Bouix, *Tractatus de Parocho,* p. 429; Deneubourg, *Étude canonique sur les vicaires paroissiaux,* p. 163; Wernz, *Jus Decretalium,* II, n. 838, III; Scherer, *Handbuch des KR,* I, 644.

[103] C. 4, X, *de officio vicarii,* I, 28.

[104] Cf. Richter, *op. cit.,* p. 229, nn. 49, 50, 52, 54, 55; Pallottini, *op. cit.,* XIII, 269, nn. 72-76 and 279, nn. 112-14; *AkKR,* XXXIX (1878), 25. Zimmermann ("Die Stellung der Pfarrkapläne," *AkKR,* XLII [1879], 416) states that all assistant priests in France and Germany who had received general delegation for the conferring of all the sacraments which do not require the episcopal order for their administration were thereby empowered to assist at marriages, whilst in Belgium and at Rome the contrary practice was followed. Wernz (*Jus Decretalium,* III, n. 838, III), on the other hand, says that assistants in Belgium, Spain, Germany, and Austria, do not usually enjoy a general delegation for assistance at matrimony, but require a special delegation in individual cases. In Paris, only the first assistant enjoyed a general delegation. The words of these two authors clearly show how variable was the practice followed in different countries, as also in the same countries at different periods.

[105] Cf. S. C. C. *in Ceneten.,* die 19 Aprilis 1834—*Thesaurus Resolutionum,* Tom. XCIV (1834), 109-121; S. C. C. *in Theatina Matrimonii,* die 16 Martii 1771; S. C. C. *in Melevitana,* die 22 Junii 1839—Pallottini, *op. cit.,* XIII, 263, n. 31; 278-79, nn. 103-04.

Sacred Congregation of the Council. In its reply it recognized the marriage as valid.[106]

Yet, in a case of comparatively recent date (1898), the principle of common error in view of a mistaken general delegation to assist at marriages—hence, not with regard to a supplied jurisdiction properly so called—was certainly accredited a far lesser degree of elasticity, if not repudiated as inoperative altogether. This becomes obvious from the reply of the Congregation of the Holy Office to a case submitted by Archbishop Chapelle of New Orleans. Because of the profoundly practical question involved, both the letter of the Archbishop and the reply of the Holy Office may be reproduced in full.

Beatissime Pater:

> Hodiernus Episcopus N. N. [Archbishop Chapelle of New Orleans] ad matrimoniorum fidelium suae jurisdictionis validitatem procurandam, ut par est, intentus, et ad pedes S. V. provolutus, quae sequuntur humillime exponit.
>
> In ista dioecesi certe viget decretum "Tametsi" Concilii Tridentini de clandestinitate Cap. "Tametsi." Pluribus autem abhinc annis inter clerum sparsa est opinio quod valide matrimoniis fidelium quilibet sacerdos dioeceseos, sacrum ministerium exercens absque *speciali* Ordinarii aut parochi delegatione, assistere valeret, vi facultatis generalis ei concessae administrandi omnia sacramenta quae ordinem episcopalem non requirunt.
>
> Plurima ergo celebrata sunt, toto istius temporis spatio, matrimonia coram sacerdotibus, qui nec ab Ordinario, nec a partium parocho delegati erant ut dictis matrimoniis assisterent.
>
> Ex indubiis testimoniis apparet Praedecessorem meum dictae opinioni adhaesisse atque repetitis vicibus pluribus

---

[106] S. C. C. *in Caesaraugustana*, die 10 Martii 1770—Richter, *op. cit.*, p. 229, n. 51; Pallottini, *op. cit.*, XIII, 165-66, nn. 88-92; *Thesaurus Resolutionum*, XXXIX, (1770), 51-56. See also Kearney, *The Principles of Delegation*, pp. 126-27, for an excellent review of this case with its consequent application.

sacerdotibus privatim declarasse dictam opinionem tuto sequi posse.

Porro dictam plurium sacerdotum istius dioeceseos opinionem nullo probabili fundamento niti, erroneam esse et decreti Concilii Tridentini Cap. "Tametsi" subversivam infrascripto Archiepiscopo videtur. Persuasum habet Ordinarium non posse delegare omnes sacerdotes dioeceseos ut assistere valeant quibuscumque matrimoniis sponsorum, qui in variis parochiis domicilium habent aut quasidomicilium. Insuper, etiamsi ius illud illi competeret, compertum est illo conceptis verbis et ex officio nunquam usum fuisse Archiepiscopum praedecessorem.

Liceat ergo sequentia dubia proponere:

I. An facultate generali administrandi omnia sacramenta quae ordinem episcopalem non requirunt, includatur facultas assistendi omnibus matrimoniis fidelium dioeceseos?

II. Quatenus negative, quid faciendum sit in casu ad revalidanda multa matrimonia contracta absque praesentia parochi proprii aut sacerdotis legitime delegati?

Feria IV, die 7 Septembris, 1898.

Ad. I. Negative, nisi agatur de vice-parochis, qui ex consuetudine dioeceseos habitualiter delegati censeantur pro propria parochia.

Ad. II. Supplicandum SSmo pro sanatione in radice ad cautelam huiusmodi matrimoniorum usque ad diem publicationis praesentis decreti per Archiepiscopum.

Sequenti autem feria VI, die 9 eiusdem mensis Sept. in audientia a SS. D. N. Leone Div. Prov. Pp. XIII R. P. D. Adsessori impertita, SSmus D. N. resolutionem EE. ac RR. Patrum adprobavit.

I. Can. Mancini, S. R. et U. Inquis. Not.

The interpretation of this decree was given a very wide extension by the *American Ecclesiastical Review*.[107] It was wrongly assumed that the *vice-parochi* were by diocesan custom to be regarded as habitually delegated for the parishes in which they were assigned. The words of the Holy Office merely indicated that if there happen to be any assistants who are regarded as possessing universal delegation in the proper parish of their appointment, then *such* assistants may indeed validly assist without any further specified delegation. The use of the subjunctive (censeantur) clearly urges this explanation.

If the *Review* [108] states that "assistant priests may be considered as having an understood right to act as authorized witnesses of all marriages, unless the pastor reserves that right to himself in exceptional cases," this statement retains its application only under such circumstances where a local, diocesan custom exists for its proper sanction. The reply of the Holy Office did not certify the existence of the custom; it solely admitted its potenial force where it certainly does exist.[109]

It is not surprising, then, to find that a number of bishops would avail themselves of the occasion presented by the promulgation of the decree *Ne Temere* to issue rather definite instructions regarding the rights of assistants in the witnessing of marriages within the parishes to which they are assigned. An instance of this is found in the joint declaration of the bishops of the province of Cincinnati (the bishop of Louisville was the only absentee) on February 13, 1908. The text of their ruling reads as follows:

> To forestall any doubts or difficulties as to the validity of the marriage ceremony, We hereby declare that all assistant priests, administrators and substitutes, who shall be appointed by us in the future, shall be vested with the full and absolute power and authority to assist at the valid

---

[107] Cf. Vol. XX (1899), 281-82 and Vol. XXXVII (1907), 527. The above text of the letter and reply was printed by this periodical in the year 1899.

[108] XXXVII (1907), 527.

[109] For a fuller study of this question see McNicholas, *The New Marriage Legislation*, p. 31, and Cronin, *The New Matrimonial Legislation*, pp. 47-56; 72-74, 201-08.

> celebration of marriage within the limits of the parishes, missions, or stations to which they shall be assigned; and We grant this same power and authority to assistants, administrators and substitutes now having faculties in Our various dioceses. But while they are thus delegated by Us without any restriction in the valid use of this power, assistants shall be dependent on the authorization of their respective pastors for the lawful exercise thereof.[110]

As in this province, so it remained for the individual provinces and dioceses elsewhere to determine the rights of assistants in the matter of authorized witnessing of marriages.[111] But, in the absence of any such joint ruling, agreed upon by the bishops, even the pastors could extend a general delegation to their assistants for the territory of their parishes. Care was to be taken, however, that the limits of the delegated power be accurately defined.[112]

Lastly, assistants enjoyed no competence, equivalent with that of the pastor, for the *official* witnessing of the *sponsalia.* The ruling of the decree "*Ne Temere*" (De Sponsalibus, I) was the following: "*Ea tantum sponsalia habentur valida et canonicas sortiuntur effectus, quae contracta fuerint per scripturam subsignatam a partibus et vel a parocho, aut a loci Ordinario, vel sal-*

---

[110] The wording is that of a copy furnished the writer by his professor in Moral Theology at St. Meinrad's Seminary, Indiana.

[111] Cronin (*op. cit.*, p. 208, footnote 1) cites the ruling of the Bishop of Hexham and Newcastle from a circular dated January 29, 1908, in which the concluding paragraph states: "Hence, after receiving official notice of their appointment, and after they [the curates] have entered upon their appointment, they may validly assist at all marriages contracted within the area of the mission, although they may not do so lawfully without the permission of the rector." He adds that similar faculties have since been granted to coadjutors (the author's preferred term for assistant priests in his book, p. 48) by many other Bishops.

[112] McNicholas (*The New Marriage Legislation*, pp. 24-25) aptly remarks that parish priests as well as the bishops could delegate parish assistants as "*parochi in ordine ad matrimonium.*" His further suggestion that assistants be delegated "*ratione officii,*" rather than "*ratione personae,*" in the parishes to which they are actually assigned offers a secure method whereby the exact limits of their competence will be manifest. An exemplary printed formula is submitted. Finally, the form-book was preferably to be drawn up in a manner that allowed both the one delegating and the one delegated to preserve a copy of the act of delegation bestowed.

tem a duobus testibus." Nor were assistants eligible for receiving a delegated power in this regard.[113] The law of the Code in canon 1017 §1 has induced no change in this discipline. Its wording equivalently retained that of the decree *Ne Temere.*[114]

Before passing to the final consideration of this chapter concerning the assistant's removal a few observations are in order on his particular right to a proper sustenance and his specific duty of parochial residence.

§I. PROPER SUSTENANCE

In the section dealing with the nomenclature of parish assistants mention was made of the terms *socii, mercenarii* and *conductitii presbyteri* as being designative appellations used over a lengthy period of time.[115] These appellations connoted not only a ministerial subordination to the pastor, but a financial dependence upon him as well. The service of assistants was one of contract. In accordance with the changes of conditions and circumstances current with the lapse of time, there was a corresponding fluctuation in the terms of their salaries.

Not least among the determining factors which gauged the amount of their salaries was the law of clerical supply and demand. When their ministry was at a premium they sensed the freedom of stipulating their own terms; when their service was little needed they felt the necessity of accepting the pastor's terms. In a similar way, when their number was copious, the standards of salary drooped; when their personnel was scant,

[113] S. C. C. *Romana et aliarum,* die 28 Martii 1908: "Ad VI. Utrum sponsalia, praeterquam coram Ordinario aut parocho, celebrari valeant etiam coram ab alterutro delegato.

R. Negative."—*ASS,* XLI (1908), 288-89.

See also *ASS, loc. cit.,* and Cronin, *op. cit.,* pp. 76-78 for the reasons underlying this decision.

[114] Can. 1017, §1: "Matrimonii promissio sive unilateralis, sive bilateralis seu sponsalitia, irrita est pro utroque foro, nisi facta fuerit per scripturam subsignatam a partibus et vel a parocho aut loci Ordinario, vel a duobus saltem testibus." Cf. Cappello, *Tractatus Canonico-moralis de Sacramentis,* III, nn. 90f and 92 9°, pp. 101, 102; Chelodi, *Ius Matrimoniale,* n. 17, p. 15; Wernz-Vidal, *Ius Canonicum,* V, n. 89, p. 108; De Smet, *De Sponsalibus et Matrimonio,* n. 10, p. 10, footnote 7; Knecht, *Handbuch des katholischen Eherechts,* p. 140.

[115] Cf. footnotes 18 and 33 of this chapter.

their pledge of assets revived. The soil to which these conditions were indigenous not infrequently produced a rank harvest of abuses. Parsimonious pastors and avaricious assistants furnish their telling commentary for that age.[116]

It was generally the parish priest who was held accountable in person for the payment of his assistant's salary. In some places, however, foundations and endowments existed for reimbursing the added ministries required at the churches. In still other regions collections accommodated this purpose. Each locality knew best how to adapt the obligation of support. Each parish could appropriate that means which secured the hope of a suitable pastoration of the existing spiritual needs.[117]

The council of Trent did not reduce these various methods in supplying the curate with a suitable income to any set norm or fixed standard. It did, however, reiterate and vindicate his claim to a congruous support,[118] and establish a sanction for its bestowal.[119] The bishops were for this reason empowered to act *"etiam tamquam apostolicae Sedis delegati."* [120]

Whatever general legislation one meets thenceforth is but a restatement of the Tridentine decrees.[121] In his Constitution *"Auctorem Fidei"* of August 28, 1794, Pope Pius VI upheld the Scriptural principle that he who serves the altar should also

---

[116] Cf. Lindner, *Die Anstellung der Hilfspriester*, p. 49.

[117] ". . . und soll drittail opfer allzeit ir sein. . . ." Or again: "Ittem der pfarrer ist schuldig ainem unterherrn alle tag drei drink wein und sein pfrient und zu der marend (Nachmittags-brot) ain kaes und prot und ain drunk wein ungever."—Lindner, *op. cit.*, p. 51, footnotes 1 and 2. Or still again:

Every man hys teythynge shall paye
  Both of smale and of grete
Of schep and swyne and other nete (horned cattle)
  Teythe of huyre and of hande (wages and handiwork)
Gotte by costome of the lande.—Davis, *Mediæval England*, p. 422.

[118] Sessio XXI, *de ref.*, c. 4: ". . . competens assignatur portio, arbitrio episcopi, ex fructibus ad ecclesiam matricem quomodocumque pertinentibus . . ."—*Canones et Decreta*, p. 128.

[119] Sessio XXI, *de ref.*, c. 4: ". . . si necesse fuerit, compellere possit populum ea subministrare, quae sufficiant ad vitam dictorum sacerdotum sustentandam; quacumque reservatione . . . vel affectione . . . non obstantibus." Or again, Sessio XXV, *de ref.*, c. 12: "Qui vero eas [decimas] aut subtrahunt aut impediunt, excommunicentur."—*Op. cit.*, pp. 128, 237.

[120] Sessio XXI, *de ref.*, c. 4—*op. cit.*, p. 127. Cf. Kearney, *The Principles of Delegation*, pp. 39-40, for an indication of the divided opinion among canonists as to the meaning of this phrase.

[121] Cf. footnote 93 of this chapter.

partake of the altar,[122] when he condemned the 54th proposition of the Synod of Pistoia which asserted that it was a shameful abuse for the ministers of the Church to receive a temporal recompense from those to whom they had ministered spiritual values.[123] The Sacred Congregation of the Council,[124] the Congregation for Bishops and Regulars,[125] and the Roman Rota [126] offer striking cases, the solution of which reveal the Church's keen and abiding sense of justice and equity in protecting and guaranteeing the assistant's right and claim to an honorable livelihood in recompense for his parochial labors.

In the present codification of her law the Church voices her command very tersely in the following words of canon 476, §1: " . . . *quibus congrua remuneratio assignetur.*" The authority, both for the enactment and the enforcement of this law rests, of course, with the ordinary of the diocese.[127]

§II. Residence

Reiffenstuel [128] formulates a classic definition of the canonical term of *residence* in the following words: "*Residere nihil aliud est quam Ecclesiae personaliter deservire in Divinis officiis.*" He makes the two concepts—formal residence and actual service—

---

122 Deuteronomy, XVIII, 1 and XXV, 4; Matthew, X, 10; Luke, X, 7; Romans, XV, 27; I Corinthians, IX, 1-15; I Timothy, V, 18; I Peter, V, 2-4.

123 Cf. *Fontes*, II, n. 475, p. 702; Denzinger—Bannwart, *Enchiridion Symbolorum et Definitionum*, n. 1554.

124 S. C. C. *in Ferentina Coadjutoriae*, die 29 Feb. 1744; S. C. C. *in Romana seu Portuen. Capellaniae*, die 16 Jan. 1768; S. C. C. *in Capenctoraten.*, die 15 Sept. 1781—Pallottini, *Collectio omnium Conclusionum et Resolutionum*, XIV, p. 517, n. 23; p. 514, n. 10; VI, p. 189, n. 41: S. C. C. *in Parisien. Emolumentorum*, die 9 Sept. 1848; S. C. C. *in Reatina Capellani Curati*, die 16 Dec. 1854 and die 22 Dec. 1855—Lingen-Reuss, *Causae Selectae in S. Cong. Cardinalium Conc. Trident. Interpretum Propositae*, n. 475, pp. 803-06; n. 498, pp. 848-51: S. C. C. *in Brixien. Congruae Parochialis*, die 22 Aug. 1874; S. C. C. *in Brixien Jurium Parochialium*, die 24 Julii 1875—*Thesaurus Resolutionum*, CXXXIII (1874), 498-505; CXXXIV (1875), 571-84.

125 *In Romana Pensionis*, die 22 Aug. 1890—*ASS*, XXIII (1890-91), 345-49.

126 Die 1 Augusti 1911—*Sacrae Romanae Rotae Decisiones*, III, n. 37, pp. 413-21.

127 Cf. cans. 1427 §3, 1429 §2, 2222 §1.

128 *Jus Canonicum Universum*, lib. III, tit. 4, n. 108.

terms of mutual complement. Residence is the *sine qua non* which must be present before anyone engaged in the care of souls in a parish can satisfy his duty of pastoral service, and conversely, pastoral service is but the sublimation of a residence conscientiously observed.

The common law before the council of Trent said little, perhaps nothing, about the duty of residence for *assistants*. It concerned itself with this duty as applicable to pastors, perpetual vicars, substitutes, and subsidiary vicars or coadjutors, which latter class comprised such priests as were appointed to lend their aid to a parish priest whose mental or physical debility prevented him from personally fulfilling all his pastoral duties.[129]

The council of Trent also formulated its laws on the duty of residence for the titular incumbents of parishes without devoting any express mention to assistants.[130]

Even later authors do little more than approach this question.[131]

It may be stated that even the provincial councils and diocesan synods up to the beginning of the last century did not much concern themselves with it. Probably the analogy of the law, as expressed for perpetual vicars and parochial coadjutors, was thought to possess the requisite sanction for vindicating the duty of residence on the part of parochial assistants. A case decided by the Sacred Congregation of the Council (July 13, 1741, ad I), which is at times adduced in confirmation of the contrary claim, does not directly touch the question of residence as obligatory on *assistants*. The priest mentioned in the case held a residential chaplaincy besides being engaged in parochial work as an assistant vicar. The duty of residence imposed

[129] In the Decretals of Gregory IX (*De officio vicarii*, I, 28; *de officio et potestate judicis delegati*, I, 29; *de clericis non residentibus in Ecclesia vel praebenda*, III, 4; *de praebendis et dignitatibus*, III, 5; *de clerico aegrotante vel debilitato*, III, 6; *de parochiis et alienis parochianis*, III, 29; *de capellis Monachorum*, III, 37) as also in the corresponding passages and titles of the additions of Boniface VIII, Clement V, and John XXII, there seems to reign a complete silence concerning the duty of residence incumbent upon assistant priests in the canonical sense of that term.

[130] Cf. Sessio VI, *de ref.*, c. 2; sessio XXIII, *de ref.*, c. 1—*Canones et Decreta*, p. 37; pp. 153-56.

[131] Cf. Barbosa, *De Officio et Potestate Episcopi*, P. III, Alleg. 63, n. 9; *Juris Ecclesiastici Universi Libri Tres*, lib. III, c. 10, n. 31; Reiffenstuel, *Jus Canonicum Universum*, lib. III, tit. 4, n. 36.

upon him by the Congregation drew its sanction not from any condition involved in his assistancy but from the status inherent in his residential benefice.[132]

It remained for the councils of the middle of the last century more definitely and specifically to enunciate the law of residence as obligatory for parish assistants.[133] Practically all the more recent synods and councils held prior to the promulgation of the Code have followed their lead. Typical as an example is the following excerpt: *"In dioecesibus nostris cum parocho habitant vicarii: sit igitur inter ipsos cor unum et anima una. Quae de parochorum residentia dicta sunt etiam de vicariis intelligenda volumus. Caveant, ergo, ne ex absentia, quantumvis brevi, ullum damnum patiantur fideles, et sui officii esse ducant ut urgente animarum cura, facile possint inveniri."*[134]

The Code does not change the discipline of the past. Parish assistants are bound to observe the law of residence in the measure in which the diocesan statutes, the laudable customs of the diocese, or the prescription of their bishop imposes it upon them.[135]

The ideal of community life has been traditionally encouraged throughout the ages of the Church,[136] yet, there never was enacted a general law to establish it as an obligation.[137] In the

---

[132] Cf. Richter, *Canones et Decreta Concilii Tridentini*, p. 37, n. 7.

[133] E.g., conc. provinciae Turonensis (1849); conc. provinciae Aquensis (1850); conc. prov. Quebecense II (1854); conc. prov. Coloniensis (1860); conc. provinciae Pragensis (1860); conc. provinciae Ultrajectensis (1865)—*Coll. Lac.*, IV, 270; IV, 985; III, 657; V, 342; V, 558; V, 796-97.. The same disciplinary legislation is implicitly contained in the II Plenary Council of Baltimore (1866), *Acta et Decreta*, nn. 111-114.

[134] Conc. Plen. Quebecense I (1909), *Acta et Decreta*, cap. 7, n. 136. See also Smith, *Elements of Ecclesiastical Law*, I, n. 665, p. 467.

[135] Can. 476 §5.

[136] Cf. c. 34, D. 5, *de Consecratione*; c. 9, X, *de vita et honestate clericorum*, III, 1; S. C. de Prop. Fide instr. (*ad Vic. Apost. Sin.*), die 18 Oct. 1883—*Collectanea*, II, n. 1606, ad V, 2; Hautcoeur, "De L'Institut des Clercs Seculiers vivant en communaute," *Revue des Sciences Ecclésiastiques*, VI (1862), 295-302; Hautcoeur, "Essai sur la vie commune au sein du Clergé," *RSE*, VI (1862), 401-25; VII (1863), 140-65; see also *NRT*, XIII (1881), 330-31.

[137] Cf. S. C. C. die 5 Maii et 24 Nov. 1742—*Thesaurus Resolutionum*, X (1742), 66-67, 139. This case, on account of the unusual attendant circumstances, furnishes an instance in which the Congregation insisted on a community of life between the *Coadiutus* and the *Coadjutor* in the same rectory.

mind of the Church community life, whenever practicable, offers noble advantages to the parochial clergy. For this reason she bids the bishops to maintain it wherever it is established and prudently to seek its introduction by their encouragement.[138] To promote its appeal and to quicken the force of its native attraction by the formation of a voluntary priestly association which tends, in as far as is feasible, to approximate its ideal in the lives of its members is a work which certainly will always invite the Church's ready commendation.[139] But to effect its realization by an act of direct legislation must with equal certainty ever remain a measure to which the Church cannot lend her countenance as long as such an act engenders the risk of infringing upon the sacred claims of human liberty.

ART. IV. REMOVAL

Since the right of removing an assistant vicar from his station at the parish church was correlated with and consequent upon the right of his appointment, it follows that a knowledge of the history of the one implies an almost equal acquaintance with the discipline of the other. There are two considerations, however, that bear particular mention: 1) Could the parish priest, arbitrarily and at will, without the existence of reason or cause, dismiss a curate from his service? 2) Could the bishop remove or transfer a curate against the wish of the pastor?

In answer to the first of these queries one must recognize a necessary distinction. If the curate was assigned by the bishop, then the bishop alone possessed the right of removing or transferring him.[140] If appointed by the parish priest, authors were not agreed whether the pastor who enjoyed the right of removing him for a just cause, could also exercise this right without the bishop's approval or consent and with no other cause than that of his arbitrary desire to do so. Berardi [141] defended their

[138] Cf. can. 134.

[139] Cf. "A Roman Institute," *AER*, LXIII (1920), 399-401; "Will you join the Apostolate," *AER*, LXXI (1924), 513-17.

[140] Cf. S. R. Rota *in Bonaëren. Remotionis*, die 5 Aprilis 1916—*AAS*, IX (1917), 85-93.

[141] *De Parocho Compendium*, n. 884, III.

right; Bouix, after quoting many authors and reproducing many decisions of the Sacred Congregation which furnish apparent reason for inclining to either opinion,[142] reserved his final judgment; Hinschius assailed their right. Since the pastor could not assume his assistant without the intervention of the bishop's approval, so also he could not dismiss him without a reason that would merit episcopal sanction.[143]

In answer to the second question it must be acknowledged that the bishop enjoyed the full right of removing or transferring an assistant—it mattered not by whom the latter was appointed—when the action was motivated by a just and reasonable cause.[144] Without such cause, however, the bishop's action of removal or transfer could be justified, at most, only when he had himself made the appointment.[145] If the pastor had assumed his own curate, the bishop's removal of him without cause became unlawful. Whilst the action of the bishop might be upheld as valid,[146] yet the cases in which it was not sustained are frequent.[147] If such a willful act of removal by the bishop was not explicitly invalidated by the letter of the law, nevertheless every sense of fairness and equity brooked its execution. It is not to be assumed that the law could countenance an extravagant procedure which would have attenuated the pastor's right to the condition of a mere delusion. The exercise of any right that permits of arbitrary contravention cannot but lapse from the status of its independence to become, in the

---

142 *Tractatus de Parocho*, pp. 636-41.

143 *System des kath. KR*, II, 321. Cf. Lindner, *Die Anstellung der Hilfspriester*, p. 70, for the opinions of additional authors.

144 See the decisions of the Congregation of the Council adduced by Richter (*Canones et Decreta Concilii Tridentini*, pp. 53-54).

145 Cf. S. C. C. *in Montis Alti Remotionis Capellani et Jurium Parochialium*, die 22 Maii 1762: ". . . Ceterum ad effectum removendi Capellanum Curatum amovibilem quaelibet sufficit levis causa, dummodo seiuncta sit ab odio et dedecore Capellani."—Pallottini, *Collectio omnium Conclusionum et Resolutionum*, VI, p. 213, n. 147.

146 Cf. Santi, *Praelectiones Juris Canonici*, lib. I, tit. 28, nn. 12-13; Wernz, *Jus Decretalium*, II, n. 838, V.

147 Cf. S. C. C. *in Spoletana Capellaniarum*, die 14 Martii 1744—Pallottini, *op. cit.*, III, p. 453, n. 106; S. C. C. *in Mediolanen.* die 16 Feb. 1867—*ASS*, III (1867-68), 449-57. See also *ASS*, III (1867-68), 506-12 for a thorough discussion of the question of *amovibilitas* and the principles of action thereby implied.

course of time, a bare concession, dependent for its operation on the unrestricted will of him who grants it.

The practical concern which these questions once offered has now become a matter of academic interest only. The Code no longer bespeaks any *direct* and *immediate* right for pastors, either in the appointment or in the removal of their assistants. The administration of their appointment, their transfer and their removal has become the exclusive right of their respective ordinaries.[148]

[148] Cans. 476 §§1, 3, 4; 477 §1; 454 §5.

CHAPTER IV

PAROCHIAL ADJUTANT VICARS FROM THE TIME OF THEIR ORIGIN TO MODERN TIMES

ART. I. LEGISLATION CONCERNING COADJUTOR BISHOPS AND *Chorepiscopi*

Similarly as the gradual formation of ecclesiastical discipline regarding assistant vicars in parochial ministrations had grown out of the legal usages current in the time when all the parishes were still administered under the direct and personal superintendence of the bishop, so also the early legislation of the Church regarding parochial adjutant vicars for permanently disabled rectors of parishes drew its origin and further development from the law regulating the appointment and subsequent status of coadjutor bishops. The fundamental principal which has always—from the very beginning—actuated the legal practice of the Church with regard to parochial legislation must be sought in her unalterable persuasion that the welfare of souls transcends all other claims.[1]

As a consequence it is to be expected that, regardless of her deeply cherished statutory enactments on relative ordination [2] which were still honored in the eleventh and twelfth centuries, the Church would adopt a practice whereby the pastoration of souls could be efficaciously consulted whenever her pastoral incumbents, the bishops, had become superannuated or incapacitated in the efficient discharge of their divine commission. There was no clash between her fixed principle of stability of appointment and her tender solicitude for an efficacious pastoration of the churches. Advanced years or infirmity of health

---

[1] S. C. Consist. decretum *"Maxima Cura,"* die 20 Aug. 1910—*AAS*, II (1910), 636 ss.

[2] Cf. footnote 34 of Chapter II.

offered no cause for the removal of a bishop thus afflicted.[3] He could continue in office with his episcopal title, rights and claims intact. The coadjutor bishop associated with him in the ministry was to receive his ultimate confirmation in office through an act of approval from the Metropolitan of the province or from the supervening provincial synod.[4] A prominent example is furnished in the person of St. Alexander, who was selected by the aged Narcissus, bishop of Jerusalem, to become his coadjutor upon the ratification of the remaining bishops of the province.[5]

Despite the intervening disciplinary legislation of the I Council of Nice (325), which proscribed the functioning of more than one bishop as the head of a diocese,[6] the contrary established custom of assuming an episcopal coadjutor to rule together with the aged or infirm bishop was not yet completely suppressed throughout the Christian world even at the end of the fourth century. This is obvious from an account furnished by St. Augustine regarding his own appointment as coadjutor to rule with Bishop Valerius over the diocese of Hippo-Regius.[7]

According to Gottlob [8] the employment of *chorepiscopi* in the Western Church during the early Middle Ages answered the purpose of coadjutor and substitute bishops.[9] The best known example is borrowed from the life of St. Boniface, the Metropolitan of Mainz. Willibald, Eoban and Lullus were

---

[3] Cf. cc. 1, 2, 3, 14, C. VII, q. 1, and c. 1, X, *de clerico aegrotante vel debilitato*, III, 6. In this citation of the Decretals Pope Saint Gregory the Great formulates the traditions which had attained the force of common law.

[4] Cf. Walter, *Lehrbuch des Kirchenrechts*, p. 278.

[5] Cf. Eusebius, *Historia Ecclesiastica*, lib. VI, cap. 9 ss.—*MPG*, XX, 541 ss.; Thomassinus, *Vetus et Nova Ecclesiae Disciplina*, P. II, lib. II, cap. 55, n. 10; Benedictus XIV, *De Synodo Dioecesana*, lib. XIII, cap. 10, n. 22; Shahan, "Alexander," *Cath. Ency.*, I, 285; Campbell, "St. Alexander," *ibid.*, I, 295.

[6] C. 8—Mansi, II, 671; Hardouin, I, 326.

[7] *Epistola 213*—*MPL*, XXXIII, 966 ss. See also c. 12, C. VII, q. 1; c. 14, X, *de officio judicis ordinarii*, I, 31; Hinschius, *System des kath. KR*, II, 39, footnotes 6 and 9.

[8] *Der abendländische Chorepiskopat*, p. 4, footnotes 1-6.

[9] Poeschl (*AkKR*, XCVII [1917], 195 ss.) thinks it is very doubtful that the office of *chorepiscopi* postulated episcopal consecration. Even at the present this question seems still to be involved in such a condition of uncertainty that the unqualified acceptance of Gottlob's opinion to the utter exclusion of that defended by Poeschl is hardly warranted.

successively appointed in the capacity of *chorepiscopi* to serve in this Metropolitan See.[10]

Almost as soon as the practice became general for bishops to avail themselves of the services of coadjutor and substitute *chorepiscopi*, abuses also appeared. As early as the year 845 a council in France upbraided the bishops for being too lavish and reckless in their grants of authorization to their *chorepiscopi*.[11] In 888 the conciliar action of Metz [12] struck a telling blow to the institution of the *chorepiscopi* throughout the western part of the Frankish Kingdom. Even the eastern part of the Kingdom no longer offered any evidence of its existence in the eleventh century.[13]

In England the office of the *chorepiscopi* continued at least for a century longer up to the time of the Norman Conquest.[14] In Ireland the last mention of them occurs in a synod celebrated by a certain Bishop Simon in 1216. The five districts formerly assigned to *chorepiscopi* were thenceforth to be designated as rural deaneries with archpriests at their head.[15]

A study of the history from which these instances are adduced, together with a consultation of C. VII, q. 1, of the *Decretum Gratiani*, proves conclusively that the Church's legislation with regard to coadjutor bishops and *chorepiscopi* was a discipline which allowed of a rather flexible interpretation in the course of the centuries.[16] Since intercommunication between the various provinces remained laborious, it followed that each province would readily elaborate its own ecclesiastical traditions and usages, and as a result cling tenaciously to them. By necessary consequence the variant circumstances thus created could best be given their proper disciplinary attention by local authority of the Metropolitan and his suffragans convened in provincial assemblies or councils. This course of action dic-

---

[10] Cf. *MGH, Epistolae*, Tom. III: *Epistolae Merowingici et Karolini Aevi*, 304, 357; c. 17, C. VIII, q. 1; Gottlob, *op. cit.*, pp. 24-25; pp. 84-87.

[11] Conc. Meldense (845), c. 44—Hardouin, IV, 1491.

[12] C. 8—Mansi, XVIII, 80.

[13] Cf. Gottlob, *op. cit.*, pp. 143-45.

[14] *MPL*, CL, 53 ss.

[15] Cf. Wilkins, I, 547.

[16] Quaestio 1 of Causa VII consists of 49 chapters or canons. It is especially the earlier chapters that bear reference to the present topic.

tated legislation for conditions that could not have been anticipated by the earlier general councils of the Church. Different provinces presented diverse conditions, and diverse conditions called for a varied form of legislation.

Furthermore, the papal letters and decrees that one finds recounted in the collection made by Gratian very frequently embody legislation for restricted territories only. They indicated the canonical norm of procedure for the particular Metropolitan to whom they were addressed, without implying the force of a universal obligation. If, then, this was the case with regard to so important a discipline as the appointment of coadjutor bishops for the efficient government and pastoration of *dioceses,* there is less reason to expect that the Church should have formulated a unified discipline for the similar needs of *parishes.* There can be no doubt that diocesan and provincial legislation for pastoral provision in parishes borrowed its norm from the laws that provided the same care in a larger measure for the dioceses.

ART. II. PAROCHIAL ADJUTANTS BEFORE THE CARLOVINGIAN REIGN

In an earlier part of this treatise [17] attention has been drawn to the practice that became current from the time that parishes began to exist separately from the bishop's cathedral. In many instances parish priests had about them a school of clerics in preparation for holy orders. Thus, in Spain we find mention of deacons at the parish churches as early as the beginning of the fourth century,[18] and in France we find all the minor and major orders of clerics represented at Laon in the sixth century.[19]

In fact, it became the universal practice for parish churches to receive aspirants to the priesthood and to offer them training for the ultimate reception of holy orders similarly as the Cathedral Church had done in the earlier centuries and still continued

[17] Cf. Chapter I, Article III, §II, under the caption "Parish Organization in the Western Churches."

[18] Cf. conc. Eliberitanum, c. 77—Mansi, II, 18; Hardouin, I, 258.

[19] Cf. Lindner, *Die Anstellung der Hilfspriester,* p. 7, footnote 1.

to do. This was the method in vogue during the early ages—and remained such until the time of the council of Trent—for the education and preparation of clerics in order to replete the diocésan ranks of the priesthood.

It is very likely that an effort was made by the parish priest to keep one or two deacons in readiness for ordination. This precaution was taken against the case in which sudden sickness or any other inability might incapacitate the parochial pastor. When the VII council of Toledo (646) ruled that, whenever mass suffered interruption, it was to be consummated by another priest in order that the sacrificial offering might be completed, it must have taken for granted the stationing of more than one priest at the various parish churches where mass was regularly celebrated.[20] A later instruction in the same ecclesiastical province is still more explicit.[21] The bishops assembled in council thought it necessary to ordain that, wherever possible, every priest offering sacrifice to God should have at his side a sacerdotal aid who could supply his stead in the event of a sudden swoon or other disturbance of health.[22]

One can trace no further *direct* legislation on this question during the immediately succeeding century. A change of conditions, however, was ushered in with regard to parish life during the close of the Merovingian and the beginning of the Carlovingian reigns which demands a little closer consideration.

Art. III. Parochial Adjutants During and After the Carlovingian Reign

It was in the beginning of this period that the "grand parishes" of the time were almost universally subjected to dis-

[20] Canon 2 of this council is reproduced by Gratian in c. 16, C. VII, q. 1. See also Mansi, X, 767; Hefele, *Conciliengeschichte*, III, 95.

[21] Cf. conc. Toletanum XI (675), c. 14—Mansi, XI, 145.

[22] ". . . cavendum ne . . . unicuique divinis officiis singulariter insistenti perniciosa passio vel quaelibet corporis valetudo occurrat, quae aut corpus subito obrui faciat, aut mentem alienatione vel terrore confundat. Pro huiusmodi ergo casibus necessarium duximus instituere ut ubi temporis, vel loci, sive cleri copia suffragatur, habeat semper quisquis ille canens Deo et sacrificans post se vicini solaminis adjutorem: ut si aliquo casu ille qui officia impleturus accedit, turbatus fuerit, vel ad terram elisus, a tergo semper habeat qui eius vicem exequatur intrepidus."—Cf. c. 15, C. VII, q. 1; Mansi, XI, 145; Hardouin, III, 1029.

memberment.[23] The oratories, chapels, and smaller churches, which had for so many years served the convenience of the nobility, were erected into parish churches for the added accommodation of the other faithful who lived near them. The general effect was that the original parishes were greatly reduced in their membership and no longer required a larger measure of service than an individual priest could offer them. His former assistants and helpers were stationed at the newly created parishes. The very multiplication of the parish churches made possible the enlistment of help from a neighboring parish in case of sudden or even prolonged need. At any rate, if the pastor's sickness became a permanent malady, then there remained always the alternative of having one of the clerics in major orders, who was in training at his own church or some other parish in the diocese, ordained by the bishop for consulting the need when it arose.

During the ninth, tenth, eleventh, and partly the twelfth centuries a harvest of abuses sprang up which called upon the Church's strictest vigilance for their eradication and ultimate suppression. The free and absolute ordination of clerics without the possession of title or benefice,[24] its obvious corrollary of clerical vagrancy,[25] the concomitant practice of simony,[26] the unwarranted division and multiplication of parishes on the one hand,[27] along with the practice of a plurality of rectors claiming title of the same churches on the other hand,[28] the non-resi-

[23] Cf. Lindner, *Die Anstellung der Hilfspriester*, p. 18.

[24] Cf. capitulare Aquisgranense (789), c. 25; synodus Francofordensis (794), c. 28; conc. Meldense (845), c. 52—Hardouin, IV, 833; 907; 1492.

[25] Cf. synod. Francofordensis (794), c. 7; synod. Arelatensis (813), c. 24; capitulare Ludovici Regis (828); synod. Parisiensis (829), c. 13—Hardouin, IV, 905; 1006; 1177 ss.; 1356.

[26] Cf. capitula Radulfi Archiepiscopi Bituricensis (849), c. 17; conc. Ticense (850), c. 29; synod. Moguntiaca I (847), c. 12; synod. Moguntiaca II (852), c. 19; iterum anno 888, c. 5—Mansi, XIV, 951-52; Hardouin, V, 25 ss.; V, 10; Mansi, XIV, 971; XVIII, 66.

[27] Cf. conc. Tolosanum (843-44), c. 7; conc. Meldense (845), c. 54; conc. Nannetense (saeculo nono), c. 8—Hardouin, IV, 1459-60; IV, 1492; Mansi, XVIII, 166. See also Lindner, *Die Anstellung der Hilfspriester*, p. 21; Thomassinus, *Vetus et Nova Ecclesiae Disciplina*, P. I, lib. II, cap. 25, nn. 9-10.

[28] Cf. conc. Aquisgranense II (836), c. 16; conc. Troslejanum (909), c. 6—Mansi, XIV, 683-84; Hardouin, VIa, 520.

dence of priests who were the canonically appointed pastors [29] and, finally, their delay in receiving the order of priesthood following their appointment [30]—all these were abuses of a rather significant nature. But the strong reform movement initiated by Pope St. Gregory VII and vigorously continued by his successors in the Papacy, especially Paschal II, Alexander III, and Celestine III, prepared the way for the glorious reign of Innocent III in which the life of the Church manifested a renewed power of spiritual influence upon the hearts of the faithful, lay and cleric alike.

When the clerical calling had once more been raised to an estate of admirable repute, the thought could again be entertained of enforcing proper provision for the honor and the sustenance due the disabled and infirm pastors in accord with the discipline insinuated by Pope St. Gregory I to Bishop Candidus.[31]

Just as the eighth century had furnished an intense and widespread activity on the part of the Monks in their missionary labors throughout the Frankish Kingdom, so the thirteenth century exhibited a similar spiritual power to the world in the personnel of the Friars Minor and Preachers whose popularity with the Christian people achieved unparalleled dimensions. Many of the churches and parishes were consequently committed to their care through incorporation with their monasteries

---

[29] Cf. Lindner, *op. cit.*, p. 28, where a number of examples are adduced in the footnotes.

[30] Cf. synod. Rhemensis (1131), c. 9; (1148), c. 10; (1157), c. 5—Mansi, XXI, 460; 716; 844.

[31] Cf. c. 2, C. VII, q. 1 and c. 1, X, *de clerico aegrotante vel debilitato*, III, 6. It is from this papal letter that the axiom "*afflictio afflictis non est addenda*" took its origin. The infirm priest or cleric was to receive the entire income of his benefice. His sickness or debility was not to curtail his continued enjoyment of the material benefits accruing to his office, for, it was beyond the right of man, in his utter lack of a certain knowledge, to judge whether the affliction visited upon the sufferer was one of honor or dishonor, of divine purgation or of divine punishment. Not only should the sufferer be spared the further affliction that man could add, but his office and his station were to be maintained in material honor and integrity, lest others be deterred from bearing the spiritual yoke of Christ for the glory of the Church.

and convents.[32] The rapid growth of the new religious orders and the unbounded trust and esteem the Christian people reposed in them accounted for their almost exclusive acquisition of the care of parish churches in many of the dioceses. This fact is very patently instanced in the words of a French provincial council of that time.[33]

But the blessing of the multiplied number of priests in the monastic orders did not continue without the development of a concomitant abuse. In this same ecclesiastical gathering the bishops saw the need of insisting by statute that *permanent* vicars be appointed at the churches incorporated with their monasteries in place of the temporary ones who had frequently been set over them for mercenary reasons. An exception to this ruling was allowed only when there was a laudable reason to vindicate a derogation from the general law.[34]

This cancerous growth of the abuse of appointing temporary vicars to the incorporated churches, both by the diocesan chapters and by the monasteries, called for strong legislation as late as the council of Constance.[35] In the meantime, while the correction of this departure from the canonical traditions of the Church was undertaken by means of repeated diocesan statutes, conciliar decrees and even papal decretals,[36] there was effected

[32] Cf. Poeschl, "Die Inkorporation und ihre geschichtliche Grundlagen," *AkKR*, CVII (1927), pp. 44-177, 497-560; CVIII (1928), pp. 24-86, for an extended historical treatment of this question. See also Hüfner, "Das Rechtsinstitut der klösterlichen Exemption in der abendländischen Kirche," *AkKR*, LXXXVI (1906), 320 ff.; 629 ff.; LXXXVII (1907), 71 ff.; 270 ff.; 462 ff.; 599 ff.

[33] Conc. Prov. Arelatense (1260), c. 1: ". . . Quia major pars Ecclesiarum Parochialium huius Provinciae ad Monachorum vel Conventuum Regularium pertinet Prioratus, de quorum collegiis aliqui censuerant in ipsis Ecclesiis continue residere, et de ipsis rationem reddere Praelatis; . . ."—Hardouin, VII, 512.

[34] *Ibid.*, c. 5: "Nec ultra Mercenariis, nisi bonis et expertis et hoc ad tempus, et ex causa dominicarum ovium, regimina committantur, quia iis gregem committi Dominicum, evangelica veritas summi pastoris ore promulgata graviter detestatur." Cf. also Conc. Germanicum (1225), c. 12—Hardouin, VII, 140, which urges the same discipline.

[35] Sessio XLIII, c. 2—Hardouin, VIII, 874.

[36] C. 1, *de capellis Monachorum*, III, 18, in VI°; and the earlier decretal of Innocent II in c. 30, X, *de praebendis et dignitatibus*, III, 5. Cf. also Bouix, *Tractatus de Parocho*, pp. 201-04; Thomassinus, *Vetus et Nova Ecclesiae Disciplina*, P. I, lib. II, cap. 27, nn. 4-6.

very little development of law with regard to the canonical discipline of appointing adjutant priests to disabled rectors of parishes. The alternative of dismissing the disabled rector who had merely temporary appointment and of designating another temporary vicar for his vacated office seemed an easy option to follow.

A council in England in the early part of the thirteenth century ordained that in all territorially extended parishes there should be two or three priests lest, in the event of prolonged sickness on the part of one or the other of them, their parishioners be denied the opportunity of attendance at the divine services and the reception of the sacraments.[37] Since no regulation was made for the parishes with restricted territorial limits, it may be assumed that the bishops considered their proximity to other parishes as sufficient guaranty of the possibility of providing seasonable relief whenever a need arose for the faithful. A similar provision was in the minds of the bishops who were gathered in the council of Poitiers in the year 1280.[38]

It was only after the Church had eventually eradicated the long-continued and malignant practice of appointing temporary vicars in the pastoration of the churches that her discipline ordained in the decretals by Popes Lucius III, Clement III, and Honorius III,[39] could tend towards efficient execution.

ART. IV. PAROCHIAL ADJUTANTS SINCE THE TIME OF THE COUNCIL OF TRENT

It remained for the council of Trent to renew, extend and amplify the canonical provisions that were to be observed by the bishops when consulting the welfare of the parochial flocks whose spiritual shepherds had succumbed to a state of permanent disability or incapacity in the discharge of their pastoral

[37] Conc. Oxoniense (1222), c. 16: ". . . pro essentialiter diffinimus, ut in singulis parochialibus ecclesiis, quarum parochia est diffusa, duo sint vel tres presbyteri, . . . ne forte, quod absit, aegrotante uno presbytero, aut altero debilitato, parochianis infirmantibus, aut divinis volentibus interesse officiis, officia debita subtrahantur, vel negentur sacramenta ecclesiastica."—Hardouin, VII, 119.

[38] Cf. c. 3—Hardouin, VII, 850.

[39] Cc. 3, 4, 6, X, *de clerico aegrotante vel debilitato*, III, 6.

functions. Because of the succinct wording of the Council in its legislation on this point, the entire chapter may be profitably reproduced here:

> Quia illiterati, et imperiti parochialium ecclesiarum rectores sacris minus apti sunt officiis, et alii propter eorum vitae turpitudinem potius destruunt, quam aedificant; episcopi, etiam tamquam apostolicae Sedis delegati, eisdem illiteratis, et imperitis, si alias honestae vitae sint, coadjutores, aut vicarios pro tempore deputare, partemque fructuum eisdem pro sufficienti victu assignare, vel aliter providere possint, quacumque appellatione, et exemptione remota. Eos vero, qui turpiter, et scandalose vivunt, postquam praemoniti fuerint, coerceant, ac castigent; et, si adhuc incorrigibiles in sua nequitia perseverent, eos beneficiis, juxta sacrorum canonum constitutiones, exemptione, et appellatione quacumque remota, privandi facultatem habeant.[40]

This chapter was practically an adaptation and an extension of the 16 canons contained in the 38th Distinction of the Gratian Collection. Of special note are cc. 5 and 9 of this Distinction which reproduced the words of Sts. Augustine and Jerome on the necessity and extent of knowledge required in priests. But it will also be noted that this chapter makes no direct mention of the needs arising in a parish when its rector became disabled because of a permanent ailment of body or mind. These cases, however, were consulted in accord with the legislation already in force from an earlier date as expressed in the decretals under the title "*de clerico aegrotante vel debilitato,*"[41] and the regulations made by Alexander III, Innocent III, and Gregory X.[42]

---

[40] Sessio XXI, *de ref.*, c. 6—*Canones et Decreta*, p. 129.

[41] Especially cc. 1, 3, 4, 6, X, *de clerico aegrotante vel debilitato*, III, 6; c. unic., *de clerico aegrotante vel debilitato*, I, 5, in VI°.

[42] C. 3, X, *de clericis non residentibus in ecclesia vel praebenda*, IV, 4 (Alexander III in Conc. Lateranensi III, anno 1179); c. 29, X, *de praebendis et dignitatibus*, III, 5 (Innocentius III in Conc. Lateranensi IV, anno 1215); c. 14, *de electione et electi potestate*, I, 6, in VI° (Gregorius X in Conc. Lugdunensi II, anno 1274). The Council of Trent based its third chapter of the VII session on reform on these decretals.

Furthermore, whilst the council of Trent did not devote a special chapter to the consideration of this particular need in parishes, its analogous legislation for the proper provision of a diocese whose bishop was permanently impeded by age or infirmity in the full exercise of his pastoral charge,[43] as also its cognate discipline in matters touching on the care of souls in parishes,[44] offered unmistakable indication of the norm that was to be followed in the efficient pastoration of the parochial churches whose actual rectors had succumbed to the disabilities consequent upon senility or the incurable maladies of body or mind.

Canonical legislation on adjutant priests for perpetually incapacitated parochial rectors remained thenceforward in a state of virtual quiescence until the time of our present codification of the Church Law. But, in order to gain a proper grasp of the import of the Tridentine Law on this point during the past four centuries, it will be very serviceable to our purpose to adduce at least a somewhat representative number of the decrees and decisions issued both by the Sacred Congregation of the Council and that for Bishops and Regulars, whilst we also keep in mind the papal constitutions that bear upon this question. Ultimately it will be useful to see what action the provincial councils took on this topic, especially those held in the last century.

The points of the law legislated by the council of Trent, and later to be confirmed by the authentic interpretations of the Roman Congregations and Papal Constitutions, may be summarized under the following headings:

1. The legally recognized causes for appointment;
2. The mode of appointment;
3. The duration of the adjutant's ministry;
4. The scope of his parochial powers;
5. The duty of residence on the part of the adjutant;

---

[43] Sessio VI, *de ref.*, c. 1; sessio VII, *de ref.*, c. 2; sessio XXIII, *de ref.*, c. 1; and particularly sessio XXV, *de ref.*, c. 7—*Canones et Decreta*, pp. 35-36; 44; 153-56; 230.

[44] Sessio VI, *de ref.*, c. 2; sessio VII, *de ref.*, cc. 3, 5, 7; sessio XIV, *de ref.*, cc. 3, 4, 10; sessio XXIV, *de ref.*, cc. 4, 13, 17, 18; sessio XXV, *de ref.*, cc. 12, 16—*op. cit.*, p. 37; pp. 44, 45, 46; 95, 96, 100; 185-86, 193-94, 197-201; 236-37, 240.

6. The adjutant's right to an appropriate salary;
7. The alternate means of insuring his support;
8. The question of perquisites and offerings;
9. The bishop's right and responsibility of ascertaining the fitness or unfitness of the parochial rector;
10. The bishop's ordinance and the possibility of redress against it;
11. The duty of residence on the part of the disabled rector;
12. The duty of personal pastoration in the functions for which the pastor remained able;
13. The *Missa pro populo;*
14. The rector's claim to the income from his benefice;
15. The remedy of parish dismemberment; and
16. The reasons justifying its application.

§I. The Legally Recognized Causes for Appointment

The causes which were recognized as reasons demanding the appointment of an adjutant vicar in a parish may be classified in four groups. Each of them bespoke a personal limitation inherent in the rector of the parish and on account of which he was rendered unequal to the task of a beneficial care for the flock entrusted to him. This deficiency manifested itself either in the body or in the mind. It was present in the body when a lingering, persistent, or incurable state of physical debility prevented a pastor from exercising the normal measure of activity required of him in virtue of his pastoral office. It was present in the mind from one of three causes: 1) Because of an abiding or incurable state produced by supervening senility, chronic mental disturbances, malignant cerebral disorders, recurring notional complexes, and the like; 2) Because of a transient or relievable condition induced by a lack of speculative mental equipment and knowledge; 3) Because of the circumstance created by a want of practical prudence and pastoral tact.[45]

[45] Richter, *Canones et Decreta Concilii Tridentini*, p. 119, nn. 1, 2; S. C. Ep. et Reg., *in Alben.*, die 15 Oct. 1601—*Fontes*, IV, n. 1611; Benedictus XIV, *Institutiones Ecclesiasticae*, IX, 16; *De Synodo Dioecesana*, lib. XIII, cap. 9, n. 21 ss., in which passages responses of the Sacred Congregation of the Council are adduced.

§II. The Mode of Appointment

The mode of appointing adjutant vicars was different from that which was conceded to parish priests in the selection of their assistant vicars. The reason for this is close at hand. Among the different classes of parochial rectors that required the aid of an adjutant vicar for the discharge of their pastoral duties were included also those whose mental capacity had completely lapsed from them. It would have been an odious distinction to grant to the others what had to be denied to them. Hence, since adaptation for the sake of uniformity was an utter impossibility on their part, the result was that all disabled rectors no longer enjoyed the option of a personal choice in the association of a vicar who was to aid their personal disability, whether its nature was mental or physical, total or partial.

If the bishop was ultimately responsible for the beneficial care of souls in all the parishes of his diocese, then it must also be he who was empowered to select and appoint a vicar who was qualified to fill the pastor's stead.[46]

§III. The Duration of the Adjutant's Ministry

The duration of the vicar's adjutancy in a parish was generally conterminous with the duration of the cause for which he was appointed. If a pastor perchance regained his health of body or strength of mind, or if his deficiency of speculative as also practical knowledge in the administration of his parish was obviated and satisfactory proof for its obviation was established by a subsequent successful examination or salutary test of experience, then the vicar's aid was no longer a necessity. As soon as the necessity for an adjutant vicar is recognized by the bishop as having ceased the adjutant's services will be made available by him in some other capacity of priestly functions.

---

[46] Innocentius XIII, const. "*Apostolici Ministerii,*" die 23 Maii 1723, §11; Benedictus XIII, const. "*In Suprema,*" die 23 Sept. 1724, §9; Benedictus XIV, const. "*Ad Militantis,*" die 30 Martii 1742, §12—*Fontes*, I, n. 280; n. 283; n. 326; S. C. C. *in Legionen.*, die 13 Dec. 1725—Pallottini, *Collectio omnium Conclusionum et Resolutionum*, XIV, p. 517, n. 22.

The council of Trent had legislated that no episcopal coadjutor was given with the right of succession unless the Roman Pontiff had first taken cognizance of the case and had confirmed his worthiness as a prospective successor for the diocese.[47] *A fortiori,* an adjutant vicar in a parish was not accredited with right of succession in the parochial office of the rector without a particular papal indult in authorization for it. Such a concession, of course, formed a rare exception.[48]

Notwithstanding this practice in the Church, canonists were not agreed when discussing the possibility of an adjutant's designation to a parish with the right of succession in office. Whilst Pope Benedict XIV in his Constitution *"Ad Militantis"* mentioned the designation of an adjutant vicar as being of temporary duration *by law,*[49] yet in his private writing as canonist of eminent rank and paramount authority he defends the view that just as the Roman Pontiff is qualified to appoint a coadjutor bishop with the right of succession, so also may he make such a concession in favor of a parochial adjutant vicar if weighty reasons indicate the decision thus reached. He sees no restrictions and inhibitions placed upon the Pope by the action of the Council.[50]

The entire question was, however, one of academic rather than practical interest in as far as the general practice of the Church was concerned with it. The right of *temporarily* appointing such a parochial vicar rested in the hands of the bishop; cases in which the bishop would have recourse to the Roman Pontiff for obtaining the grant of an appointment with the right of succession were indeed extremely rare.[51]

---

[47] Sessio XXV, *de ref.*, c. 7—*Canones et Decreta*, p. 230.

[48] Cf. S. C. C. *in Albiganen.*, die 1 Sept. 1663—Pallottini, *op. cit.*, XIV, p. 517, n. 24.

[49] Cf. §12: "Item a deputatione Coadjutorum aut Vicariorum *pro tempore*, . . . juxta praescriptum eiusdem Concilii d. sess. 21, *de Ref.*, cap. 6."—*Fontes*, I, n. 326. The italics are indicated by the writer.

[50] Cf. *De Synodo Dioecesana*, lib. XIII, cap. 10, nn. 25-30.

[51] Cf. Lämmer, *Kirchenrecht*, pp. 257-61, 283-84.

§IV. THE SCOPE OF HIS PAROCHIAL POWERS

The scope of powers with which the adjutant vicar was invested during the term of his adjutancy had to be measured by the norm indicated in the bishop's letter of appointment. If the appointment had in view the duty of a complete and unrestricted assumption of parochial functions because the rector of the parish was rendered totally incapable of lending his services either by actively sharing in the work or by directing its fulfillment, then the vicar possessed fixed and ordinary powers as ample as those which were conceded to the office of rector itself. If the rector was still able to perform a share or a distinct sphere of the work personally, then he remained personally obligated as the pastor of his flock to be responsible for its performance. The aid given by the adjutant was then of a subordinate and subsidiary character. The parish priest was fully qualified to reserve such functions to his own personal execution as he was able to perform in his own person, and hence, in these matters the adjutant was fully subject to his pastor's instruction and direction for their administration.

Even then when the infirm rector on the one hand enjoyed the full possession of his mental faculties, and was moreover endowed with all the intellectual and moral requirements of pastoral knowledge, tact, and prudence, but was physically unequal to the task of personally undertaking any of the functions, his direction and his instruction to his adjutant would define the limits of the latter's powers in the parish, unless the bishop had granted ampler faculties in the notice of his assignment.

Outside of the case when the adjutant was assigned for the purpose of assuming both the temporal and the spiritual administration of the parish, the extent of his partial powers and the authority with which he could execute them were left dependent on the authorization committed by the rector himself unless the bishop in his appointment had definitely indicated a different norm of procedure. The presumption of the law favored the rector's continued personal responsibility in the administration of parochial matters until the bishop, upon proper investigation or examination, limited his normal powers and committed the functions thus subtracted to the exercise of another who then functioned vicariously for him.[52]

§V. The Duty of Residence on the Part of the Adjutant

The duty of constant residence in the parish on the part of the adjutant vicar is readily deducible from the very purpose of his appointment. Whilst the infirm rector continued in his office as titular and actual parish priest, the adjutant was associated with him for the sake of supplying or integrating the pastoral activity for which the rector had become either totally or partially disabled. The vicar's personal option of absenting himself from the parish for even a restricted period of time would have wrought havoc for the surety of a beneficial pastoral administration of the parish. Hence, the nature of the duties committed to the adjutant argues the necessity of his unbroken residence in the parish wherein he was assigned as an aid to his incapacitated pastor.[53]

Not only the council of Trent,[54] but also the later official responses and decrees of the Roman Congregations and constitutions of the Popes are silent about the vicar's right to the enjoyment of a vacation during the period of his adjutancy. It is possible that the discipline established for the coadjutor canons at cathedral and collegiate chapters was in this regard appropriated as a norm also for parochial adjutants. Richter [55] adduces two decrees of the Sacred Congregation of the Council from which it appears manifest that those who supplied the place of permanently disabled canons in cathedral and collegiate chapters enjoyed neither the special indult granted to the latter

---

52 The fact that none of the decisions of the Sacred Congregation of the Council treat this question *ex professo* reveals that, beyond the very general presumption of the law already indicated, no definite principle was established whereby all cases could be judged. The solution of each case constituted its own individual norm without any further indications. Individual circumstances created an individual status to which no general norm could be applied.

53 Cf. S. C. Ep. et Reg., *in Nicoteren.*, die 7 Sept. 1619—*Fontes*, IV, n. 1704; Benedictus XIV, *Institutiones Ecclesiasticae*, XVII, nn. 1-28.

54 Sessio XXI, *de ref.*, c. 6—*Canones et Decreta*, p. 129.

55 *Canones et Decreta Concilii Tridentini*, p. 360, nn. 90-91.

with regard to recreational vacations, once the canons themselves had made use of it, nor the privilege of substituting some other priest or cleric in their own station during a contemplated absence.[56] One may conclude, therefore, that if the adjacent vicar was to enjoy the leave of a vacation during the period of his temporary appointment, his reasons were to be submitted to his bishop and favorably adjudged by him in each particular instance before the adjutant could bespeak any right upon the use of a vacation.

§VI. THE ADJUTANT'S RIGHT TO AN APPROPRIATE SALARY

The right of an adjutant to the claim of an appropriate salary for his term of service is founded upon the natural law of justice. One of the strongest traditions prevalent in the history of the Church throughout all the centuries of her existence is the sense of justice and equity that she has ever manifested in behalf of her ordained ministers of religion. She was never content with the support that her clergy might procure for themselves through the medium of their own initiative and enterprise by engaging themselves in honorable work outside the ministry; rather, she considered the very possibility of procuring a livelihood in this manner as a probable obstacle in the way of an efficient discharge of the pastoral duties committed to them. For this reason she demanded that every pastoral charge have connected with it the means of a secure material support. This was effected either by the income accruing from a benefice or through a specified salary for the one who did not possess a benefice. As long as the beneficial income was sufficient to supply the needs of the beneficiary together with his adjutant or assistant priests, no other method for the proper remuneration of the clergy in their spiritual ministrations was urged by the Church.[57] Her demand rather was that no cleric

[56] *Ibid.*, S. C. C. *in Civitaten.*, die 20 Mart. 1745: "Canonicos Coadjutores gaudere posse indulto vacationis quod recreationis causa canonicis tributum est, si coadjuti eo non utantur . . .;" S. C. C. *in Spoletana ad dubium II*, die 28 Feb. 1795: "Canonicum Coadjutorem alium substituere non posse in chorale officium."

[57] S. C. C. *in Seguntina*, mense Oct., 1589—Richter, *Canones et Decreta Concilii Tridentini*, p. 114, n. 15.

was to be admitted to sacred orders or given a pastoral station or incumbency unless his proper support was safeguarded by the possession of a benefice or an equivalent source of income.[58] If the income from the parochial benefice was insufficient, then the bishop was within his right to bestow an additional income derived from the possession of a simple benefice. Because this second benefice made no requirement of residence, its holding was entirely compatible with the possession of the first.[59] This method was sanctioned not only by the council of Trent but also by the repeated decisions of the Congregation of the Council.[60]

The primary means of securing the adjutant's proper support were drawn from the beneficial income of the parish priest in whose aid this vicar was employed. This is evident from the ruling of the council of Trent itself.[61] It is expressed again in the constitutions of the Popes.[62] The chief determinant of the parish priest's duty to maintain his pastoral aid out of his own beneficial income may be traced to the principle of equity: "*Cuius est emolumentum, eius debet esse et onus.*" [63]

The portion or share that was allotted to these vicars was variable at different times. Very likely the norm that was

---

[58] S. C. C. die 23 Maii 1609; S. C. C. die 29 Nov. 1670; Benedictus XIV, *Institutiones Ecclesiasticae*, XXVI, nn. 7-8.

[59] Sessio XXIV, *de ref.*, c. 17—*Canones et Decreta*, p. 197.

[60] Cf. Benedictus XIV, *Institutiones Ecclesiasticae*, *loc. cit.*

[61] Sessio XXI, *de ref.*, c. 6—*Canones et Decreta*, p. 129: "Episcopi, etiam tamquam apostolicae Sedis delegati, . . . partem fructuum eisdem [adjutoribus] pro sufficienti victu assignare, vel aliter providere possint, quacumque appellatione, et exemptione remota."

[62] Innocentius XIII, const. "*Apostolici Ministerii*," die 23 Maii 1723, §11; Benedictus XIII, const. "*In Supremo*," die 23 Sept. 1724, §9; Benedictus XIV, const. "*Ad Militantis*," die 30 Mart. 1742, §12—*Fontes*, I, n. 280; n. 283; n. 326. The first two constitutions use the same words since the second was but an extension of Pope Innocent's original constitution to the bishops in Spain. The words are: "*Archiepiscopi, et Episcopi per alios a se deputandos, sumptibus Parochorum minus idoneorum opportune suppleri curent.*" The last one almost literally repeats the words of the Tridentine Council: "*Cum assignatione partis fructuum pro sufficienti illorum* [adjutorum] *victu.*"

[63] Cf. Reg. 55, R. J., in VI°. The same principle is here enunciated with a wider scope so as to include its converse application: "Qui sentit onus, sentire debet commodum, et e contra." See also *ASS*, VIII (1875), 696, where this principle is stated in still another form: "Qui commodum sentit, debet et incommodum persentire."

established for them received its specification more or less in proportionate accord with the practice in vogue regarding the *actual* vicars who administered parishes for communities or monasteries in whom the parochial title to the church was vested. The ruling of the council of Trent had fixed the third part of the income from the benefice for them;[64] Pius V defined their portion within maximum and minimum limits;[65] Gregory XIII, in turn, modified this ordinance somewhat,[66] and Clement XIV reconstructed it on a new basis for Sardinia.[67] In this constitution the ratio was changed from one-third to one-fourth of the beneficial income.

§VII. The Alternate Means of Insuring His Support

When the revenues of the parochial benefice were so insignificant that a just and honorable salary could not be provided from this income alone, then the bishop was called on to make proper provision in some other way. This was usually accomplished by attaching the responsibility of support to the people of the respective parishes wherein this need existed.[68] This remedy could be enforced, if there were need of constraint, by the threat and execution of ecclesiastical penalties according to the specifications of the Tridentine Council.[69]

---

[64] Sessio VII, *de ref.*, c. 7—*Canones et Decreta*, p. 46.

[65] Const. "*Ad Exequendum*," die 1 Nov. 1567—*Bullarium Romanum*, VII, 628-30; Ferraris, *Bibliotheca*, VII, 595-96.

[66] Const. "*In Tanta Rerum*," die 1 Mart. 1573—*Bullarium Romanum*, VIII, 39-41.

[67] Ep. encycl. "*Inter Multiplices*," die 21 Sept. 1769, §14—*Fontes*, II, n. 466.

[68] Two very early undated decisions of the Congregation of the Council to this effect are listed by Pallottini, *Collectio omnium Conclusionum et Resolutionum*, XIV, p. 514 (*In Novarien.*, et *In Cremen.*). Further decrees of the same Congregation may be found in Pallottini, *op. cit.*, XIV, p. 419, n. 32; XIV, p. 514, n. 10; VI, p. 189, n. 41. See also Richter, *Canones et Decreta Concilii Tridentini*, p. 119, n. 4; p. 460, n. 4.

[69] Sessio XXV, *de ref.*, c. 12—*Canones et Decreta*, p. 237: "Qui vero eas [decimas] aut subtrahunt, aut impediunt, excommunicentur; nec ab hoc crimine, nisi plena restitutione secuta, absolvantur." Cf. also sessio XXI, *de ref.*, c. 7; sessio XXIV, *de ref.*, c. 13—*op. cit.*, pp. 130; 193.

§VIII. THE QUESTION OF PERQUISITES AND OFFERINGS

The perquisites and offerings received from the faithful on the occasion of a spiritual ministry yielded to the parish priest personally, and in their entirety, unless custom or usage in a certain locality, or the expressed will of the donor specified otherwise for the portion exceeding the customary or stipulated offering.[70]

Since it was the burden of the parish priest to support his helpers in the ministry, it remained also his right to accept the offerings of the faithful whereby this duty was facilitated for him. He was the pastor of the flock, the spiritual father of his parochial family, and therefore the material marks of honor and pecuniary pledges of esteem that were offered belonged by right of office and acknowledged trust to him.[71] The authors are unanimous in according him this right, although they freely admit that, in circumstances, his primary right of justice might eventuate in a secondary duty of Christian charity towards the vicars associated with him in a participated pastoral obligation.[72]

§IX. THE BISHOP'S RIGHT AND RESPONSIBILITY OF ASCERTAINING THE FITNESS OR UNFITNESS OF THE PAROCHIAL RECTOR

Having considered the rights and duties that made up the parochial adjutant's sphere of pastoral activity, there are next to be considered the right and the responsibility of the bishop in making such an assignment to a disabled pastor. First of all, the bishop, as the pastor of his diocese, was responsible for the salutary administration of the care of souls in all the par-

---

[70] Reiffenstuel, *Jus Canonicum Universum*, lib. III, tit. 30, n. 190. This author cites the authority of a great number of noted canonists who find this teaching incorporated in the *Decretum Gratiani* and the later Decretals. The silence of the council of Trent in this matter leaves the discipline of the past unaltered with regard to the future.

[71] S. C. C. *in Senogallien.*, die 24 Maii 1710; S. C. C. *Emolumentorum Funeralium*, die 2 Maii 1711—Pallottini, *op. cit.*, XIV, p. 622, n. 26.

[72] Cf. Reiffenstuel, *op. cit.*, *loc. cit.*, nn. 193-95; Engel, *Collegium universi juris canonici*, lib. III, tit. 30, n. 69; Van Espen, *Jus Ecclesiasticum Universum*, P. II, tit. 33, cap. 10.

ishes within his territorial jurisdiction.[73] For this reason he was to make an annual visitation, if possible, in all the churches of his diocese, to ascertain the status of conditions within the individual parishes.[74] On the occasion of these official pastoral visits, from which no parochial benefices were exempt,[75] he was authorized to examine the parish discipline in all matters that pertained to the proper upkeep of the churches and the well-ordered fulfillment of the pastoral duties connected with the parochial title or office.[76]

To this end it was necessary that he should be fully empowered with the right of appointing parish rectors or instituting the parochial incumbent nominated or presented by the competent religious superior or lay patron in the case of parochial churches which were incorporated with religious institutes or affected by the privilege of lay patronage. It was his right as well as his responsibility to certify the fitness of all prospective parochial beneficiaries by the test of a previous examination conducted by responsible authorities.[77]

The duty of episcopal vigilance was not absolved by this initial act of examination. His annual visitations were but the continued exercise of this same duty. Hence, whenever a parochial rector was involved in a grave suspicion of unfitness which might jeopardize the material or spiritual well-being of a parish, the bishop was fortified with the power of the Holy See to make proper provision in the case.[78]

---

[73] Sessio VI, *de ref.*, c. 2—*Canones et Decreta*, p. 37: ". . . quibus casibus nihilominus officium sit episcoporum, tamquam in hac parte a Sede apostolica delegatorum providere, ut . . . cura animarum nullatenus negligatur: nemini, quoad hoc, privilegio, seu exemptione quacumque suffragante." Cf. also sessio VII, *de ref.*, cc. 5, 7—*op. cit.*, pp. 45, 47.

[74] Sessio XXIV, *de ref.*, c. 3—*op. cit.*, pp. 183-85; sessio VII, *de ref.*, c. 4—*op. cit.*, p. 38.

[75] Sessio XXIV, *de ref.*, c. 9—*op. cit.*, pp. 188-89.

[76] Sessio XXIV, *de ref.*, c. 13—*op. cit.*, pp. 193-94; sessio XXIV, *de ref.*, c. 3—*op. cit.*, pp. 183-85.

[77] Sessio XXIV, *de ref.*, c. 18—*op. cit.*, p. 200.

[78] Sessio XXI, *de ref.*, c. 6—*op. cit.*, p. 129. See especially S. C. C. *in Pampilonen.*, die 15 Jan. 1667 et die 22 Sept. 1668—Benedictus XIV, *Institutiones Ecclesiasticae*, IX, n. 16—where the following points of note are established: 1) The bishop's right of re-examining the rector consequent upon his initial approval, whenever a grave suspicion of incompetence should later arise; 2) his right of proceeding to this examination even apart from the official act of visitation; 3) his right of acting in this regard without

§X. THE BISHOP'S ORDINANCE AND THE POSSIBILITY OF REDRESS AGAINST IT

The decision reached by the bishop admitted of no suspensive appeal, nor could it be evaded by the plea of exemption.[79] The bishop's decree had to be obeyed. Since he had acted as a delegate of the Apostolic See, the only conceivable appeal or recourse would have been that which remanded the case to the same Apostolic See for final adjudication whilst the bishop's decree was imposed as binding for the interim. The certain principle of the law, namely, that anyone who felt himself aggrieved could appeal from an ordinance with the effect of suspending its application, was not conceded in such cases where the law denied the benefit of appeal. The question therefore arises: What did the law concerning the appointment of parochial adjutants stipulate in this regard?

This kind of appointment was conditioned upon a number of causes as already described. When the bishop assigned an adjutant because of the rector's supervening infirmity of body or debility of mind, the law of the older decretals still regulated his procedure. No mention is made in these papal ordinances and laws that the bishop was to act with a power delegated from the Holy See. Moreover, the council of Trent is altogether silent about this particular question. Hence, it seems necessary to conclude that when the bishop had provided in these two cases by the appointment of an adjutant vicar, the way still remained open for appeal or recourse according as the bishop's execution had been undertaken by judicial sentence or preceptive decree.

If the pastor was no longer in possession of the rational use of his mind, then, of course, neither an appeal nor a recourse could come into question. He was then barred from the use of this privilege of the law, not because of any legal prohibition, but because of his utter incapacity for the placing of human acts. If his mind retained possession of its rational functions,

---

the necessity of previous *judicial* proof in warrant of the current suspicion; 4) his lack of right to resort to an examination in the absence of an objectively grave suspicion. Cf. also *De Synodo Dioecesana*, lib. XIII, c. 9, n. 21, where additional responses are cited.

[79] Sessio XXI, *de ref.*, c. 6—*Canones et Decreta*, p. 129.

then he could avail himself of the prerogative of the law which allowed him the benefit of appeal or recourse in accord with the nature of the case.[80] In the interval of the pending appeal or recourse the bishop was permitted to enforce execution of his act of appointment only in case the rector had neglected to make some other proper provision for the care of souls within his parish.[81]

Whenever a parish required the continuous services of a priest in addition to those which could be afforded by the rector himself, and the circumstances were such that it remained doubtful whether the appointee should be assigned not merely as an assistant vicar but rather as a parochial adjutant, then the presumption of the law favored the appointment of an assistant priest as long as the need of an adjutant had not become an established and recognized fact. This principle of law was evidenced in a decision rendered by the Sacred Congregation of the Council. On account of its decisive importance in indicating a norm of procedure in similar cases, it will prove helpful to reproduce its attendant circumstances, in at least a summary form together with the decision that followed.

A pastor, 77 years of age, presided over a parish in which two churches about 1,000 paces apart required his pastoral attendance. He had the help of an assistant vicar in his parochial work. In his advanced years he had lost the normal keenness of his senses. His absent-mindedness betrayed itself repeatedly and his impaired hearing wrought more than trifling embarrassment for the parishioners. His vicar also was not without his shortcomings. His reputation was not altogether unblemished, especially at the church where he resided, although no general complaints were registered against him at the second church where he also ministered to the parochial needs.

The bishop's action in removing the vicar and appointing another opened the way for a long-continued series of ecclesiastical trials. April 20th, May 8th, and November 6, 1761, had already marked three stages of the legal procedure, but the pastor was still pressing his claim and right of retaining titular possession of the parish, and, by consequence, that of associat-

80 Cf. Bouix, *Tractatus de Parocho*, p. 426.

81 S. C. Ep. et Reg. *in Aquen.*, die 30 Nov. 1582—*Fontes*, IV, n. 1399.

ing a vicar of his own choice in place of the one appointed by the bishop. On November 26th the bishop wrote to the Sacred Congregation: "*Hisce propterea malis opportuna medela a Concilio Tridentino praescripta occurere satagens, remoto inviso Capellano, alium morigeratum, et ab Examinatoribus Synodalibus ad Curam animarum idoneum repertum, nuperrime deputavi.*" The Sacred Congregation reviewed the case on July 24, 1762. Its answer was: "*Non proposita, cum reliquis.*" On August 21st of the same year when the case came up for a second hearing the Congregation issued an "*Iterum proponatur.*" On January 22, 1763, the pending case was again prorogued without a final answer. The case was then subjected to a final hearing by the Congregation of the Council on February 26, 1763. The questions and the responses published were the following:

> I. An sit locus remotioni Capellani, ita ut deveniendum sit ad electionem novi Capellani Curati?
>
> II. An constet de attentatis, et quomodo sint purganda, in casu?
>
> Ad I. Arbitrio et Conscientiae Episcopi: et in casu denegatae reintegrationis Pompanii, Episcopus praefigat terminum Parocho ad eligendum alium Capellanum ab eodem Episcopo approbandum, et ad mentem, et amplius.
>
> Ad II. Affirmative per viam nullitatis, et amplius.[82]

A number of guiding principles are set into clear relief by this response. For the two cases mentioned (infirmity of body and debility of mind [barring insanity]), it clearly established: 1) The possibility of appeal on the part of the pastor; 2) the right of appeal *in suspensivo* if suitable provision had been made by the pastor for the needs of the parish in the meantime; 3) the corresponding duty of the bishop to refrain from executing his sentence or judgment except in a case where the security of divine worship demanded executive action; 4) the use of these same rights by the pastor and the observance of this same duty by the bishop when the case was one of recourse instead of

---

[82] *Thesaurus Resolutionum*, Tom. XXXI (1762), 155-58; 165-66; Tom. XXXII (1763), 8-9; 27.

appeal;[83] 5) the presumption of law that a pastor could select and assume a parochial *assistant* vicar for his needed help in the administration of his parish as long as it was not clearly established and plainly recognized beyond the question of reasonable doubt that he required the aid of a parochial *adjutant* vicar, who was to be assigned by the bishop for the proper pastoration of souls under his charge.

This last mentioned principle must be specially noted. When the bishop appointed an adjutant, this action necessarily constituted an implied affirmation of the personal limitations of the pastor. But, the dictates both of equity and of charity demanded that no pastor's disabilities, whether culpable or inculpable, be made the subject of unnecessary revelation as long as there was a well-grounded hope of securing the proper care for his flock through other equivalent means which more efficiently safeguarded the esteem due him by precluding the occasion for perplexing surmises on the part of the people. Once the lack of his physical competence and mental vigor, lost without any fault of his own, could be placed beyond the pale of doubt, then also it became more readily possible not only to silence unjustified innuendos, but also to soothe misguided resentments on the part of parishioners, since their pastor's condition was then recognized by all reputable people as demanding the aid of an adjutant in their midst. Judged by the merits of natural equity and Christian charity, this reason, more than any other, must have played a deciding part in the normation of this principle whereby the law postulated the appointment of an assistant priest until the need of an adjutant was plainly and indubitably indicated.[84]

When the bishop had determined upon the appointment of an adjutant to a pastor whose lack of intellectual knowledge or

[83] Cf. cans. 1569 §2, 1889 §2, for the distinction between recourse and appeal according to current legislation. The discipline before the present Code had not reached the same clarified differentiation of legal procedure against matters expedited by episcopal precept or decree on the one hand, and executed by judicial declaration or sentence on the other.

[84] Benedict XIV, in his constitution "*Etsi Pastoralis*" of May 26, 1742, c. 5, n. 9 (*Fontes*, I, n. 328), had already adopted the same norm of legal conduct in providing for parishes whose rectors labored under the handicap of unfamiliarity with the language of some of their parishioners.

experience disqualified his unaided services from giving the assurance required for a beneficial administration in the parish, then all avenue of redress by law was closed to the pastor. In cases of this nature the bishop was empowered by the Council of Trent to act as a delegate of the Holy See. No further appeal or recourse was possible save that which transmitted the cause from the delegate to his Superior for a final judgment, whilst the subject remained bound in the interim to respect the decision of the bishop. A contrary decision by the Holy See—an event not so likely—was the only alternative by which such a pastor could be freed from compliance with the bishop's provision.[85]

§XI. The Duty of Residence on the Part of the Disabled Rector

The pastor who was given such a vicar in aid was not exempt from the duty of personal residence in the parish. Examples of responses from the Sacred Congregation of the Council on the pastor's duty of residence could be multiplied almost indefinitely. Pope Benedict XIV[86] cites an abundance of decisions, all of which treat of some phase or other bearing on the law of residence for parochial rectors. Richter[87] and Pallottini[88] adduce an additional number of responses touching on this question. These official answers were nothing more than a declaration, adaptation, and enforcement of the law of residence as it was formulated in the council of Trent.[89] Since a permanently infirm or disabled parish priest was fully permitted to retain title to his parish,[90] the law on residence remained the same for him as for the able-bodied and active titular incumbents of parish churches.

---

[85] Sessio XXI, *de ref.*, c. 6—*Canones et Decreta*, p. 129; Bouix, *Tractatus de Parocho*, p. 427.

[86] *Institutiones Ecclesiasticae*, XVII, nn. 1-28 and CVII, n. 2; *De Synodo Dioecesana*, lib. VII, cap. 1, nn. 2-6 and lib. XIII, c. 19, nn. 2-10.

[87] *Canones et Decreta Concilii Tridentini*, pp. 37-38.

[88] *Collectio omnium Conclusionum et Resolutionum*, v. *Parochus*, §XI, "Parochus quoad Residentiam et Absentiam."

[89] Sessio XXIII, *de ref.*, c. 1—*Canones et Decreta*, pp. 155-56.

[90] Cf. cc. 1, 3, 4, 6, X, *de clerico aegrotante vel debilitato*, III, 6.

As early as the year 1573 we find confirmation of this principle by a declaration of the Congregation of the Council in the following case:

> Quaeritur: "Si aliqua Parochia sub tanta coeli inclementia constituta sit, ut nemo, nisi indigena in eadem sede absque vitae discrimine immorari possit, alibi degere Rectori licet?"
>
> Responditur: "Non posse. Si tamen Rector infirmus esset, et in loco Parochiali curari non posset defectu Medicorum, vel medicinarum, tunc posse ab Ordinario dari delationem 3 aut 4 mensium, ut in locis vicinioribus maneat recuperandae sanitatis causa, posito interea ab ipso Ordinario in Parochiali idoneo Vicario cum congrua portione ex reditibus ejusdem parochiae."[91]

In 1619 there is found a case still more characteristic. On July 27th an aged and infirm bishop had been granted permanent leave of absence from his diocese on condition of his supplying an able and suitable coadjutor in his place. On September 7th of the same year, upon more diligent consideration of the case, Pope Paul V instructed the Sacred Congregation of Bishops and Regulars to notify and remind the bishop that his duty of residence would *not* cease with the provision of a coadjutor, but that he was obliged to remain at his Church in order to satisfy the duty of his pastoral office.[92] Although this case deals with the residence required of a bishop, yet it has the same force for parochial rectors whom the council of Trent had placed under the same obligation. Its words are: "*Eadem omnino, etiam quoad culpam, amissionem fructuum, et poenas de curatis inferioribus, et aliis quibuscumque, qui beneficium aliquid ecclesiasticum, curam animarum habens, obtinet, sacrosancta Synodus declarat et decernit.*" [93] In a word, neither old age, nor broken health, nor yet the assurance that a neighboring pastor could sufficiently provide for the few members of the

---

[91] S. C. C. *in Regien.*, anno 1573—Benedictus XIV, *Institutiones Ecclesiasticae*, XVII, n. 14; Pallottini, *op. cit.*, XIV, pp. 726-27, n. 77.

[92] S. C. Ep. et Reg. *in Nicoteren.*, die 7 Sept. 1619—*Fontes*, IV, n. 1704.

[93] Sessio XXIII, *de ref.*, c. 1—*Canones et Decreta*, p. 155.

parish, was a valid excuse from the law which demanded personal residence on the part of all beneficiaries entrusted with the care of souls.[94]

§XII. THE DUTY OF PERSONAL PASTORATION IN THE FUNCTIONS FOR WHICH THE PASTOR REMAINS ABLE

Despite his age and infirmity, the rector was held responsible for a personal pastoration in all the functions that were not beyond the scope of his ability to perform. Being the pastor of his people, he could not be exempted from the personal ministration of the sacraments whenever lawfully asked by the faithful to confer them, or whenever a condition of sufficient bodily health and mental energy made possible his acquiescence with their pious wishes.[95]

§XIII. THE *Missa Pro Populo*

The *Missa pro populo* also remained his personal obligation. This is evident from the ruling of the council of Trent,[96] which, however, did not specify the particular days on which this obligation became an actual and necessary duty.[97] The law of custom attached this duty to the Sundays and Feast Days of Obligation. But since the practice soon varied with regard to the observance of certain feasts as days on which there was an obligation of assisting at mass and of abstaining from servile works, Pope Urban VIII found it necessary to regulate which days were thenceforth to be observed universally as Holydays of Obligation.[98] About a century later Pope Benedict

---

[94] Benedictus XIV, *Institutiones Ecclesiasticae*, XVII, n. 16.

[95] S. C. C. *in Grossetana*, die 16 Sept. 1645—Richter, *Canones et Decreta Concilii Tridentini*, p. 39, n. 19; S. C. C. *in Nicien.*, die 7 Oct. 1604; S. C. C. *in Sabinen. Jurium Parochialium*, die 10 Mart. 1742—Pallottini, *op. cit.*, XIV, p. 513, n. 2; pp. 627-28, n. 13.

[96] Sessio XXIII, *de ref.*, c. 1—*Canones et Decreta*, p. 153: "Cum praecepto divino mandatum sit omnibus, quibus animarum cura commissa est, oves suas agnoscere, pro his sacrificium offerre, . . ."

[97] Sessio XXIII, *de ref.*, c. 1—*Canones et Decreta*, p. 153-54—merely enjoins the celebration of the mass without inculcating its obligation under the term *Missa pro populo*.

[98] Urbanus VIII, const. "*Universa*," die 13 Sept. 1624, §2—*Fontes*, I, n. 226.

XIV issued an encyclical letter to the hierarchy of Italy reminding them of the special days on which the obligation of the *Missa pro populo* was incumbent upon all who had the care of souls committed to them.[99] This instruction was in accord with the decisions of the Congregation of the Council which antedated this papal ordinance.[100] Later legislation on this point formulated by Pope Leo XIII in his Apostolic Letter *"In Suprema"* of June 10, 1882,[101] as well as the action of the Sacred Congregation of the Council in its repeated decisions,[102] inculcated the application of the *Missa pro populo* as a personal and real obligation for all canonically constituted parish priests. No excuse was offered by the meagerness of their financial revenues from the parishes. If their condition of health prevented them from a personal fulfillment of this obligation, the burden of the duty still remained their own, for in such cases they had to supply a stipend to another who was to offer and apply the mass in their stead.

§XIV. The Rector's Claim to the Income from His Benefice

Just as the burden of the *Missa pro populo* remained a personal obligation for all parish priests who still retained the title to their parishes although their weakened condition of body or mind required the services of an adjutant, so all the other burdens of parochial activity still adhered to their office. Since, as a consequence of this, they were also personally under the obligation to supply a suitable salary to their adjutant vicars out of their own financial resources, it is evident that the material emoluments accruing to their office, whether from the revenues of their parochial benefice or from the perquisites and offerings of the faithful, yielded in their entirety to them. They had

99 Benedictus XIV, ep. encycl. *"Cum Semper Oblatas,"* die 19 Aug. 1744, §7—*Fontes*, I, n. 345.

100 Benedictus XIV, *Institutiones Ecclesiasticae*, X, nn. 4-7.

101 Especially §§1, 5, 6, 7, 9—*Fontes*, III, n. 585.

102 S. C. C. die 23 April. 1853—*Jus Pontificium*, VI (1927), 116; S. C. C. die 9 Dec. 1865—*ASS*, II (1866), 90-92; S. C. C. die 14 Dec. 1872—*AkKR*, XXIX (1873), 466; S. C. C. die 9 April. 1892—*ASS*, XXIV (1892), 661-69.

full and exclusive claim to all the beneficiary concomitants of their parochial office because the responsibility of the parochial burdens postulated the enjoyment of all the parochial benefits.[103]

§XV. The Remedy of Parish Dismemberment

In exceptional cases and under extraordinary circumstances the appointment of an adjutant vicar to a disabled parochial rector would have created untoward conditions which, far from promoting the interests of the parish, might have directly militated against their furtherance by this ordinary provision. For this reason the council of Trent did not neglect to place in the hands of the bishop a proper remedy for these unusual situations. According to the nature of the need in each parish the bishop could, in the capacity of a delegate for the Apostolic See,[104] avail himself of the various methods permitted him by law. These methods consisted mainly of the division or erection,[105] the union,[106] the suppression or transfer[107] of benefices in order to ensure proper provision for the beneficiaries dependent upon them for their means of honorable support.

§XVI. The Reasons Justifying Its Application

The reasons justifying this procedure on the part of the bishop were offered, on the one hand, by the presence of such conditions within a parish as might be created by insufficiency of revenues[108] or diminution of its membership,[109] and on the other, by the pressure of such causes as the barriers of distance or the accession of an overflowing parochial population.[110] But, even in such cases the bishop's act was invalid unless he had

---

103 Cf. Reg. 55, R. J., in VI°.

104 Sessio XXI, *de ref.*, c. 5—*Canones et Decreta*, p. 128.

105 Sessio XXI, *de ref.*, c. 4—*op. cit.*, p. 128.

106 Sessio XXI, *de ref.*, c. 5; Sessio XXIV, *de ref.*, c. 13—*op. cit.*, pp. 128-29; 193-94.

107 Sessio XXI, *de ref.*, c. 7—*op. cit.*, p. 130.

108 Sessio XXIII, *de ref.*, c. 13—*op. cit.*, p. 193.

109 S. C. C. *in Veliterna Servitii seu Parochialis*, die 17 Junii 1702—Pallottini, *op. cit.*, XIV, pp. 520-21, n. 46.

110 Sessio XXI, *de ref.*, c. 4—*Canones et Decreta*, p. 128.

first received a hearing from the parish rector, or his proxy, before proceeding to final action.[111]

The existence of embittered quarrels, factious hatreds, or confirmed enmities within a parish, were not frequently recognized as sufficient causes for proceeding to a dismemberment of the parish.[112] Generally speaking, the bishop could efficaciously exercise the needed redress in such circumstances by the infliction of spiritual penalties on the guilty ones, thus effecting their return to submission and compliance with the decrees. It was only when every other resource of his episcopal authority lacked efficiency in achieving its aim that the dismemberment of a parish might be invoked as a last resort for safeguarding the spiritual welfare of the people. *Salus animarum suprema lex.* Therefore, all means that remained within the realm of moral right and pastoral prudence admitted of being made subservient to the procurement of this sovereign aim.

Art. V. Legislation of the Provincial Councils of the Past Centuries

After this discussion of the law of the council of Trent on adjutant vicars and the points of law correlated with it, the closing remarks of this chapter may be limited to a review of the legislation ordained by the provincial councils, especially those of the past century, which concerned themselves with this question. One need hardly expect to find any new legislation in the acts and decrees of these councils. The Ecumenical Council of Trent had been sufficiently explicit to consult the needs of the centuries that followed. Yet, because its legislation was of such a nature that it liberally entrusted the selection of certain ways and means for its enforcement into the hands of the bishops, the possibility of a varied discipline in the various countries becomes manifest.

---

[111] E.g., S. C. C. *in Cassanen. Dismembrationis,* die 3 et 17 Dec., 1740—*Thesaurus Resolutionum,* Tom. IX (1740), 74-76 and 85.

[112] S. C. C. *in Vintimilien, Dismembrationis,* die 8 Aug., 1818—Pallottini, *op. cit.,* VIII, 6. 595, n. 268: ". . . Nam ob utriusque Populi rixas et odia, quae sola perpetua dissociatio compescere valet, *aliquando* conceditur dismembratio." Italics in the quotation are those of the writer.

If the instances in which the councils make direct mention of adjutant vicars are few, this fact is possibly due to the circumstance that the appointment of adjutants in a diocese scarcely ever constituted more than a very limited number of cases. It is altogether likely that in centuries past, as in our own day, a considerable number of parish priests, whose advanced years and broken health rendered them unequal to the task of administering their parishes singly and unaided, availed themselves of the option of resignation from the tenure of their office in preference to the alternative of accepting an adjutant whose grant of independent action, in even one or the other of the parochial activities which were once their very own, might furnish a test that impinged heavily upon their human sensibilities. At no time could it be a pleasant experience for them to be constrained to admit their irrelievable limitations when formerly their activity had measured up to the strictest demands. But, trying as this circumstance was, it could be accompanied by the redeeming consciousness that theirs was a condition not of their own deliberate choice or making. Yet, their second alternative—that of admitting an adjutant vicar into their own pastoral domain together with the resultant necessity of making themselves the constant spectators of their own continued disability—still remained a test for human courage. To invite its deliberate occurrence, even though it was occasioned by merely passive choice, might serve all the more to intensify the realization of their distraught feelings. If a choice had to be made, the option of avoiding this second alternative seemed the happier preference.

Nevertheless, there were also instances in which this human element was not so pronounced. Furthermore, in these cases, justice and equity demanded that the partially incapacitated pastor be sustained in his right by which he sought, in the hope of receiving the material recompense that was his due, to continue furnishing whatever benefit his waning strength could still supply; hence, there always was, as there will always be, need of legal adaptation for these eventualities.

A number of provincial councils of the past century make no direct mention of adjutant vicars in parishes. They speak solely of vicars who are appointed in parishes for the sake of integrating by their assistance the work which is objectively too extensive to be accomplished without their help. It is indeed certain that assistant vicars are plainly referred to in these passages, yet, it is not so readily denied that adjutant vicars may also be implied. Whatever legislation there may be contained in the acts and decrees of these councils, it is by way of analogy with the law concerning assistant priests, rather than by a direct and exclusive statute applicable to adjutant priests alone, that any mention is included of the latter. Among these councils may be mentioned the following: Paris, Rheims, Tours, Rouen, Bordeaux, Aix-la-Chapelle and Toulouse.[113]

Other councils like those of Cassel, Bourges and Ravenna use the term *"adjutor,"* but in its context this word is evidently employed to signify an assistant priest or curate.[114] Recognizing the relative infrequency for the application of a specific law concerning adjutant priests, these councils left its disposition in the personal judgment of the bishops whenever emergencies arose.

There were, however, a few provincial councils which drew up specific legislation on this point. The councils of Rouen, Bordeaux, and Aquileia,[115] made provision for this need shortly after the council of Trent, by recognizing that in cases where the removal of the *"illiterati, et impediti parochialium ecclesiarum rectores"* would occasion spiritual harm to the parishes or disturb the order of peace in the communities, the bishops were to assign adjutant vicars for the proper administration of the parochial functions. At the close of the following century the provincial council of Naples in the year 1699 [116] reminded the pastors, who had *coadjutores* appointed to them, of the duty to perform personally whatever pastoral work they were still able to do, since they were not freed of all pastoral obligations by the appointment of such a pastoral aid. Their *coadjutores*

[113] Cf. *Coll. Lac.*, IV, 15a, 140-41, 266c and d, 526b, 587, 984, 1044. These councils were celebrated in the years 1849-1850.

[114] *Coll. Lac.*, III, 832; IV, 1098; VI, 195. These councils were held in 1850, 1853, and 1855 respectively. Cf. also Chapter III, footnotes 23 and 32.

[115] Conc. Prov. Rothomagense (1581); Conc. Prov. Burdigalense (1583); Conc. Prov. Aquileiense (1596)—Hardouin, X, 1237; 1357; 1895-96.

[116] Tit. 9, cap. 4, n. 9—*Coll. Lac.*, I, 225.

were assigned not as complete substitutes in their office, but as supply priests for the fulfillment of the ministries to which they could no longer give personal attention.

In the early eighteenth century a provincial synod was celebrated in the city of Bahia in Brazil. One of its primary aims was the rehabilitation of priestly learning. With regard to the *vicarii et coadjutores* it demanded a triennial examination in the matters pertaining to their ministry. The synod seems to refer to both classes of parochial vicars when it uses these two terms, for, whilst it speaks first of the help afforded a pastor in the administration of the sacraments, it next mentions the aid given him for the integration of his personal office as pastor. If the examination proved unsatisfactory, a time-limit was set during which these *vicarii et coadjutores* were to equip themselves with the needed knowledge and furnish proof of its acquisition in a subsequent examination before they were to be appointed unconditionally to any parochial station or ministry.[117]

In the last century the councils of Albi (1850), Vienna (1858), Prague (1860), Cologne (1863), and the Republic of Colombia (1868) all present statutory legislation on the question of adjutant vicars. The first of these ordains that all vicars exercise a merely delegated jurisdiction. It recognizes the fact, however, that these vicars have their powers delegated to them *ad universitatem causarum* and that in consequence of this they are to supply the pastor *quasi ex officio* whenever he is absent or otherwise hindered or prevented from the fulfillment of his pastoral duties.[118] There is hardly any doubt that the council had both adjutant and assistant vicars in mind when it drew up this legislative decree.

The council of the Province of Vienna simply notes that all pastoral duties remain a personal obligation for the parish priests unless his infirmity or unless his infirmity or old age demand the services of a colaborer for a partial or total supply-pastoration in the parochial ministry.[119]

---

[117] Synodus Bahiensis (1707), lib. III, tit. 29—*Coll. Lac.*, I, 855.

[118] Conc. Prov. Albiense (1850), tit. II, n. 9—*Coll. Lac.*, IV, 416.

[119] Conc. Provinciae Viennensis (1858), tit. II, cap. 8—*Coll. Lac.*, V, 157.

The decrees of the council of Prague hold the rural deans responsible for making tentative provision for a stricken pastor who lacks the services of an *adjutor.* They are then to bring notification to the bishop of their act in order that the bishop may make definite provision for the future.[120]

The enactment of the Provincial Council of Cologne is the most specific of any of the decrees formulated by the contemporary councils. In treating of the adjutant vicar it speaks of the requisites for his assignment, the manner of his appointment, the assurance of a suitable salary for him, and the extent of his jurisdictional and pastoral powers.[121]

The last council to be cited acquaints us with the discipline prevalent in the Republic of Colombia in the second half of the last century. Its legislation was a departure from the current practice elsewhere maintained in so far as it permitted an incapacitated parish priest to exercise his own choice, not indeed in determining when there was need of an adjutant vicar, but in selecting him after the bishop had indicated this mode of provision in the case. The act of nomination by the pastor required a corresponding act of admission on the part of the bishop. A schedule of the prospective vicar's obligations and consequent rights was to be submitted to the bishop, whose personal sanction sealed the agreement with a mutually binding power for both the pastor and the vicar.[122] If the pastor did not use his faculty of selecting the needed adjutant, then the

---

120 Conc. Prov. Pragense (1860), tit. VI, cap. 8—*Coll. Lac.*, V, 564.

121 Conc. Provinciae Colocensis (1863), tit. II, cap. 6—*op. cit.*, V, 636: "Jus dandi ex causis canonicis parocho administratorem temporaneum Episcopo competit, qui debet etiam invito dare quando parochus ex aliqua perenni corporis vel animi infirmitate ultro parochiam suam debite regere nequit, aut senio gravatus vel alias adeo impeditus perpetuo sit, ut officium suum utiliter exercere non valeat; potest vero dari administrator illi parocho quem Episcopus necessaria ad officium suum scientia destitutum compererit. Portionem congruam administratori per parochum cedendam, partes item agendorum in cura pastorali definit Episcopus."

122 Decreta Synodi Provincialis Neo-granatensis (1868), tit. II, cap. 8—*op. cit.*, VI, 483-84: "Episcoporum proinde erit efficere, ut parochi coadjutorem sibi adjungant, quoties infirmitate vel senectute ita laborant, ut ministerii oneribus haud valeant satisfacere, . . . aut vel quoties tanta erit parochi aut ignorantia aut vitae inhonestas, ut ministerium cadat . . . . Electio documento roborata, in quo onera, quae vicario committuntur, tempus et merces adsignata, inscripta sint, Episcopi sanctioni submittatur, qua obtenta, partes ad implementum obligantur."

bishop himself appointed him and specified his sphere of duties and rights. A vicar thus appointed became removable at the wish and the behest of the bishop.[123]

The legislation of the Church on adjutant vicars towards the close of the last century is ably summarized by Kober.[124] According to this author an adjutant was assigned:

1) When the pastor suffered from total and continued unfitness of body or mind. The contrary will of the pastor notwithstanding, the bishop could then appoint an adjutant vicar. The bishop could also regulate the amplitude of the latter's parochial powers and specify his share in the parochial beneficial income. The pastor received what was necessary for his honorable sustenance. The benefice became vacant only with the death or resignation of its titular incumbent. But the bishop remained free to dismiss the adjutant even prior to this contingency.

2) When the pastor, apart from any personal fault or criminal negligence, lacked the intellectual and mental qualifications required of him as the spiritual shepherd of his Christian flock. In this case the bishop could not execute an appointment as long as proper proof against the pastor was not established. The mouthing abroad of serious suspicions constituted legal ground for an examination that could be undertaken either at the time of the bishop's visitation of the parish, or even outside of such official visit. For his pastoral activity the adjutant's sphere of powers was specified according to the need of the functions he was called upon to supply. He was removable at will by the bishop. His ministry furthermore ceased as soon as his pastor had rendered sufficient proof of his personal pastoral capacity.

3) When the pastor, without the perpetration of any criminal act, had nevertheless estranged the confidence of his people by misguided zeal, brusque demeanor or any similar defect of priestly character to the extent that his ministry not only offered no hope of success, but even indicated the fear of a contrary result. The bishop was then empowered to remove the pastor

---

[123] *Ibid.*

[124] "Hilfspriester," *Herder-Kirchenlexicon,* V, 2097.

temporarily and, in the interim, to provide for the parish through the services of a supply vicar.[125]

ART. VI. NOTES OF COMPARISON BETWEEN PAST AND PRESENT DISCIPLINE

A comparison instituted between the Post-Tridentine discipline and that of the present Code reveals a remarkable similarity and in many points a near-identity. The point of substantial *juridical* difference between them consists in this that now the local ordinary is empowered to execute this measure of pastoral need altogether in view of his ordinary jurisdiction as the pastor of his diocese, when formerly there acceded to the bishop the delegated power of the Apostolic See.[126]

The diversity of juridical effects emanating from the dual possibility of recourse or appeal, as implied by this grant of the Tridentine Council together with the legislation of the Decretals which integrated it, has been considered in a previous section of this chapter.[127] The action of recourse or appeal which under the current legislation is available against the preceptive decree or judicial sentence of the local ordinary must, of course, follow the ruling of the pertinent canons of the IV Book of the Code.[128] The cases in which either the one or the other of these two modes of legal redress becomes potentially operative cover a wide range of possibilities in relation to the subject under discussion.[129]

---

[125] *Ibid.*: "Wenn der Pfarrer, ohne sich eines eigentlichen Verbrechens schuldig gemacht zu haben, durch unerleuchteten Eifer, durch schroffes Auftreten oder aus irgend einem anderen Grunde sich die Gemüther in einer Weise entfremdete, dass keine gedeihliche Wirksamkeit zu hoffen, sonderen das directe Gegenteil zu fürchten ist, so kann ihn der Bischof provisorisch vom Orte seiner Thätigkeit entfernen und die Seelsorge einsteweilen durch einen Vikar verwalten lassen."

[126] Cf. Stutz, *Der Geist des Codex iuris canonici*, pp. 270-71, together with the authors there cited by him. The discussion centers about the meaning to be attached to the two phrases so frequently recurring in the sessions of the Council of Trent: "*Tamquam apostolici Sedis delegati*" and "*Etiam tamquam apostolici Sedis delegati.*"

[127] Cf. Art. IV, §X.

[128] Cf. cans. 1569-71; 1879-91.

[129] Cf. cans. 192 §3, 475 §4, 1333 §2, 1340 §3, 1428 §3, 2146 §§1-3, 2153 §1, etc.

The substantial contrast between the old law and the present discipline consists in the more efficient means now conceded to local ordinaries for securing a fruitful pastoral ministry in the parochial churches of their dioceses. The decree *"Maxima Cura"* of the Sacred Congregation of the Consistory, issued on August 20, 1910,[130] established a notable departure from the legal practice and discipline of the past.[131] At the same time it offered a basis for the legislation now canonized in the Code.[132] It is in accord with these canonical norms that diocesan authority will now proceed.

---

[130] *AAS*, II (1910), 636-48.

[131] Cf. Sebastianelli, "Inamovibilitas Parochi," *Analecta Ecclesiastica*, IV (1896), 43-45 and 83-87, for a comprehensive statement of the method of legal procedure in the removal of pastors as based upon the ruling of the Council of Trent.

[132] Cf. cans. 2142-94.

PART II

PRESENT LEGISLATION

CHAPTER V

TEXTUAL IMPORT OF CANONS 475 §1 AND 476 §§1-2

CANON 475

§1. Si parochus ob senectutem, mentis vitium, imperitiam, caecitatem aliamve permanentem causam suis muniis rite obeundis impar evaserit, Ordinarius loci det vicarium adiutorem, praesentatum a Superiore, si de paroecia agatur religiosis concredita, qui suppleat eius vicem, assignata eidem congrua fructuum portione, nisi aliter provisum sit.

CANON 476

§1. Si parochus propter populi multitudinem aliasve causas nequeat, judicio Ordinarii, solus convenientem curam gerere paroeciae, eidem detur unus vel plures vicarii cooperatores, quibus congrua remuneratio assignatur.

§2. Vicarii cooperatores constitui possunt sive pro universa paroecia, sive pro determinata paroeciae parte.

ART. I. EXPLANATION OF TERMINOLOGY

§I. THE APELLATION OF THE *Vicarius Adiutor*

The specific designation by which the vicar mentioned in canon 475 §1 is differentiated from all other vicars is to be found in the word *adiutor*. This term reveals a great similarity, one might even say a near-identity, with the term *coadiutor* that is used in designating a titular bishop assigned in aid of an infirm or decrepit episcopal local ordinary. The etymon of both words is the same. The traditional usage of the Church from the time of the Tridentine Council had employed the term *coadiutor* for bishops and priests alike who were assigned in personal aid of their episcopal and parochial incumbents in office. The difference of terminology now employed by the Code may have been motivated for possibly two reasons: 1) Because of a real difference in the *potential* scope of their functions;[1] and 2) because of the inequality of their honor and dignity in the Church.

The Church is not wont to relinquish the traditional usage of words which have become time-honored in her acceptance of them. Hence, the term *coadiutor* was also retained by her. But, since its general use as applied to bishops dated back to times preceding the council of Trent,[2] while its adoption as referring to priests became common only with this Ecumenical Council,[3] the spirit of traditional propriety and equity suggested that the term *coadiutor* be reserved rather for the bishop, not only because of his priority of claim to it, but also because of his precedence over the priest in the rank of ecclesiastical honor and dignity.

The reservation of this term for bishops postulated the selection of another word for the priests whose functions were similar to theirs. The choice fell upon the word *adiutor* as being best suited to convey the kindred idea attaching to his parochial ministry. On the one hand, the term is similar and even near-identical in meaning with that of *coadiutor*, and thus succeeds most aptly in its indication of the like work imposed. On the other hand, the term marks an appropriate deviation which likewise bespeaks a relative limitation of meaning and thus achieves its purpose of delineating the corresponding restriction of potential powers in the parochial ministry.

Authors who have written commentaries on the Code in the English language are not at one in their appellation of the *adiutor*. Augustine[4] uses the words *coadjutor* and *assistant*.

---

[1] Cf. cans. 351 §§1-2 and 475 §§2-3.

[2] C. 5, X, *de clerico aegrotante vel debilitato*, III, 6; c. unic., *de clerico aegrotante vel debilitato*, III, 5, in VI°.

[3] Sessio XXI, *de ref.*, c. 6—*Canones et Decreta*, p. 129.

[4] *A Commentary of Canon Law*, II, 568-70; *The Pastor according to the New Code of Canon Law*, p. 45; *Rights and Duties of Ordinaries*, p. 182, n. 4; *The Canonical and Civil Status of Catholic Parishes in the United States*, p. 217.

Ayrinhac [5] refers to him as a "vicar coadjutor, called also sometimes administrator." In a subsequent passage he calls him a *vicar adjutor*. Woywod [6] employs the term *assistant vicar*, or simply *vicar*. This lack of uniformity in the choice of an English term corresponding to the Latin terminology readily shows the difficulty of finding an appropriate and at the same time suitable word for the appellation used in the Code.

It might seem that the use of any one of the several words employed is not sufficiently precise to warrant standard acceptance. To use the word *coadjutor* clashes with the wording of the Code which appropriates this term for bishops only. To adopt the appellation of *assistant* or *assistant vicar* confuses the issue with parochial curates who are frequently, and indeed very correctly, called by these same names. To accept the term *administrator* creates a like ambiguity since this word is by better right reserved as the equivalent of *vicarius oeconomus*.[7] To appropriate a mere transliteration of the Latin term *adiutor* by calling him an *adjutor* seems commendable only then when no English equivalent can be found in its place. And finally, to employ the generic expression of *vicar* without any properly qualifying adjective or adjectival noun leaves the word quite so unspecified as to fall short of gaining its native, specific purpose.

The terms mentioned by these authors fail to achieve their proper aim because of their overlapping, ambiguous, or inoperative tendencies. The terms *coadjutor, administrator, assistant*, and *assistant vicar*, trespass upon alien territory; the word *adjutor* tarries upon neutral soil; the name *vicar* without any added specification simply recoils upon its indeterminate self.

As stated, the choice of a definitely precise and properly familiar term presents its difficulty. The term selected should embrace within itself the enlarged concept of a personal aid permanently rendered. It should also be so closely allied with the Latin form in its construction as to leave it recognizable in its English adaptation.

Free from any desire to discredit his masters, the writer has earnestly sought to meet these requirements. It appears to him

[5] *Constitution of the Church in the new Code of Canon Law*, nn. 298-99, pp. 358-59.

[6] *A Practical Commentary on the Code of Canon Law*, I, 172-73.

[7] Cf. Ayrinhac, *op. cit.*, nn. 294-95, pp. 354-56.

that the term *adjutant vicar*, or simply *adjutant* might not prove ill-chosen. Abstracting from the military signification which in common parlance attaches to the term, usage may well appropriate it, and that without any infringement on the exactitudes of lexicographers, in the sense of the person of a priest engaged by his appointment in the aid of his pastor. The hope that the selection of this term will furnish the requisite clarity and exactness of expression suggests its constant use henceforth throughout the present treatise.

§II. The Appellation of the *Vicarius Cooperator*

Much less difficulty attaches to the effort of finding an appropriate equivalent for the Latin *vicarius cooperator*. Although he is known by various appellations in our country, the more common words used in designation of his identity are the terms *curate* and *assistant*. The use of either of them in any section whatsoever of the country would not open the way for any misapprehension of meaning. If in some restricted areas the terms *assistant priest, assistant vicar*, or *parochial vicar* seem to enjoy equal, if not prevalent, favor of usage, the added variety of appellation occasioned by their use does not becloud the ultimate issue of clarity since the conjoint form of their expression tends to specify their meaning even more definitely.

The Latin term *vicarius cooperator* is a most precise appellation. It implies a dual concept: on the one hand, the word *vicarius* points to a potential capacity of subordinate substitution; on the other hand, that of *cooperator* supplies the needed determinant to specify him as belonging to that class of vicars who are associated as co-workers with their parish priests for the quantitative integration of the pastoral work.[8] Yet, the use

[8] The following authors reflect the varied nomenclature in the vernaculars of the different European countries: Vermeersch-Creusen, *Epitome Iuris Canonici*, I. n. 520, p. 330; Eichmann, *Lehrbuch des Kirchenrechts*, pp. 210-11; Hilling, *Personenrecht*, p. 228; Hilling, "Cooperator: Eine einheitliche Amtsbezeichnung," *AkKR*, IC (1919), 146-47; De Meester, *Juris Canonici et Juris Canonico-civilis Compendium*, II, n. 877; Schäfer, *Die Kirchenämter*, II Band, *Pfarrer und Pfarrvikare*, pp. 100-04; Freising, "Rechte des Pfarrers über die sogenannten Hilfsgeistlichen, *LQS*, LVI (1903), 801-07; Rettenbacher, "Der Kooperator nach dem Codex Juris," *LQS*, LXXII (1919), 337-48; "Gibt es amovibile Beneficiaten?", *ibid.*,

of such a term as *associate pastor* would surely overdraw the relationship existing between the parish priest and his sacerdotal helper to the latter's unmerited recognition. The terms *curate* and *assistant* have gained a currency of stabilized meaning, and hence their signification has become unmistakable in English-speaking countries.[9]

In Europe the vernacular equivalent of *vicarius cooperator* has achieved uniformity in its use in most of the countries. In Spain he is the *coadjutor*,[10] in France and Belgium the *vicaire*,[11] in the Netherlands the *onderpastoor*,[12] and in Italy the *vice-curato* or *sotto-curato*.[13] In the central countries of Europe, notably in Switzerland, Germany, and Austria, the usage is still quite variant in the German language.[14]

481-83; Grosam, "Die Anstellung der Kooperatoren durch die Ordinarien nach Anhörung der Pfarrer," *LQS*, LXXIV (1921), 305-06; Mair, "Beichtsjurisdiktion der pfarrlichen Vikare," *LQS*, LXXII (1919), 237-42; Haring, "Die Jurisdiktion des Pfarrvikars," *LQS*, LXXV (1922), 22-27; "Die Bestellung des pfarrlichen Hilfspriesters," *LQS*, LXXVI (1923), 335-37; "Bestellung der Hilfspriester," *LQS*, LXXX (1927), 788; "Die Trauung durch einen 'inaudito parocho' bestellten Hilfspriester," *LQS*, LXXXII (1929), 126-27; Schneider, "Über die Jurisdiktion und Anstellung der Pfarrvikare," *Th Gl*, XVII (1925), 55 ff.; Cronin, *The New Matrimonial Legislation*, pp. 47-48; Stutz, *Der Geist des Codex iuris canonici*, p. 40. See also *AkKR*, CI (1921), 52.

[9] Cronin, *op. cit.*, *loc. cit.*, deprecates the use of the term *curate*. He refers to this appellation as "a singular inversion of the true and canonical signification of the word." His argument has weight in the light of the current usage in France of *curé* and in Italy of *curato* to designate those who have the care of souls. Cf. "De Canone 1427 et de Vicariis Perpetuis," *Periodica*, XIV (1925), pp. (17)-(18), for a discussion of the term *curatus*. However, the author's substitution of the term *coadjutor* has become equally inadmissible since the promulgation of the Code.

[10] Cf. Muñiz, *Derecho Parroquial*, II, n. 498, footnote 1; Melo, *De Exemptione Regularium*, p. 91. The term adopted for the *adiutor* is *regente*. See footnote 128 of next chapter.

[11] Cf. Vermeersch-Creusen, *Epitome Iuris Canonici*, I, n. 520, p. 330.

[12] *Ibid.*

[13] Cf. Cronin, *op. cit.*, p. 48.

[14] Cf. Hilling, "Cooperator: Eine einheitliche Amtsbezeichnung," *AkKR*, IC (1919), 146-47. Stutz (*Der Geist des Codex iuris canonici*, p. 40) offers what appears to be a model adaptation of the terms *vicarii adiutores* and *vicarii cooperatores* when he uses the respective words *Pfarrgehilfe* and *Pfarrhelfer*. See Köstler, *Wörterbuch zum Codex Iuris Canonici*, v. *vicarius cooperator*, p. 367.

Art. II. Motives of Appointment

§I. The Assignment of the *Vicarius Adiutor*

Canon 475 §1 enumerates a number of causes that incapacitate the pastoral activity of a parish priest to the extent that an adjutant vicar becomes necessary for him. Some of these causes are mentioned explicitly, both because of their more common occurrence as also because of their aptitude for the exemplification of additional causes. The four disabilities listed by name are the following: senility, mental debility, pastoral incompetency, and blindness. It is obvious that each one of these implies the existence of an actual personal disability. But, in addition, in each case the disability mentioned is of such a nature that its existence is not merely transitory, but actually permanent and abiding for the person affected by it. Hence, when the canon continues with the phrase *"aliamve permanentem causam,"* the potential causes here included must all be understood to involve both the note of personal disability together with the connotation of its continued perdurance.[15]

A. Personal Disability of the Parish Priest

The first element is that of personal disability.[16] Now, disability may be occasioned in two ways. It may arise when one's powers and faculties suffer deterioration or impairment so that they are no longer equal to the performance of a task or the fulfillment of an office whose objective requirements have not been increased beyond the original measure of capacity requisite for their discharge. It may also result when one's powers and faculties not only suffer no deterioration or impairment, but even achieve an improvement or enhancement, and yet are no longer equal to the performance of a task or the fulfillment of

[15] Cf. Wernz-Vidal, *Ius Canonicum*, II, *De Personis*, n. 743, p. 801; De Meester, *Compendium*, II, n. 872, p. 336, footnote 1. Additional causes mentioned by way of example by these two authors are: aberration of the mind, amnesia, paralysis, deafness, loss of speech.

[16] Cf. Vermeersch-Creusen, *Epitome Iuris Canonici*, I, n. 519, p. 330; Hilling, *Personenrecht*, p. 226; Eichmann, *Lehrbuch des Kirchenrechts*, §83, n. 4, p. 210.

an office whose objective requirements have been increased beyond either the original or also the acquired measure of capacity to discharge them. In the first instance the disability arises not from a change of external circumstances, but purely from a lapse of inherent capacity. In the second it originates not with the person himself but because of the changed circumstances surrounding him. Broadly speaking, the deficiency thus resulting may be called a personal disability, but in the prior case it proceeds from within the person himself whilst in the latter it accrues to him from without.

This consideration naturally suggests the question: Does canon 475 §1 intend to embrace both sets of circumstances as constituting a personal disability in the parish priest? Both the wording of this canon and the norms established in canon 476 §§1-2 for the appointment of curates or assistant priests can be said to indicate a solidly negative reply.

First of all, the causes expressly mentioned as requiring the appointment of an adjutant are all of such a nature that the deficiency created by them in a disabled parish priest indicates a purely inherent lapse of capacity. But, since these explicit causes are set up to furnish a directive norm of judgment in determining other implied causes, the inference is that no cause affords a reason for the appointment of an adjutant which does not manifest a strictly personal impairment and active deterioration of the fitness and competency formerly enjoyed. A deficiency accruing passively through the medium of newly arising needs in a parish, regardless of their nature, does not argue a lapse of the pastor's normal powers, but an accession of work so constituted in quality or quantity as to out-measure the scope of his normal capacity. Hence, in this case provision should be made according to canon 476 §1 by the appointment of an assistant priest or parochial curate who will integrate the parochial ministry which has outgrown his pastor's normal powers.

Another circumstance that adds weight to this interpretation is the fact that the construction of canon 475 §1 is cast in the active voice of the verb.[17] The word *parochus* is made the subject of the sentence. Consequently, whatever impairment of parochial administrative capacity arises is represented as deriving

---

[17] "Si parochus . . . impar evaserit."

its actualization from his own person as its efficient cause. If the law had intended to be more inclusive in its enumeration of contributing causes for the appointment of an adjutant vicar it could readily have availed itself of an impersonal grammatical construction, or at least it could have shaped the sentence in a passive mold, which would then admit the action of external agencies as well as the factors at work within the person himself into the realm of canonical determinants of an adjutant's appointment. Grammatically, the canon excludes the equalization of externally operative causes with internally impairing agencies even though both factors produce a parallel result of need in the parish.

In order to exemplify the above, a number of cases may be adduced. It can happen that the establishment of a new industrial project in a parish will occasion the influx of a foreign-speaking parochial population. The inability of their parish priest to offer them the necessary spiritual care results not from the fact that the population is increased, but from his unfamiliarity with their foreign tongue. His pastoral ministry suffers indeed from a handicap, for he remains no longer able to provide a suitable pastoral care for all the members of his flock. But his essential, usual and normal competency as a pastor of souls remains unaffected by the fact that an accidental, unusual and abnormal contingency makes ampler qualification necessary for the full and unaided pastoration of his parish. This case therefore demands not the appointment of an adjutant vicar but of a curate or assistant priest who, because he is conversant with the language and the customs of this class of the parish, will help to integrate the work which is beyond the pastor's normal power of fulfillment.[18]

Furthermore, canon 476 §2 makes provision for just such a case as is here considered when it suggests that the appointment of a curate can stipulate his work for the entire parish or for a determined part or portion thereof. The "*determinata paroeciae pars*" mentioned in this canon should not be restricted to a meaning that implies division of the territory only. The phrase

---

[18] Cf. Augustine, *Commentary*, II, 573, and Ayrinhac, *Constitution of the Church*, p. 362; see also Benedictus XIV, const. "*Etsi Pastoralis*," die 26 Maii 1742, §V, n. IX—*Fontes*, I, n. 328, p. 741.

as it stands is not qualified in any way. Hence, it ought rather to be taken as referring to any kind of equitable and feasible division possible. But, an apportionment of a particular part of the parish which results from the presence of different language groups can be made as equitably and feasibly as a division which relies upon territorial boundaries. Consequently, the case is one which requires the services of an *assistant* in the parish.

Other cases implying a similar limitation of a parish priest's individual competency in the full administration of the parochial duties can arise. While the extent of the parochial territory and the number of parishioners resident therein may not in themselves, either singly or conjointly, demand an ampler care than an individual priest can supply, yet there may be other factors that do make such a demand.[19] Among them may be mentioned the following: A pastor's inconstant health, his advancement in years, the multiplication of his various pastoral duties and increased demands in the administrative government of the parish. The two last conditions can depend upon a variety of circumstances. Such, for instance, would be the presence of hospitals, asylums, or other similar institutions within the confines of the parish if there were no special chaplain appointed for them, the added burdens of stricter school supervision, an enlarged programme in the formation and direction of new parochial societies or confraternities, the organization of needed social and charitable agencies, the possible necessity of erecting a new parish building for the accommodation and furtherance of these newly undertaken activities, and finally, the increased frequentation of the sacraments because of the fuller flowering of religious life and activity in the parish.[20]

The limitations thus created in the ability of an individual pastor to supply the needed pastoral care do not call for the assignment of an adjutant, for they are not the result of an inherent lapse of a former personal competency, but rather the consequence of external contingencies and adjuncts which extend the realm of pastoral activities beyond the scope of an individual normal ability to fulfill them. Hence, such and similar needs will be consulted by the appointment of a curate or

[19] Schäfer, *Die Kirchenämter*, II Band, *Pfarrer und Pfarrevikare*, p. 100.

[20] Cf. Schäfer, *ibid.*; Augustine, *Commentary*, II, 573.

parish assistant whose association with the pastor makes possible the consummation of a work which has outgrown the normal capacities of an individual pastoration.

B. Permanency of Its Duration

Besides the element of personal disability in a parish priest there must accede also the circumstance of its continued and permanent duration before there is need of an adjutant for him. Ailments which temporarily incapacitate his personal abilities, or even chronic infirmities as long as they still offer a solid hope of successful treatment and subsequent cure, are not sufficient reasons for the appointment of an adjutant vicar. Such temporary or even protracted emergencies can be given their proper attention by the employment of a substitute or the assignment of an assistant vicar.[21]

The wording of the Code[22] leaves room for no other conclusion since both the explicit and the implied disabilities arising from an impairment of bodily health and mental vigor are in their very nature indicated as permanent and perduring. The sole instance in which the Code allows the appointment of an adjutant when the parish priest's incompetency is not necessarily of a permanent nature is in the case of his lack of suitable pastoral qualifications. This actual pastoral defect in his official person may result from a number of causes among which might be numbered such as the following: inexperience, imprudence, improvidence, notorious unrefinement, extreme uncontrol of temper and a brusque uncouthness of action and demeanor, whether in his official or in his personal relations, towards the people of his parish. This is the practical and unfolded meaning of the word *imperitia* used by the Code.[23]

Of their nature these defects are not irremediable. Yet, since a pastor's activity could easily be so vitiated by any one of them

---

[21] Cf. Cocchi, *Commentarium in Codicem Iuris Canonici*, lib. II, *De Personis*, Pars I, n. 364, p. 441: "In casu infirmitatis temporaneae potius assumendus est vicarius substitutus vel etiam cooperator." Ayrinhac, *Constitution of the Church*, n. 298, p. 358: "Under the present law temporary inability would not ordinarily justify this measure [i.e., the appointment of an adjutant], as it might suffice to have a vicar co-operator."

[22] Cf. can. 475 §1.

[23] Cf. Augustine, *Commentary*, II, 570.

that either the spiritual or temporal welfare of the parish might not only lack the proper furtherance of its interests, but even suffer actual harm and detriment, it becomes necessary that some other priest be appointed to supply the personal deficiencies of the parochial incumbent until such time when the latter can give proper and satisfying assurance of a salutary government of the parish by his own unaided efforts. Since the priest appointed for this interim must supply not merely a quantitative but also a qualitative defect in the administration of the parish, it will be an adjutant who is assigned. If the pastor within a reasonable time limit, granted him by the prudent judgment of his local ordinary, cannot furnish proof of his personal fitness and qualification for the unaided resumption of his pastoral duties, or if, moreover, proper provision for the parish can no longer be made by the appointment of an adjutant, then the local ordinary will proceed to his removal or transfer.[24]

§II. The Assignment of the *Vicarius Cooperator*

After the foregoing discussion, which involved mention of the *vicarius cooperator* in its negative treatment, little remains to be said concerning the conditions that postulate or motivate the appointment of assistants to parochial churches. Canon 476 §1 makes *explicit* mention of only one cause when it uses the phrase *propter populi multitudinem.* But the canon obviously has in mind the possibility of a number of similar causes when it adds the phrase *aliasve causas.* This phrase furnishes a further illustrative enumeration by way of necessary connection and inseparable kinship with the single cause directly expressed. The indication of the law is plain; it has in mind any and all such objective conditions by reason of which the functions of the pastoral care exceed the measure of normal capacity that an individual pastor can afford.[25]

[24] Cf. cans. 475 §4, 2142-2161. Of especial note are cans. 2146 §§1 and 3, 2147 §2 1°, 2151, 2152 §1, 2153 §§1-2.

[25] Cf. Chelodi, *Ius de Personis*, n. 231, p. 383; Wernz-Vidal, *Ius Canonicum*, II, n. 744, p. 803; Prümmer, *Manuale Iuris Canonici*, Q. 165, p. 224; Koeniger, *Katholisches Kirchenrecht*, §41, n. 5, p. 238: "Der Pfarrkaplan . . . der zu dauernder Aushilfe für grössere Pfarreien, zuweilen nur für einen bestimmten Bezirk derselben, vom Ortsordinarius nach An-

A. Local and Real Needs of the Parish

Vermeersch [26] draws a line of clear distinction between the reasons and causes that necessitate the appointment of adjutants and assistants for parochial aid. The reasons demanding the assignment of an adjutant must be sought in the *personal* and *perduring* pastoral deficiencies of a *parish priest;* the causes postulating the appointment of an assistant must be looked for in the *local* and *real* agencies of need existing in a *parish.* Only such causes can come into consideration for the appointment of an assistant which presuppose that a full pastoral care within the parish can no longer be guaranteed by the normal and unimpaired abilities of its pastoral incumbent. It is insufficiency of the personal office, and not deficiency in the official person of the parish priest that is involved when local and real agencies of need call for an associate helper in the fulfillment of the pastoral work. This fact is given distinctive recognition in the past century by one of the provincial councils which declares that parish assistants are appointed *"in partem ministerii, non muneris pastoralis."* [27] This same idea was oftentimes expressed in a similar way when it was said that assistants are appointed *"non in partem curae, sed ad participationem officii."* [28]

B. Transiency of Their Duration

The parochial needs which require alleviation and relief through the appointment of an assistant pastoral helper are not always such as to indicate continued permanent duration. In some instances one can readily foresee that the special contingencies creating the present need will be of comparatively short duration. A parish priest may be confronted with the task of

hörung des Pfarrers (C. Conc. 13 Nov. 1920) ernannt, bei Klosterpfarreien durch den Obern nach Anhörung des parochus actualis (vic. perp.) vorgeschlagen und vom Ordinarius approbiert wird; . . ." The *larger parishes* may exist as such either because of territorial extension or because of a populous membership.

[26] *Epitome Iuris Canonici,* n. 519, p. 330.

[27] Conc. Provinciae Auscitanae (1851), c. VII, n. 54—*Coll. Lac.,* IV, 1180.

[28] *Coll. Lac.,* IV, 140, 266, 416-17, 587, 833, 984, 1098, 1180. Cf. passages indicated in footnotes 59 and 99 of Chapter III.

erecting a parochial school or some other parish unit. During the planning, the progress and the execution of this work, too many demands may be made upon his time and energy to allow him to meet all the other requirements of his pastoral care. Once the work is completed he may again be in a position to attend to his pastoral duties unaided and alone.

Similar conditions of a mere temporary need of added pastoral help can arise in parishes contiguous to the multiplied places of seasonal resort. To escape from the rigor of cold or the oppression of heat, to safeguard themselves against the contracting of unpleasant ailments from which they are not immune in their native clime during certain months of the year, to enjoy the invigoration of a more salubrious climate during the days or weeks of their vacations, or possibly even to give vent to their religious feelings by a continued visit at some noted shrine or place of pilgrimage, people will be absent from their home parishes over extended periods of time. During the interval of their absence they will necessarily shift the responsibility of their spiritual care to the parishes where they temporarily reside. On account of the largely increased membership that will thus be occasioned in these parishes, additional pastoral agencies are required for the proper spiritual care of the faithful temporarily resident there. The need continues for the relatively short time during which residence at these places holds a popular appeal and then subsides until its seasonal recurrence the following year. These intermittent recurrences of an enlarged pastoral ministry in the respective parishes can under almost all circumstances be properly met by the appointment of additional pastoral agencies in the persons of assistant priests whose ministry adapts itself to temporary as well as permanent needs in the parishes to which they are assigned.

The temporary need of any unusual diversification, amplification or intensification of pastoral activity may make necessary the continuous association of additional pastoral help for the interim until the need be relieved. Such unusual diversification could be required by reason of the influx of a foreign parochial population. The zealous parish priest can hope to furnish a proper pastoration for this portion of his flock only after he has made himself conversant with the language, the thought, the traditions and the customs of this people. Until such time he will recognize the need of an associate helper in his work. As soon as he has acquired the requisite abilities to meet this new element of pastoral administration he will no longer have need of an assistant and the work can then be committed once more to his individual pastoral care.

A merely temporary amplification of his pastoral duties could result from the fact that a transient and floating population will be resident in his parish for the number of months or even years that are required for the actualization of some gigantic industrial, commercial or governmental project. It may be plainly foreseen that this new element of population will move on to another part of the country as soon as the present project is completed.

A transient intensification of pastoral duties could originate from the circumstance that a new programme of parochial activity, such as the thorough and complete organization of the various parish groups into parochial sodalities or societies, needed introduction into a parish. The patient labor and assiduous application required to achieve success in this laudable endeavor might make such strenuous demands upon the parish priest that his whole-hearted devotion to this cause would not allow a concurrent dedication of his pasoral energies to the more ordinary, though equally necessary, duties of his pastoral charge. Here, too, as in the foregoing cases, the temporary assistance required by him will be met by the appointment of a parochial curate whose duty in a parish is to integrate the obligations of the pastoral office whether the need be admittedly transient or prospectively permanent.

The existence of a presently passing need is indeed not a feasible reason for the definite appointment of an assistant to a parish. The need should connote rather a *condition* than a mere *act* of emergency. But to insist that an appointment should be made only then when there is *permanent* need of added help would be placing too restrictive an interpretation on canon 476 §1 which merely specifies that if the parish priest alone cannot exercise habitually a proper care for the parish, then the ordinary is to join with him the one or more needed assistants. The word *gerere* used in the canon bespeaks at least a somewhat continued state of emergency, but it seems also equally plain that it does not indicate or stress either the prospective or absolute permanency of its duration. Hence, when Vidal [29] states that an assistant is appointed in view of some *permanent* cause, or always in relation to a particular parish which presents a special *permanent* condition of need, the lines seem to be drawn more narrowly than intended by the canon in question. To appropriate this interpretation in an effort to furnish conclusive proof that all assistants possess a canonical office in view of their objective stability of appointment certainly falls short as a reason of comprehensive force and universal application.[30]

The foregoing discussion of the canonical terminology used in appellation of parochial adjutants and assistants together with the extended enumeration of the potential causes that may contribute to the need of their appointment opens the way for the next consideration—*the manner* of their appointment as regulated by the Code.

Every canonical act of parochial appointment presupposes the existence of a canonical need. The certification of the existent need depends upon the prudent judgment of authority. The authority by which these acts of judgment are to be exercised is vested in the local diocesan ordinary. It is his right and office, within the legal confines of the sacred canons, to govern his diocese in matters both spiritual and temporal with a legislative, judicial, and coercive power.[31] The right to exercise this power which is innate in his office necessarily implies the right of exercising a native judgment from which alone a motivation of act can flow.

---

[29] *Ius Canonicum*, II, *De Personis*, n. 739, II, e, p. 797.

[30] Cf. *AER*, LXXVII (1927), p. 311, where, in reply to an objection raised against his previous article (*AER*, art. "Benefice of Assistant Pastorate," LXXVII [1927], pp. 74-79) the writer in the *Review* used this very argument. He contends that an assistant has a canonical office because his allotted station in the parish is endowed with objective perpetuity *in specie*, pointing to the teaching of Vidal as above indicated in substantiation of his statement. See Schwentner, "Über die Erteilung der allgemeinen Vollmacht zur Eheassistenz," *Th Gl*, XIX (1927), 518 ff., for a clear treatment on the delegated nature of an assistant's powers.

[31] Cf. can. 335 §1.

Moreover, by a priority of legally acknowledged right the local ordinary is competent in the matter of collating benefices and conferring offices throughout the territory of his diocese.[32] *A fortiori*, he enjoys the same right with regard to the assignment of any parochial ministry in his diocese.

Both rights—the certifying of the judgment and the sealing of the appointment—are vindicated for the local diocesan ordinary relative to the assignment of parochial adjutants and assistants in canons 475 §1 and 476 §§1-4. The discussion of the following chapters will be concerned with the *manner* in which this dual right of the local ordinary is to be exercised.

[32] Cf. cans. 1432 §1 and 152.

CHAPTER VI

THE MANNER OF APPOINTING ADJUTANTS

CANON 475

§1. Si parochus . . . impar evaserit, Ordinarius loci det vicarium adiutorem, praesentatum a Superiore, si de paroecia agatur religiosis concredita, qui suppleat eius vicem, assignata eidem congrua fructuum portione, nisi aliter provisum sit.

ART. I. FREE APPOINTMENT BY THE LOCAL ORDINARY

Excepting the cases where the local ordinary can proceed to the institution of an adjutant only upon a previous act of presentation by a religious superior, the appointment of an adjutant is an act of free collation reserved to the local ordinary. Since the term *local ordinary* must be accepted in its diversified and extended meaning,[1] unless an explicit stipulation in the Code,[2] or the context in which this term is used [3] concentrates and restricts its signification, the question may be asked whether this term is in our present connection to be accepted in its natural and unlimited or in its legally arbitrary and limited sense.

Canon 475 §1 simply uses the term *local ordinary* without any further specification or restriction. In virtue of this canon alone one could not say that any limitation of meaning was

---

[1] Can. 198 §1.

[2] Cf. can. 198 §§1-2. Dugan (*The Judiciary Department of the Diocesan Curia*, pp. 27-28), Stutz (*Der Geist des Codex iuris canonici*, pp. 286-95) and Chelodi (*Ius de Personis*, n. 200, pp. 331-32) tabulate a list in which are indicated the various canons in the Code limiting the rights and powers of the vicar general despite his rank and position as a local ordinary.

[3] E.g., can. 831 §1 in connection with 1303 §3; can. 1999 §3 together with can. 2002; etc.

indicated. But, since in canon 455 the Code offers a general instruction about the mode of provision for pastoral offices and ministries, it is in the light of this general ruling that one must fix the meaning of this term which is subsequently employed when mention is made of the competent authority for the act of appointment to the various subsidiary pastoral charges.[4] Therefore, canon 475 §1 also uses the term *local ordinary* in that scope of meaning which is attached to it by canon 455.

In reading this canon it must be noted that the appointment of an adjutant may occur within the compass of three distinct sets of circumstances. A local ordinary may govern his ecclesiastical territory under one of the following three conditions: 1) *Sede plena;* 2) *sede vacante;* 3) *sede impedita.* For each one of these eventualities canon 475 §1 indicates the proper and competent authority for appointment by its use of the term *local ordinary.*

§I. *Sede Plena*

The first paragraph of canon 455 considers the case of a diocese, a vicariate or prefecture apostolic, and an abbacy or prelature *nullius, sede plena.* Accordingly, the competent local ordinary will be either the bishop,[5] the apostolic administrator,[6] the vicar or prefect apostolic,[7] the abbot or prelate *nullius,*[8] or finally, their coadjutors when they enjoy the requisite rights and powers.[9]

§II. *Sede Vacante*

The second paragraph of canon 455 regulates the procedure of appointment, *sede vacante.* In a diocese that has become vacant,[10] the powers of appointment and the rights of institu-

[4] Cans. 472-78.

[5] Can. 335 §1.

[6] Cans. 312, 315, 316 §1.

[7] Can. 294 §§1-2.

[8] Can. 323 §§1-2.

[9] Cans. 351 §2, 309 §1.

[10] Can. 430 §1: "Sedis episcopalis vacat Episcopi morte, renuntiatione a Romano Pontifice acceptata, translatione ac provisione intimata." This canon is practically a restatement of the general ruling of canon 183 §1. But, compare can. 429 §5 with can. 188 to note the lines of departure from the general law.

tion in office as intimated by canon 455 §2 1°-2° devolve either upon the diocesan chapter,[11] the vicar capitular (in dioceses which have no chapter, the administrator),[12] or the apostolic administrator.[13] In a vicariate or prefecture apostolic these same powers and rights are transferred either to the pro-vicar or pro-prefect, or to their properly designated successors in office, or finally, if no canonical provision was made, to the senior missionary in the respective territory.[14] In an abbacy or prelacy *nullius* the transfer of government will pass to the chapter, to the vicar capitular or to the administrator appointed by the Metropolitan.[15] The coadjutor with the right of succession [16] cannot, properly speaking, be classified under this category. There is indeed a factual vacancy before he assumes office, but this vacancy is by its very nature of momentary duration only. The fact of vacancy is not a continued condition; it is a mere point of transition. One and the same moment of time contains within itself both the predecessor's lapse from and the successor's entry upon an office which suffers no practical interruption in its actual incumbency.

§III. *Sede Impedita*

The third eventuality contemplated by canon 455 §2 is had when a local ordinary rules over an ecclesiastical territory, *sede impedita.* The various elements constitutive of this condition are mentioned in canon 429 §1. Ayrinhac paraphrases it thus: "A bishop becomes physically impeded when one of the following causes prevents him from ruling his diocese and communicating even by letter with his subjects: captivity, whether in the hands of pagans, heretics, or schismatics, of external enemies or internal foes and fellow-citizens; relegation or exclusion from the diocese, exile, inability, whether due to bodily or men-

[11] Can. 435 §1: ". . . ante deputationem Vicarii Capitularis."

[12] Cans. 430 §3 1°, 432; 426 §5, 431 §2. In can. 426 §5 the Code uses the term *Vicarius Capitularis*, but the context evidently has in mind the administrator spoken of in can. 431 §2.

[13] Cans. 312, 313 §2, 315 §§1-2, 431 §1.

[14] Cans. 309 §§2-4, 310 §2.

[15] Cans. 435 §1; 327 §1; 432 §3, 285.

[16] Cans. 353, 355.

tal infirmity, culpable or inculpable." [17] That the Code applies this same canon for other local ordinaries besides bishops becomes manifest from canons 309 §2 and 327 §2 which directly invoke canon 429 for vicars or prefects apostolic and abbots or prelates *nullius* respectively.

When these conditions of impediment obtain in a *diocese*, then the office of local ordinary attaches either to a coadjutor,[18] to an apostolic administrator,[19] to the vicar general, to some other ecclesiastic appointed by the bishop,[20] or to one deputed by the Holy See in cases of moral emergencies.[21] If the jurisdiction of the apostolic administrator be in turn impeded, or if he lapse from office, then canon 429 is also to be invoked. Finally, if the vicar general or the ecclesiastic specially deputed by the bishop suffer a similar impediment of jurisdiction or lapse from office, then the chapter will constitute a vicar who assumes the government of the diocese with powers equivalent to those possessed by the vicar capitular.[22]

ART. II. THE EXCEPTIVE NORM OF CANON 430 §2

Incidentally it may be mentioned that canon 430 §2 excepts only the collation of ecclesiastical offices and benefices from the general rule—it matters not whether the vacancy in the episcopal office results *sede plena* or *sede impedita*—in virtue of which all the acts of the vicar general will have full valor up to the time when he receives certain notification of the effected vacancy. The exception here specified may not be interpreted as covering the entire period of his provisional tenure of office. Such an explanation would run counter to the inclusiveness of his implied rights as granted by canons 429 §1 and 455 §§2-3.[23]

---

[17] *Constitution of the Church*, n. 215, p. 268.

[18] Can. 353 §3.

[19] Can. 313 §2, 315 §2.

[20] Can. 429 §§1-2.

[21] Can. 429 §5.

[22] Cf. cans. 429 §3, 435 §§1-2, 66 §2.

[23] Cf. Stutz, *Der Geist des Codex iuris canonici*, p. 311, footnotes 3-5. The author manifestly questions the need of the vicar general to wait for a year from the time when the episcopal see became impeded before proceeding to the collation of benefices and offices. "Ob erst, wenn die Behinderung ein Jahr lang gedauert hat? Nach dem Wortlaut des can. 455 §2 und 3 müsste man das annehmen. Jedoch der Grundsatz des can. 436, dass sede

The exception constituted by canon 430 §2 rescinds only such acts of free appointment to benefices and offices which were placed by the vicar general during the time elapsed between the term of *actual vacancy* in the episcopal office and the term of his own *authentic information* concerning it. The restriction is one of uniform application whether the vacancy occurs *sede impedita* or *sede plena.* In the cases where these acts of collation are undertaken by the vicar general *sede impedita,* no general or special mandate is required in qualification for his acts.[24] Canon 429 §1 commits the government of the diocese to him in virtue of his office as vicar general.[25]

Eichmann is very definite when he speaks of the differentiation of powers enjoyed by the vicar general and the alternate episcopal deputy in the government of a diocese, *sede impedita.*[26] Koeniger,[27] Coronata,[28] and Wernz-Vidal,[29] by their use of the particle *aut* or some other construction of equivalent force, also indicate the former's power as ordinary and the latter's as delegated. Such an interpretation furnishes indeed a full compliance with the spirit of the Code in the light of which it is obvious that the government of a diocese is always, whenever possible, to be vested in the hands of an authority who can act with ordinary power.

In cases where the collation of benefices and offices, or any other act which requires a special mandate, is undertaken by the vicar general in virtue of such a particular authorization, his

---

vacante nihil innovetur, und die Ausnahme davon, die bisher nach Jahresfrist oder nach längerer Dauer der Stuhlerledigung auf Grund ausserordentlicher päpstlicher Vollmachten eintrat, in Zukunft aber von Gesetzes wegen eintreten soll, kommt bei behindertem Stuhl nicht in Betracht."—*Ibid.*, footnote 5.

[24] Cf. c. 3, *de temporibus ordinationum,* I, 9, in VI°; Prümmer, *Manuale Iuris Canonici,* Q. 132, 3c, p. 179; and especially Stutz *op. cit.*, pp. 288, 289, 292, 310, 311, 315, 323-29.

[25] ". . . dioecesis regimen, nisi Sancta Sedes aliter providerit, penes Episcopi Vicarium Generalem vel alium virum ecclesiasticum ab Episcopo delegatum esto."

[26] Cf. *Lehrbuch des Kirchenrechts,* §80, I, 1, p. 196: "Sind solche Vorkehrungen nicht getroffen worden, so steht die Diözesanregierung bei dem Generalvikar *als dem alter ego des Bischofs*, oder einer anderen vom Bischof hierzu delegierten kirchlichen Persönlichkeit."

[27] *Katholisches Kirchenrecht,* §39, p. 217.

[28] *Institutiones Iuris Canonici,* I, n. 457, p. 529.

[29] *Ius Canonicum,* II, *De Personis,* n. 705, p. 756.

act is exercised with a merely delegated power.[30] But whether his act proceeds from an ordinary power *sede impedita*, or whether it derives its valor from a delegated (mandated) power *sede plena*, its exercise continues with full canonical efficacy until it is in some way recalled.[31] For the act of collation of ecclesiastical offices and benefices, whether ordinary or delegated, it ceases with the moment when the episcopal see becomes actually vacant. For all the other acts it lapses only with the certain and authentic intimation of the fact of the vacancy.[32]

When the impedient circumstances enumerated in canon 429 §1 affect the status of a vicariate or prefecture apostolic, then the proper government of the territory by a local ordinary devolves upon the pro-vicar or pro-prefect. Should he in turn be similarly impeded, his office will be supplied by an ecclesiastic whom he has previously deputed as his potential successor. If no provision has been made in either of these ways, then the senior missionary becomes *ipso facto* the provisional head of the vicariate or prefecture apostolic. He will have the full *use* of all the ordinary and delegated faculties (with the exception, of course, of such as were granted in respect of person) of the vicar or prefect apostolic.[33]

Concerning the powers and rights of a vicar delegate who may be selected and deputed by the local ordinaries of missionary territories, the special instruction of the Sacred Congregation for the Propagation of the Faith will have to be observed.[34]

First of all, his powers are merely delegated like to those of the senior ecclesiastic who succeeds to the government of a vicariate or prefecure apostolic in default of the designation of an

---

[30] Cf. Kearney, *The Principles of Delegation*, pp. 72-74, for a discussion of the divided thought of canonists on this question, and the solid reasons advanced for concluding against the opinions of Stutz, Maroto, Vidal, De Meester, Eichmann, Coronata, Blat, Ayrinhac, etc., in favor of the interpretation offered by Hilling, Vermeersch, Creusen, Cocchi, Claeys Bouuaert-Simenon, Koeniger, Prümmer, Augustine, and others.

[31] Cf. cans. 371, 430 §2, 183, 207, 208.

[32] Cf. can. 430 §§1-3.

[33] Cans. 309 §§1-4, 310 §2.

[34] Cf. Epistola S. C. de Prop. Fide, die 8 Dec. 1919—*AAS*, XII (1920), 120.

administrator by the titular or pro-titular of the respective territory.[35]

Furthermore, since the practical measure of his powers is identical with that of a vicar general, he is not competent in such matters for which the latter requires a special mandate. Over and above the powers thus detached by the common law,[36] the extent of his powers and faculties may be further lessened by particular reservations on the part of the titular or pro-titular of the territory.[37] But, in all likelihood, a vicar delegate would have precedence over the senior ecclesiastic relative to the question of a potential right to take over the provisional government of a vicariate or prefecture apostolic, when no one has been nominated by either the titular or the pro-titular as a prospective successor in the vacant or impeded see.[38]

Finally, whilst the exercise of powers enjoyed by the vicar delegate runs parallel to that of the vicar general, yet, his very status as a delegate will make his relationship with the one who presides over the mission territory as its local ordinary divergent from that of a vicar general to his diocesan ordinary in a number of cases.[39]

The rules laid down in canon 429 §1 for impeded dioceses and vicariates or prefectures apostolic must also be followed as an analogous norm when like conditions arise in an abbacy or

---

[35] Cf. cans. 309 §4 and 310 §2; Kearney, *The Principles of Delegation*, pp. 61-62, who correctly disavows the opinion of Hilling (*AkKR*, CIV [1924], 186) that an administrator thus specified by the law of the Code enjoys ordinary power. See also Schwentner, "Über die Erteilung der allgemeinen Vollmachten zur Eheassistenz," *Th Gl*, XIX (1927), 514, who puts both the vicar delegate and the senior ecclesiastic in his capacity of administrator into the class of local ordinaries. But, it seems obvious that the very appellation of "*Vicarius Delegatus*," and the manifest wording of the two canons cited must invalidate this classification.

[36] Cf. Stutz, *Der Geist des Codex iuris canonici*, pp. 286-95; Eichmann, *Lehrbuch des Kirchenrechts*, §75, pp. 186-87; Dugan, *The Judiciary Department of the Diocesan Curia*, pp. 27-28, for a compilation of the cases wherein the vicar general cannot act except with a special mandate.

[37] Cf. *Periodica*, XVII (1928), 70* and 74*.

[38] *Ibid.*, p. 76*.

[39] *Loc. cit.* Concerning the canonical status of the vicar delegate constituted in the letter of the Sacred Congregation on Dec. 8, 1919, see Vromant, "De Vicario delegato in territorio Missionum," *Periodica*, XVII (1928), 68*-78*; Toso, "Summa de Officio et Potestate Vicarii Generalis," *Jus Pont.*, VII (1927), 141; Vermeersch, *Periodica*, IX (1920), (25)-(33).

prelacy *nullius*. This becomes manifest from the legislation of the Code itself.[40]

When the condition of *sedes impedita* is verified in dioceses, in vicariates or prefectures apostolic, and in abbacies or prelacies *nullius*, the needs of these ecclesiastical territories allow of a diversified manner of procedure in the designation or the deputation of the ecclesiastical persons called upon to assume the provisional tenure of office. The person thus presiding over a territory, *sede impedita,* may be either a local ordinary, a vicar delegate, or a special deputy. In the first instance he acts within a sphere of ordinary powers; in the two latter instances he proceeds with delegated powers. The efficacy and the extent of the powers of these two separate classes will alike be regulated by the specifications of canon 430.

Art. III. The Special Application of Canon 430 §2

The two ecclesiastical ministries of parochial adjutants and parochial assistants fall within the group of parochial vicars, mentioned in canon 455 §2 1°, whose appointment may be undertaken by the one who rules over an ecclesiastical territory *sede vacante aut impedita,* or by the vicar general, *sede impedita.* Because of the intimate relation existing between the norm regulating the appointment of adjutants and that governing the appointment of assistants, the discussion can be clarified by considering both classes of these parochial ministries in the present connection. It may be asked then, whether such acts of appointment are valid: 1) When they are made in the interval elapsing between the actual vacancy and its subsequent intimation, *sede impedita;* 2) when they are executed during the time current between the appointment of the new local ordinary and his subsequent occupancy of office, *sede vacante.*

§I. The Interval Between Actual and Intimated Vacancy

The importance of the first query becomes obvious when one inquires whether or not parochial adjutancies and assistancies

[40] Cf. cans. 327 §2, 285.

possess the canonical status of ecclesiastical offices or benefices. If they do, all acts of appointment to their incumbency, *sede impedita,* will have to be ruled by the *exceptive* norm and *limited* competency indicated in canon 430 §2. If they do not, such acts become negotiable, *sede impedita,* according to the *ordinary* norm and *liberal* competency indicated for all the other acts in the same canon. But, with regard to appointments made, *sede vacante,* by the vicar capitular or diocesan administrator, one and the same norm of action regulates the validity of appointments once the see has continued vacant for a year, regardless of whether they imply the subsequent corporal institution in a benefice, the conferment of an ecclesiastical office, or the assignment to a mere diocesan or parochial ministry.[41]

A. Appointment Relative to Ecclesiastical Benefices

Adjutants and assistants, excepting, of course, the case contained in canon 477 §2, are not incumbents of ecclesiastical benefices. Canon 1412 1° and 3° raises an efficient canonical barrier against all the encroachments of contrary or contradictory contentions. Moreover, if canons 145 §§1-2 and 1409 could, perchance, leave uncertified the vindication of this same deduction, canon 1438 would efficiently stand by to reinforce and to integrate the native legal virility of these two canons in the preciseness of their definitions. Hence, the act of appointment of adjutants and assistants, *sede impedita,* up to the time of the authentic intimation of vacancy, suffers no restriction on the score of its being a collation of an ecclesiastical benefice.[42]

B. Appointment Relative to Ecclesiastical Offices

But, does the act of appointment fall under the restriction of canon 430 §2 relative to the conferring of ecclesiastical offices?

[41] Cf. cans. 334 §§2-3, 430 §3, 443 §§1-2.

[42] Cf. Woywod, "The Profession of Faith," *HPR,* XXVIII (1928), 1179-87. On p. 1186 the author states: "Under this system [of voluntary offerings] not only the position of pastor, but also that of assistant priests, could be erected into a benefice by decree of the bishop." In its context this statement plainly requires the existence of an objectively permanent office to which must be added a specific decree of erection before the essential conditions for the constitution of an ecclesiastical benefice are verified. The very indication in the cited passage of a mere possibility relative to an assistant's beneficed status is equivalent to an implicit denial of its present actuality.

This question has been answered differently by different authors, in as far as some of them militantly maintain that the parochial ministries of adjutants and assistants constitute ecclesiastical offices, whilst others just as bravely deny this. Discussion over this point has been earnest and spirited; arguments have been heaped on either side. In the end, perhaps, one would have to acknowledge that at times some of them have launched too far adrift from safe canonical moorings to inspire a feeling of legal serenity in their immediate environment, or even to invite a sense of generous forbearance with their competitive hazards. When the law of the Code offers legal security within its own harbor wherein one will not have to encounter the likely perils of conflicting opinions far at sea, it seems not only expedient, but imperative as well, to remain close at anchor for the sake of abiding under the egis of the law.

A fact admitted by all canonists is that an ecclesiastical office cannot exist without the inherence of at least some participation in ecclesiastical power, whether of orders or of jurisdiction.[48] This necessarily follows from the Code's own definition of an ecclesiastical office in canon 145 §1. Now, all ecclesiastical power possessed by ecclesiastical persons is classified under two categories: delegated power and ordinary power. An ecclesiastical person may come into possession of ecclesiastical power in a twofold way: 1) By a direct commission of power to his person; 2) by a direct participation in a potential capacity established and sanctioned by the law itself. The nature of the power possessed receives its specification from the mode in which it is acquired. If the exercise of power is made available for a person, not through the link of an official capacity existing outside of himself, but through the medium of his own individual personality, then that power is called delegated. If the potentiality of its exercise is rooted, not in the person through whom it becomes operative, but in his official post with which the law itself has associated it, then that power is called ordinary. Canon 197 §1 describes ordinary power to be that which by the law itself has been connected with an ecclesiastical office; delegated, that which is committed to a person. Thus, whenever power is not connected by the law itself with an ecclesias-

[48] Cf. Maroto, *Institutiones Iuris Canonici*, I, n. 579, pp. 675-76.

tical office, it cannot be ordinary; it must be delegated. In other words, all delegated power exists altogether apart from any inherent connection by law with an ecclesiastical office.[44]

Ordinary power presupposes two essential facts for its constitution: 1) The existence of an ecclesiastical office with an inherent participation of ecclesiastical power; 2) the communication of this power to the office by the law through whose legal efficacy the office was also created. Hence, it manifestly appears alien to the concept of ordinary power to suppose the creation or generic erection of an office by the common law, and thereupon to admit the specification of its inherent powers by the authority of particular law. It is one thing if a local diocesan ordinary notably limits or circumscribes the ordinary powers of an individual person who is the incumbent of an office which has been generically constituted by the common law; it is quite another if the same ordinary attempts a substantial restriction of the innate capacity of the office itself. The first is conditionally permissible; the second is absolutely inadmissible.

1. The Status of Parochial Assistants

Now, if one were to assume that the ministry of parochial assistants constitutes an ecclesiastical office,[45] and therefore endows it with ordinary powers,[46] one would at the same time

[44] Cf. Oietti, "De Natura Potestatis Ordinariorum secundum Codicem," *Greg.* VI (1925), 436-41. This author demands an intrinsic, essential and natural bond between office and power before admitting the *potestas ipso iure officio adnexa* to be an ordinary power. This requirement appears altogether too strict. See Kearney, *The Principles of Delegation*, pp. 62-71, for an able refutation of this claim.

[45] Cf. *op. cit.*, I, n. 582, pp. 678-79.

[46] The interrelation of an ecclesiastical office and its inherent ordinary power is so essentially intimate, that the one is inconceivable without the other. Even the authors—without a single exception in the knowledge of the writer—who contend that a parochial assistancy is an ecclesiastical office make no effort to deny this legal consequence, despite the difficulties its admission must raise for them.

Vermeersch-Creusen (*Epitome Iuris Canonici*, II, n. 742, p. 462), in enumerating the essential elements required for the constitution of an ecclesiastical benefice, make the following observation concerning an ecclesiastical office: "Cum agitur de officio *sacro*, potissimum designat potestatem quandam iurisdictionis, *praesertim nomine proprio exercendam. Sufficit tamen etiam potestas delegata.*" In another passage (*op. cit.*, I, n. 522, p. 331) they say: "Episcopus posset declarare in synodo vel extra synodum iurisdictionem

have to admit that there has been established by the common law an ecclesiastical office whose sphere of ordinary powers becomes variable not only by a restriction on the part of the diocesan statutes or the precept of the local diocesan ordinary, but also at the behest of an individual parish priest at any time when the two preceding agencies have failed to determine the limits of power inherent in the office. This actually is the very assumption formulated by Coronata.[47]

Also many other authors [48] declare themselves for the opinion that a parochial assistant possesses an ecclesiastical office and that, in consequence, he enjoys at least the radical potentiality of an ordinary-vicarious power in the exercise of his subordinate parochial ministry. They are careful not to make their statement absolute and unconditional because of the evident possible limitations lurking in the clause *"nisi aliud expresse caveatur"* contained in canon 476 §6.

Now, the wording of the Code in canon 476 §6 indicates a fourfold alternate gradation in accordance with which one

---

ipsa nominatione Vicarii concessam intelligi." Possibly they wish to acknowledge the bishop's capacity for elevating an assistant's ministry into the estate of an ecclesiastical office. At any rate, the statement implies an admission that an assistant does not automatically acquire jurisdiction in virtue of the mere act of appointment. His ministry, therefore, falls short of the essential requirement of an ecclesiastical office which postulates an inherent participation in at least some degree of jurisdiction whenever the power of orders does not supply a constitutive element in its content (*op. cit.*, I, n. 227, p. 181). Hence, despite their opinion that a delegated power suffices for the content of an ecclesiastical office, they nevertheless appear to disclaim the existence of an ecclesiastical office in the case of an assistant vicar, precisely because his ministry lacks the endowment of ordinary power (*op. cit.*, I, n. 522, p. 331).

[47] *Institutiones Iuris Canonici*, I, n. 492, p. 578. See especially footnote 6 on this page for the author's citation of other writers who share this opinion with him.

[48] Cf. Augustine, *A Commentary on Canon Law*, II, 572; Bargilliat, *Praelectiones Juris Canonici*, II, n. 1174, p. 200; Raus, "Wähler und Gewählte, gelegentlich der Diözesansynode," *LQS*, LXXV (1922), 477-81; Rettenbacher, "Der Kooperator nach dem Codex Juris," *LQS*, LXXII (1919), 337-48; especially p. 342; Haring, "Die Jurisdiktion des Pfarrvikars," *LQS*, LXXV (1922), 22-27; Schäfer, *Die Kirchenämter*, II Band, *Pfarrer und Pfarrvikare*, pp. 101-03; Fanfani, *De Iure Parochorum*, n. 251 B 6°, pp. 231-32 and n. 454, p. 381; Hilling, *Das Personenrecht*, p. 85, where the author speaks of the *office* of the assistant, and p. 228, where he says: "Die Jurisdiktion der Kooperatoren ist teils eine ordinaria (vicaria), teils eine delegata, . . . " etc.; on p. 89, however, he states: "Die Hilfsgeistlichen haben eine potestas delegata pro foro interno."

will deduce the rights and obligations of an assistant. The endowments of his powers are to be derived: 1) From the diocesan statutes; 2) from the letter of the ordinary; 3) from the commission of his pastor; and 4) *nisi aliud expresse caveatur*, from the duty which is his by reason of his station, namely, to supply the stead of his pastor and to assist him in the complete parochial ministry, the application of the *Missa pro populo* alone remaining excepted. Palpably, the correct interpretation of this canon is bound up with the following basic issue: Does the fourth member constitute the leading directive norm, so that all the other members must follow after in the mere capacity of potential exceptive norms, or do the three preceding members alternately establish the decisive rule, so that the fourth member need only accrue in the capacity of a suppletive norm when all the other preferred agencies lie dormant? In other words, does the legal presumption of canon 476 §6 favor the potential primacy of particular law and precept, or does it reserve the right of priority to the common law of the Code?

The above cited authors accord precedence to the common law. In so doing, however, they permit its directive norm to be overruled by the statutes of the diocese, by the precepts of the local ordinary, and by the mandates of the pastor. For this reason it is also found necessary to interpret canon 1096 §1 in a singularly restricted application. It is exclusively made to fit the case where a curate's right of assistance at all the marriages contracted within the parish has been restricted by particular law, only later to be granted to him again by way of general delegation through some other, or perhaps the identical agency of that particular law.[49] Surely, in the light of such an interpretation the common law of the Code on this point might as well have been left unenacted, since it has not only no effective force, but even directly legalizes multiple opportunities for contravening any sanction it might have.

The second interpretation concedes the presumption of primacy to the particular law. In so doing, it looks upon the

---

[49] ". . . qui [nempe can. 1096 §1] tamen facile interpretatur de casu quo ex iure particulari potestas cooperatorum assistendi matrimonio restricta fuerit: etenim etiam in hoc casu cooperator delegari potest generaliter ad assistendum matrimoniis."—Coronata, *loc. cit.*

ruling added by the common law in the fourth member of the paragraph as a mere suppletive norm to provide for the contingency resulting from a lack of all particular legislation or ordinance. The very liberality of its grant, in virtue of which an assistant becomes empowered, by a *delegatio a iure*, subordinately to share with his pastor the entire parochial care, save the application of the *Missa pro populo*, reacts as an efficient sanction for inducing the specific legislation or preceptive ordinance whereby the assistant's measure of delegated powers and faculties will be aptly adapted for the particular needs of the parishes throughout the diocese. If one understands the meaning of canon 476 §6 in this light, then it is also easy to see the natural connection which canon 1096 §1 can and must have with it. Certainly, the suppletive norm of the Code, relative to the proper specification of an assistant's rights and powers, is not without its impressive legal import and effective sanction when one adheres to the present interpretation.

No further effort need be made to adduce arguments in substantiation of this conclusion. It seems entirely sufficient in itself. Moreover, the testimony of authors who maintain that assistants have no other but delegated powers, and consequently no strict ecclesiastical office, could be multiplied on all sides.[50] If, then, an assistant possesses neither a benefice [51] nor an ecclesiastical office, the vicar general, or any other ecclesiastical person, who rules over a diocese or an ecclesiastical territory *sede impedita*, will be competent in the appointment of parochial

[50] Cf. Ayrinhac, *Constitution of the Church*, n. 303, p. 362; Woywod, *A Practical Commentary on the Code of Canon Law*, I, n. 357, p. 174; Schwentner, "Über die Erteilung der allgemeinen Vollmachten zur Eheassistenz," *Th Gl*, XIX (1927), 518 ss., and "Die Grundsätze des Codex Iuris Canonici über die Delegatio (c. 199) und die Entscheidungen der Codex-Kommission über die delegatio zur Eheassistenz," *ibid.*, XXII (1930), 54-59; Mair, "Beichtsjurisdiktion der pfarrlichen Vikare," *LQS*, LXXII (1919), 237-42; Eichmann, *Lehrbuch des Kirchenrechts*, §83, 5, p. 211, and *Prozessrecht des Codex Iuris Canonici*, §109, p. 261; Muñiz, *Derecho Parroquial*, II, n. 498, especially footnote 1; De Meester, *Juris Canonici et Juris Canonico-civilis Compendium*, II, n. 881, pp. 340-42; Cocchi, *Commentarium in Codicem Iuris Canonici*, lib. II, P. I, n. 369, p. 445; Vermeersch-Creusen, *Epitome Iuris Canonici*, I, n. 552, p. 331; Chelodi, *Ius de Personis*, n. 232, p. 384: "Vi officii et iure communi cooperator *nullam* iurisdictionem aut potestatem habet." See especially *IER* (5th series), XXXI (1928), 634-37.

[51] The exception of can. 477 §2 must ever be borne in mind.

assistants not only up to the time of actual vacancy of the see, but until he has received certain and authentic intimation of it.[52]

2. The Status of Parochial Adjutants

In order to determine whether the adjutant's ministry constitutes an ecclesiastical office in the strict canonical sense, a distinction must be made concerning the various forms his ministry may assume. He may be appointed to supply the pastor either in whole or in part. If his ministry consists of a merely partial integration, it may again take one of two forms. He may be called upon to assume the execution of one or the other integral element of the parochial functions, for example, the work in the confessional, or the attendance to everything relating to marriages within the parish, or, he may be instructed to aid the pastor only in as far as individual occasions of need may require. In the latter instance his ministry will closely approximate that of a parochial assistant. Each of these three possibilities calls for separate consideration.

a. Total Integration

If the adjutant's service is one of total supplementation, his rights and duties become equal to those of the pastor. The single exception to this otherwise all-inclusive statement is concerned with the application of the *Missa pro populo*.[53] The equality of his status with that of a canonical parish priest is further confirmed by other express passages in the Code.[54] The ordinary power that is thus acknowledged for him bespeaks the necessity of an office in which to inhere. Hence, it is certain beyond all doubt that adjutants of this class are the incumbents of strict ecclesiastical offices. Their appointment, therefore, is not sustained when executed by the vicar general, *sede impedita*, at any time subsequent to the actual moment of vacancy in the impeded see.

[52] Cans. 430 §2 and 455 §2 1° and §3.
[53] Cf. can. 475, §2.
[54] Cf. cans. 451 §2 2°, 873, 899 §3.

b. PARTIAL INTEGRATION

The second class of adjutants are those whose supply-pastoration embraces one or the other distinct integral element or portion of the pastoral functions. The two above mentioned examples relating to the sacraments of penance and of matrimony will be kept in mind for later illustration.

First of all, it is to be remarked that no conclusive argument can be drawn from the wording of canon 475 §2 [55] to establish with certainty that an adjutant must, *under all conditions,* act with merely delegated powers whenever he supplies his pastor in part only.[56] Although the use of the phrase *"ex litteris deputationis"* might suggest this interpretation at first glance, yet the word *deputatio* is not universally interchangeable with the term *delegatio.* This is obvious from certain canons in the Code which use it in a sense much ampler than that suggested by the word *delegatio.*[57] One may therefore not depend exclusively upon any strictly etymological investigation of the word *deputatio* in order to determine whether an adjutant's power is delegated or ordinary.

ADEQUATED REPLACEMENT

Canon 451 §2 2° states that parochial vicars—hence, also the parochial adjutant—share equal rights with those of a pastor if they are endowed with full parochial power. Canon 873 §1 states that for the hearing of confessions those also enjoy ordinary power who are in a pastor's stead. Does the wording

[55] ". . . si vero [vicarius adiutor] suppleat ex parte dumtaxat, eius iura et obligationes desumantur *ex litteris deputationis.*"

[56] The expression "in part only" is taken here in its twofold sense as above explained.

[57] Cf. can. 139 §4, where the term *"deputati"* is used in reference to civil officials; cans. 433 §1, 434 §§1 and 3, where the verbal form is employed with relation to the constitution of a vicar capitular in office; can. 435 §1, where the parity of this meaning is retained; can. 1359 §§1-4, where the nounal form is employed in designation of a certain class of seminary officials. The last paragraph of can. 1359 obliges the bishop to seek counsel of these *deputati* in matters of greater moment. It is hardly conceivable that the Code would impose a duty on the bishop to requisition the advice of his own *delegates.* See also Köstler, *Wörterbuch zum Codex Iuris Canonici,* v. *deputare,* p. 114.

of these canons find application only when the adjutant assumes the entire care of *all* the parochial functions and offices? Or, rather, is it also verified when he is assigned for the entire care of merely one or the other, or possibly an incomplete number, of the total list of pastoral duties and incumbencies? A negative reply to the first, and an affirmative reply to the second of these queries seems to offer the correct interpretation.

For the sake of illustrating this statement, an appeal may now be made to the two particular cases above mentioned.

Case I. An adjutant is instructed in the letter of his deputation to betake himself to a parish where he will supply the ministry of a parish priest whose defective hearing entirely incapacitates him for lending his services in the confessional in an approvable manner. The adjutant is authorized exclusively for this single constituent of the parochial ministry, yet, in such a way that he alone—in the place of his pastor—will have the care of all matters relating to the sacred tribunal. Did he receive a delegated, or did he acquire an ordinary jurisdiction in the commitment of this authorization?

If he did not acquire the pastor's ordinary jurisdiction in the confessional, then it would remain for the local ordinary to communicate to him the special powers of canons 899 §3, 1044-45 and 1245 §1, in addition to the simple delegation for the hearing of confessions, since the lack of these powers on the part of the adjutant would leave the effectiveness of his services in the confessional considerably retrenched. Whilst it is true that the powers of dispensing granted by canons 1044-45 and 1245 §1 do not form a necessary part of the content of jurisdiction for the hearing of confessions, yet the frequency with which the use of these powers or at least the request for their use enters into the realm of the confessional would make it highly desirable, if not morally urgent, that the adjutant be specially empowered with them. If the local ordinary should have failed to grant all of these faculties, and had at the same time limited the pastor's capacity to confer any of them upon his adjutant, the issue would manifestly effect for the people of the parish a deprivation not countenanced by the common law of the Code. The Code wishes parishioners to enjoy the efficacious right of profiting by the special powers which are by law attached to the office of a parish priest, or him who functions *loco parochi*. Hence it follows that it would also be the mind of the Code that anyone who is called upon officially to replace the deficiency or incapacity of a pastor in the sacred tribunal of penance should also enjoy rights and powers equal to those which have lapsed from him. This intention bespeaks nothing short of ordinary jurisdiction for the adjutant thus supplying his pastor.

Thus, also, even if the pastor is left unimpeded by the local ordinary for the transmission of his own ordinary powers to his adjutant by way of delegation, the latter's powers in the confessional, *loco parochi*, would still remain incomplete in as far as a pastor is not able to delegate the particular confessional jurisdiction implied in canon 899 §3.[58] The fortuity of such an incompleteness in the capacity of the adjutant for supplying the fullness of his pastor's lapsed powers in the confessional is efficiently offset by the admission that the adjutant's deputation under such circumstances qualifies him with all the ordinary jurisdiction that was erstwhile exercised by the pastor in this definite but restricted sphere.

Moreover, when canons 873 §1 and 899 §3 use the phrases *"aliique qui loco parochi sunt"* and *"aliive qui parochorum nomine in iure censentur,"* they are to be understood in accordance with the norm of canon 451 §2 which includes under the class of parish priests, relative to the nature of their pastoral capacities, not only quasi-pastors, but also all parochial vicars who are endowed with a full parochial power. Now, this fullness of power lends itself to a twofold concept: the one, absolute; the other, relative. In relation to the adjutant it is absolute when he assumes the full charge of all the essential parochial functions; it is relative when he assumes the full charge of some, or at least one, of the essential parochial functions. In either case, however, his integration is full, exhaustive, un-

[58] Cf. Pont. Com. Int., die 16 Oct. 1919—*AAS*, XI (1919), 477. See also Kelly, *The Jurisdiction of the Simple Confessor*, p. 202. In view of the above decision by the Pontifical Commission he arrives at the unwarranted conclusion that the exercise of any faculty enjoyed by the pastor in virtue of his office may not be delegated by him for use in the internal sacramental forum. But, see also Haring, "Delegation pfarrlicher Dispensvollmachten," *LQS*, LXXIX (1926), 594-95, and Leitner, *Handbuch des kath. KR*, IV, 313.

conditional and exclusive within the sphere of pastoral authority deputed to him.

To endow him with the prerogative of ordinary power it is not required that an adjutant's pastoral capacity be equivalent to that of the pastoral office in the totality of its several constituents; it suffices that it be equivalent in the fullness of that particular integral portion of it that he may be called on to supply in the place of his pastor.

The correctness of this conclusion appears beyond dispute. It receives a legal confirmation and a decisive approval from the Code itself in the analogous legislation concerning substitute vicars. Canon 474 states that substitutes constituted in accordance with canons 465 §§4-5 and 1923 §2 fill the place of the pastor in everything regarding the care of souls as long as the local ordinary or the pastor has excepted nothing from it. The meaning of this canon is not that the ordinary's or pastor's exception of one or the other integral portion of the pastoral activity disbars the substitute from still occupying the place of the pastor for the elements not excepted; its meaning simply is that such a positively intimated exception will reduce the fullness or completeness of his substitution from an absolute to a relative one, leaving him still *loco parochi*, but in a limited sphere.[59] If this ruling obtains for a substitute who supplies the *physical* absence of a parish priest, on what score is one justified in denying its application when an adjutant supplies the *moral* absence of a pastor? The pastor's personal incapacity for assuming the performance of some particular essential function of his office is in effect the same as an absent pastor's lack of ability to acquit the same function.

The wording of canon 475 §2 merely states that when an adjutant's powers are cast in a limited sphere, the nature and extent of his rights and obligations are to be determined from the instruction contained in the letter of his appointment. It appears altogether unwarranted to deduce therefrom that, be-

[59] Cf. Schwentner, "Über die Erteilung der allgemeinen Vollmacht zur Eheassistenz," *Th Gl*, XIX (1927), 522-24, for a lucid discussion on the nature and extent of a substitute's powers of active delegation for assistance at matrimony. See also Claeys-Bouuaert, "De vicariis substitutis," *Jus Pont.*, VII (1927), 72-81, for a concise treatise on the law of the Code for substitute vicars.

cause his powers are limited in numerical extent, they must automatically sink to the level of mere delegated powers. The need for an adjutant to function with ordinary power remains identical whether he supplies *in toto* or *in parte* in the sense here understood.[60] If the law wished to accord merely delegated powers to an adjutant appointed for such a partial integration, it could readily have clarified its meaning as it did in the case of parochial assistants.[61]

It is to be admitted, therefore, that the law grants ordinary power to adjutants not only then when they supply the parochial activity in its entirety, but also when they integrate, with an exclusive right, merely one or the other essential portion of it. This interpretation will, no doubt, find its full application in the case where an adjutant will have entrusted to him the care of all the matters connected with the sacred tribunal of penance. His capacity for the fulfillment of this duty will be rooted in ordinary power in virtue of his office.

Case II. Ad adjutant is instructed to assume in the parish to which he is appointed the care of all matters relating to the sacrament of matrimony. The need of such an appointment might be occasioned by the fact that the faithful of the parish have suffered a series of disedifying or unpropitious experiences in their dealings with their pastor on this point of the *cura animarum.* The possibility of the existence of such an inauspicious situation easily arises when the investigations of the *status liber* and the attendant pre-nuptial instructions habitually evince a lack of pastoral prudence, of delicate refinement, and of discerning tact, to say nothing of the case where they eventuate in an outright compromise of priestly dignity. The consideration of the present case cannot be dispatched as futile by invoking the expedient of a removal from office in such a supposition of defective pastoration. The removal from office because of a pastor's display of untactfulness is sanctioned by the law only

[60] "Ubi lex non distinguit, nec nos distinguere debemus." "Ubi eadem est ratio, ibi eadem esse debet iuris dispositio." Reg. 46, R. J., in VI°: "Is, qui in ius succedit alterius, eo iure, qui ille, uti debebit."

[61] Reg. 57, R. J., in VI°: "Contra eum, qui legem dicere potest apertius, est interpretatio facienda." Reg. 88, R. J., in VI°: "Certum est, quod is committit in legem, qui legis verba complectens, contra legis nititur voluntatem."

then when the good of souls in the parish can no longer be properly consulted by the appointment of an adjutant.[62] When an adjutant is appointed precisely for the sake of meeting this singular need, will he function in his capacity with ordinary or with delegated power?

If he acts with ordinary power, then his capacity for this particular pastoral function is equivalent to that enjoyed by any parish priest. If he must proceed with solely delegated power, then his ability becomes restricted to a degree of utter inefficiency in trying to meet the requirements of this integral and essential portion of the pastoral activity exclusively confided to him.

A general delegation for authorized assistance at all the marriages taking place within a parish can be made operative for parochial assistants only. The text of canon 1096 §1 [63] is so explicit in this regard that all authors who claim that an adjutant under the present supposition has merely delegated power, resort to an explanation whereby they postulate an identity of assistant and adjutant in order to qualify the latter for receiving such a general delegation. This is a rather taxing test for canon 1096 §1 which prides itself in anything but legal elasticity or flexibility. To subject it, nevertheless, to such a legal strain is, in the writer's mind, a mode of procedure with no canonical warrant.[64] If any canon is express in formulating its incapacitating clause, canon 1096 §1 indubitably passes that test. It disdains to give quarter to any *dubium iuris*.[65]

Hence, in the light of this unmistakable import of canon 1096 §1, which precludes the possibility of a general delegation for assistance at marriages except when parochial curates are made the recipients of it, and in view of the analogous legislation of canon 474, which includes the possibility of a substitute functioning *loco parochi* even when his sphere of pastoral activity has been definitely restricted, one arrives at the conclu-

---

[62] Cf. cans. 2147 §2 1° and 475 §1 and §4.

[63] "Licentia assistendi matrimonio concessa ad normam can. 1095 §2, dari expresse debet sacerdoti determinato ad matrimonium determinatum, exclusis quibuslibet delegationibus generalibus, nisi agatur de vicariis cooperatoribus pro paroecia cui addicti sunt; *secus irrita est.*"

[64] Cf. cans. 17 §2, 18, 20.

[65] Cf. cans. 11 and 15.

sion that an adjutant possesses ordinary power when he replaces his pastor in the execution of the particular pastoral function which embraces all the pastoral duties centering in the sacrament of matrimony. If, then, the adjutant's power is ordinary, it must also be admitted that he is the incumbent of an ecclesiastical office.

The necessary induction from the consideration of the above two particular cases is the following: The vicar general, or any other ecclesiastic, who rules over a diocese or ecclesiastical territory, *sede impedita,* can appoint parochial adjutants, when they are assumed for supplying an integral portion of the pastoral functions, only up to that time which marks the occurrence of the actual vacancy in the see. Any such appointment that is undertaken in the interval elapsing between the actual vacancy and its subsequent intimation loses all canonical force and legal efficacy, since it constitutes an act which falls under the ruling of the exception mentioned in canon 430 §2, in virtue of which a collation of ecclesiastical offices is not sustained by the law.

Subordinated Replacement

Lastly, there remains the consideration of the case of an adjutant appointed with the instruction to aid his pastor only in so far as individual occasions of need may require his suppletive help. Under this supposition the one who confers the appointment cannot, without attendant difficulty, and possibly even confusing consequences, *predetermine* the exact limits of the adjutant's potential activity. Practically, the measure and the extent of the latter's suppletive functions will be left to the pastor's own determination. Under these circumstances, is the adjutant's power ordinary or delegated?

Since the adjutant's services are here required only at such times when the pastor will also be able to delegate the power for their execution, it is evident that there exists no need for the possession of ordinary power by the adjutant. He functions in view of the individual mandates received from his pastor over and above the general diocesan faculties that the local ordinary may previously have committed to his person. Such mandates are nothing more than separate acts of delegation.

Therefore, the adjutant's capacity for action remains rooted within the exclusive sphere of the delegated powers indicated for him. If he has no other than delegated powers, his ministry is not an ecclesiastical office. In consequence, his appointment may be undertaken, *sede impedita,* up to the time when information concerning the fact of actual vacancy has been communicated to the one in whose hands the temporary government of the diocese or ecclesiastical territory has continued to abide.

§II. The Interval Between Appointive and Canonical Occupancy

What is to be said concerning the appointments of adjutants or assistants which may take place, *sede vacante,* during the time current between the preconization of the incoming local ordinary and his subsequent occupancy of office? How long may such acts of appointment be exercised by the one who rules *sede vacante?* The answer is easy. It is supplied by the Code in canons 455 §2 1°, 311, 318 §2, 355 §3, 430 §3, and 443 §2. The duration of the various administrative offices indicated by these canons continues uninterrupted in its fullest efficacy up to the time when the newly appointed local ordinary has actually taken canonical possession of his office in the act of presenting for inspection to the temporary administrator,[66] to the diocesan chapter,[67] or to the body of diocesan consultors,[68] the letters patent of the Sacred Congregation for the Propagation of the Faith, the apostolic bulls, and the apostolic letters respectively.

The Code contains no prohibition against the appointment of parochial adjutants or assistants by the incumbent of the administrative office at any time throughout the entire term of vacancy in the see. The only exception made consists of the conferment of a parochial office of free collation *in titulum.* Such an appointment can be executed by the temporary incumbent only after the see has continued vacant for the full term

[66] Cf. cans. 293 §2 and 309 §§1-4.

[67] Cf. can. 334 §§2-3.

[68] Cf. can. 427.

of one year. He then enjoys the right of executing an appointment even though the parish may have been vacant for a much shorter span of time.[69] Thus the appointment of all classes of parochial adjutants and assistants, including the adjutant who supplies *in toto* according to canon 475 §2 and the assistant who holds a beneficed office according to canon 477 §2, is negotiable by the incumbent of the administrative office from the time when it passes into the hands of his successor through the medium of canonical occupancy of the office.

The powers possessed by the vicar general with regard to the appointment of parochial adjutants and assistants under the various aspects of occupancy *(sedes plena)*, quasi-vacancy *(sedes impedita)*, and unintimated vacancy *(sedes vacans)* of an episcopal see are limited to a restricted sphere. As a local ordinary he is competent for these acts exclusively in virtue of canon 429 §1. As a delegate he becomes competent when he receives a special commission or mandate in virtue of canon 455 §3.[70] This special authorization may be extended to embrace both the power of constituting other classes of parochial vicars, and the right of confirming an act of election, or acknowledging an act of presentation, or approving an act of nomination in their regard, thereby to grant them ultimate institution in their office or station whenever their assignment to a given post must be effected through the mediation of such agencies.[71]

Furthermore, when granting his vicar general such authorization by special mandate, the bishop is under no obligation of circumscribing its exercise within restricted local, temporal, or numerical limits. He may grant it to his vicar general either at the time when the latter assumes his office, or at any time during his term of incumbency. Precisely because he is a vicar

---

[69] Cf. cans. 455 §2 3°, 458, 152, 155.

[70] Cf. cans. 152 and 1466 §2. The removal of these vicars by the vicar general also requires a special mandate in virtue of canon 477 §1.

[71] Cf. cans. 455 §3, 152, 368 §1, 1432 §2, 1466 §2. The other classes of parochial vicars are enumerated in cans. 472-74. The vicar of canon 471 may be preferably termed a *parish vicar*, the more clearly to differentiate him from the vicars mentioned in the succeeding canons. His rights and powers approximate those of titular parish priests.

general, the bishop may select him for the execution of many acts not natively inherent in his vicarial office.[72]

The only cases when a vicar general will enjoy competency in the appointment of adjutants or assistants are offered when the distinct conditions of canons 429 §1 *(sede impedita)* and 455 §3 *(cum speciali mandato)* are verified. At no other time is he ever competent. The entire question of competency in the act of appointing or instituting adjutants and assistants is basically settled by canon 455. *Sede plena,* this right belongs to the titular local ordinary; *sede vacante,* to the administrative incumbent; *sede impedita,* to the vicar general or such other ecclesiastical personality who may be assumed for the temporary government of the diocesan or vicariate territory. Outside of these stipulations this right can accrue to the capacity of the vicar general or the vicar delegate only by special mandate for such time and under such circumstances as may therein be specified.

ART. IV. APPOINTMENT IN SECULAR INCORPORATED PARISHES

The incorporation of a parochial church with a moral person or a juridic personality invests the habitual pastoral title of such a church in the moral body with which the parish has become united.[73] Such a union or incorporation creates for the habitual pastor certain rights relative to the appointment of the actual vicar or incumbent of the incorporated parish church. These rights are indicated by the terms *nomination* and *presentation*.[74]

When there is question of a parish which is entrusted to a religious house or institute, the proper religious superior enjoys

[72] Cf. Vermeersch-Creusen, *Epitome Iuris Canonici,* I, n. 436, 3, p. 284; De Meester, *Juris Canonici et Juris Canonico-civilis Compendium,* II, n. 730, p. 188; Wernz, *Ius Decretalium,* II, n. 805, pp. 627 ss.

[73] Cans. 452 §§1-2, 471 §§1-2, 1423 §2. Cf. Poeschl, "Die Inkorporation und ihre geschichtliche Grundlagen," *AkKR,* CVII (1927), 44, 177, 497-560; CVIII (1928), 24-86; Scherer, "Incorporatio plena oder minus plena," *AkKR,* LIII (1885), 105-25; Hinschius, *System des kath. KR,* II, 436-55, for a comprehensive historical conspectus of the question of incorporation; Wernz-Vidal, *Ius Canonicum,* II, *De Personis,* n. 154, pp. 180-82, for an admirable classification of the various kinds of union and incorporation of benefices and parishes.

[74] Cans. 456, 471 §2, 1425 §§1-2.

the right of presentation also with regard to parochial adjutants.[75] In this same connection the question may be asked whether a diocesan cathedral or collegiate chapter, or any other secular juridic personality in whom the habitual title to a parish is vested, enjoys the equal right of presenting an adjutant in personal aid of the actual vicar with the subsequent approval of the local ordinary.

The particular section of the Code which treats expressly of canonical chapters is altogether silent about such a right.[76] Rather, canon 415 §5 insists that the members of the chapter are to remember that charity obliges them to lend their help in the way the local ordinary will determine, whenever the parish vicar lacks the necessary help that would be afforded by the appointment of an adjutant or an assistant vicar in his aid. Now, if the local ordinary possesses an independent right to specify how the chapter is to lend its services when the number of canons may be too small to furnish one or the other of its members for the constant ministry of a parochial adjutancy or assistancy, then with even more reason should he be free to proceed with equal independence when their numbers are sufficient to allow of the appointment of an adjutant or an assistant from their ranks. That the bishop is to select the adjutant as well as the assistant in a capitular parochial church from the body of the canons is indicated by the Code in canon 420 §1 4°.[77]

Besides these considerations which bespeak the diocesan ordinary's right of appointing an adjutant or an assistant [78] in a capitular parish church, or in any other parochial benefice united with a collegiate chapter *quoad temporalia tantum*,[79] it must be recalled that canon 475 §1, which treats expressly of the right of presentation and appointment of adjutants, accords this right

---

[75] Can. 475 §1.

[76] Cf. cans. 391-422.

[77] Cf. Chelodi, *Ius de Personis*, n. 212, p. 353, footnote 4, which indicates also under what conditions and to what degree canons who are appointed for pastoral work in churches other than the capitular parish church will share in the fruits and daily distributions of the chapter.

[78] Can. 420 §1 4° uses the term *coadiutor*. That this term is here used to convey the comprehensive idea of both adjutant and assistant is further confirmed by a similar usage in can. 415 §5.

[79] Can. 1423 §2.

of presentation neither to cathedral nor to collegiate chapters, nor to any other secular moral personalities with whom parishes might be incorporated. The very silence of this canon concerning any such enjoyment of right by them is the strongest proof that it is not possessed by any of these moral ecclesiastical bodies. Hence, since the Code in canon 420 §1 4° appears to reserve the appointment of adjutants and assistants in capitular parishes as an act of free collation to the local ordinary, and especially since canon 475 §1 does not expressly extend to cathedral or collegiate chapters, or other secular moral ecclesiastical personalities, the right of presentation which it so clearly accords to the religious superior, it must be concluded that in all these situations the local ordinary enjoys the unconditional right of free collation in the appointment of the needed adjutants.

ART. V. CLASSIFICATION OF PARISHES ENTRUSTED TO RELIGIOUS

The manner in which adjutants are appointed is determined by the circumstances inherent in the nature of the parochial benefice at which their services are required. As is well known, parochial benefices may be classified under two general categories: secular and religious.[80] They are called *secular* when the exclusive right to their incumbency is vested in the clergy of the diocese; they are called *religious* when the enjoyment of this same determinate right appertains to the clergy of a religious institute. Hence, canon 1442 enunciates the principle that secular benefices are to be given to the members of the diocesan clergy and that religious benefices are to be conferred upon members of that particular institute to which these benefices belong.

Parochial benefices belong with *full right* to a religious house or institute when they have been completely incorporated with it by an indult of the Holy See.[81] But, the Code uses a variety

[80] Can. 1411 2°: "Beneficia ecclesiastica dicuntur saecularia vel religiosa, prout ad solos clericos saeculares vel solos clericos religiosos spectant; omnia autem beneficia, erecta extra ecclesias vel domus religiosorum in dubio saecularia esse praesumuntur."

[81] Cf. cans. 452 §1, 1423 §2, 1425 §2.

of terminology when it speaks of parishes whose administration or care is placed in the charge or committed to the trust of religious orders or congregations.[82] It is evident that not all the cases and conditions contemplated bespeak a *pleno iure* incorporation. Thus, mention is made of the parishes which are incorporated with a religious house in regard to the temporalities only.[83] Furthermore, there is the possibility of an even less intimate bond of union or relationship in cases where a bishop, in virtue of special faculties, assigns to the religious clergy the care of certain parishes for whose pastoration the number of his diocesan clergy does not suffice.[84] Hence, it becomes readily intelligible that when the Code wishes to speak of parishes which may in any way soever be entrusted to the care of religious—whether *pleno* or *semi-pleno iure*, whether *perpetually* or *temporarily*—it avails itself of a very general and comprehensive form of expression by referring to such parishes as "*religiosis concreditae.*" [85]

---

[82] Can. 452 §2: "*Persona moralis*, cui paroecia sit *pleno iure unita*, ..." Can. 456: "Ad paroecias *religiosis concreditas*, ..." Can. 471 §1: "Si paroecia *pleno iure fuerit unita domui religiosae*, ..." Can. 472 2°: ". . . si tandem agatur de *paroecia religiosis concredita*, ..." Can. 475 §1: ". . . si de *paroecia* agatur *religiosis concredita*, ..." Can. 630 §4: ". . . si *ecclesia* [parochialis] sit *communitatis religiosae*; . . . ." Can 1423 §2: "Nequeunt vero [Ordinarii locorum] *paroeciam unire cum . . . ecclesiis religiosorum*. . . ." Can. 1425 §1: "Si a Sede Apostolica *paroecia domui religiosae uniatur ad temporalia tantum* quod attinet, ..." Can. 1425 §2: "Sin autem *pleno iure, paroecia fit religiosa*, ..." Can. 1427 §5: "Divisa *paroecia quae ad aliquam religionem iure spectat, vicaria perpetua aut paroecia* noviter erecta *non est religiosa*; . . . ." Can. 1442: ". . . *religiosa* [beneficia etiam paroecialia] *sodalibus* [conferenda sunt] *illius religionis, ad quam beneficia* [paroecialia] *spectant*."

[83] Cf. can. 1425 §1.

[84] The special faculties granted by the Sacred Consistorial Congregation on May 6, 1919, to Apostolic Nuncios, Internuncios and Delegates include the following one: "Concedendi in casibus particularibus, vel ad tempus, Ordinariis dioecesanis facultatem praeficiendi paroeciis religiosos in defectu sacerdotum saecularium, de consensu tamen suorum Superiorum, et cum clausula ut saltem duo alii religiosi cum parocho cohabitent, servatisque in reliquis sacrorum canonum dispositionibus." Cf. Vermeersch-Creusen, *Epitome Iuris Canonici*, I, 527; Augustine, *Commentary*, I, 277. This faculty is listed under Section V, n. 48.

[85] E.g., cans. 472 2°, 475 §1. Cf. Blat, *Commentarium Textus Codicis Iuris Canonici*, lib. II, *De Personis*, n. 504, p. 489; Augustine, *Canonical and Civil Status of Catholic Parishes*, pp. 188-89.

One can speak, then, of a threefold relationship; first, the full incorporation which establishes for the religious institute certain rights with regard both to the spiritualities and the temporalities of the incorporated parish;[86] secondly, the partial incorporation which restricts these rights to the sphere of temporalities only;[87] and thirdly, a mere concession in trust, which entirely abstracts from the more generous rights accruing through full or partial incorporation, by granting to the religious house or institute no further rights than those enjoyed by the superior in presenting or in approving a priest of his own religious community as the prospective appointee and his subsequent right, concurrent with that of the local ordinary, in removing that religious from his post of duty. These rights of the religious superior are primarily motivated by his priority of claim to the obedience of his religious subject in view of the latter's personal subordination by vow.[88]

ART. VI. PRESENTATION BY THE RELIGIOUS SUPERIOR

Bearing in mind the threefold manner in which parishes may be entrusted to religious or to a religious house or institute, a number of questions arise for discussion. They may conveniently be summarized under the following three headings: 1) Which particular religious superior is intimated by canon 475 §1 as enjoying the right of presenting an adjutant when the latter's services are required by a permanently disabled parish priest or parish vicar in a parish which is entrusted to religious? 2) Has the religious superior a strict obligation of selecting the prospective appointee from the clerical membership of his own religious community, or is he free to present a candidate selected from the ranks of the diocesan priesthood? 3) Can the religious superior exercise his right of presentation only when the parish is a religious parochial benefice, or does he enjoy the same right relative to secular parishes which are partially incorporated with his house or institute, or which are merely given in trust to it?

[86] Can. 1425 §2.

[87] Can. 1425 §1.

[88] Cf. cans. 454 §5, 472 1°, 487, 608 §1, 630 §1: Blat. *op. cit., loc. cit.;* see also footnote 84 above.

§I. The Active Subject of Presentation

If one inspects canon 475 §1 it is found that the law mentions merely a presentation made by the *superior*. No qualifying phrase of any kind is added for the sake of a more definite specification. In itself, then, the wording employed in the canon is not so clear that one would have to arrive at an exclusive interpretation. The word *superior*, unmodified in its immediate context, admits of a variable explanation.

Religious superiors are classified either as major or as minor superiors.[89] Major religious superiors are in turn distinguished into various classes.[90] Minor religious superiors are generally also local superiors.[91] Hence, in seeking to establish the definite limits within which this term must be confined for its proper canonical interpretation, one must invoke the guiding principle of canon 18. This canon directs that in cases of doubt and obscurity in any given text the parallel passages of the Code must be inspected. If even these be wanting, then the purpose and the circumstances of the law along with the mind of the law-giver must prove the deciding factor of interpretation.

The context of canon 475 §1 offers no further indication than that the superior there mentioned is he who has the government of the religious to whom the care of the parish has been entrusted. Consequently, any effort at a conclusive interpretation still remains confronted with the question of whether the law contemplates the local superior of an individual religious house, or the major superior, for instance, the one who rules over an entire province of the institute. Relying merely upon the possible norm insinuated in this canon, one would have to ask whether the care of the parish was committed to the members of a local community or whether it was entrusted to

---

[89] Cf. cans. 504, 505.

[90] Cf. can. 488 8°.

[91] The wording of canons 505 and 488 8° would seem to leave room for a class of superiors mediate in station between the minor local superiors mentioned in canon 505 and the major provincial superiors of canon 488 8°. As vicars, they possess a power *"ad instar provincialium."* Their powers in this capacity would, then, extend beyond the local limits of a given religious house.

the membership of an entire province. In accord with the original stipulation entered upon by the local ordinary and the religious institute the right of presentation would then devolve upon the local or provincial superior respectively. But this norm alone scarcely offers sufficient security if it is found that in parallel cases and under similar conditions the Code has specified a more definite method of procedure. It is not difficult to indicate passages in which this is done.

When there is question of presenting a prospective appointee for the exercise of the pastoral office in a parish entrusted to religious, the right of presentation is enjoyed by that superior whom the constitutions of the institute acknowledge as the competent authority in this regard.[92]

Moreover, when a religious is presented for the office of parish vicar in a parish which is fully incorporated with some religious house, the one competent in the act of presentation is the superior of that particular local community.[93]

Again, when a local diocesan ordinary assigns a religious as an administrator to a vacant parish the execution of his act is conditioned on the consent he receives from the superior of this religious;[94] in a similar way the consent of the local ordinary alone does not suffice for the appointment of a substitute by the religious parish priest who contemplates a vacation for longer than a week, since the substitute selected must be approved both by the local ordinary and by the religious superior. In both these instances the natural inference would seem to suggest the immediate local superior rather than the major or provincial superior.[95]

Finally, when the Code speaks of the appointment of an assistant, taken from the ranks of the religious clergy, the right

---

92 Can. 456.

93 Cans. 471 §§1-2, 1425 §2; cf. Pistocchi, *De Re Beneficiali*, p. 102.

94 Can. 472 1°.

95 Cans. 472 1° and 465 §4. Concerning the necessity of this double approval it must be remembered that a substitute appointed by a religious parish priest or parish vicar can validly assist at matrimony and can, moreover, delegate some other specified priest validly to assist at a determinate marriage, after the local ordinary's approval has been obtained for him by the pastor. The pastor's neglect to obtain also the approval of his religious superior will not invalidate these acts of the substitute. Cf. Pont. Com. Int., die 14 Julii 1922, ad V, n. 3; die 20 Maii 1923, ad V, n. 3—*AAS*, XIV (1922), 527; *AAS*, XVI (1924), 114.

of presenting him for appointment belongs to that religious superior whose competency for this act is defined by the constitutions of the religious institute.[96]

From the enumeration of these various cases where the appointment to parish work by the local diocesan ordinary is conditioned upon a previous act of presentation by a religious superior, the following points become evident: First, when there is question of the appointment of parish priests or parochial assistants, the constitutions of the respective religious institute will indicate the competent religious superior for the act of presentation. Secondly, when there is occasion for the appointment of a parish vicar or substitute, and again, when there is need of the consent of the religious superior for the appointment of a parish administrator taken from the ranks of the religious clergy, the context of the various canons seems to point to the local rather than the provincial or major superior as being qualified for executing the right of presentation.[97] Since both of these norms are rather specific in comparison with the covert indication of canon 475 §1, and since this latter canon calls for an analogous exercise of authority on the part of the religious superior, it seems conformable to all the tenets of correct interpretation, first of all to infer the proper superior's competency in the right of an adjutant's presentation from the specification of the approved constitutions of the institute. In default of such specification, the competency for presentation might rest either with the major superior of the province or

[96] Can. 476 §4.

[97] Augustine, *Canonical and Civil Status of Catholic Parishes*, p. 191, has the following: "Can. 456 rules that, for parishes entrusted to religious, the superior who enjoys this right by virtue of his constitutions, shall present a priest of his own institute to the local Ordinary for investiture. We believe, that generally speaking, only the "*superiores maiores*" mentioned in can. 488 are here intended . . . . If the respective constitutions provide otherwise (either extending or restricting the power of the superiors) they must be followed." It must be noted that can. 456 treats specifically of the presentation of religious who are appointed in parishes to assume the rôle of a *parish priest*; one is hardly justified in view of can. 456 *alone* to transfer its interpretation to can 475 §1 and thus apply its norm for the presentation of adjutants. Besides, the Code (cans. 471 §1, 1425) allows the incorporation of a parish with a "*domus religiosa.*" But, since the government of such a house or *local* community of the institute rests ordinarily in the hands of a *local* superior, one may rightfully question the exclusiveness of the norm indicated by the author here cited.

the local superior of the house or community to which the care of the parish has been explicitly entrusted.[98] If none of the above norms could be invoked, one would next have to rely on whatever original agreement, whether stipulated or implied, might have been made between the diocesan ordinary and the religious institute when first the parish was entrusted to the latter's administration or care. In a case where even such a disposition remained unavailable for the specification of the proper superior regarding the right of presentation, the suppletive force of legitimate custom or legal prescription would have to be adopted as a determinant for the proper course of action.[99]

§II. The Passive Subject of Presentation

Since the Code has clearly differentiated the religious from the secular parishes and has constituted a definite norm in the method of appointing actual pastors or parish vicars in these parochial benefices,[100] it may be asked whether the law of the Church urges a similar norm of procedure when adjutants are appointed for their ministry of parochial aid in these parishes. In other words, has the religious superior, who enjoys the right of presenting the adjutant, a strict obligation always to select the prospective appointee from the clerical membership of his own religious community, or is he ever free to present a candidate selected from the ranks of the diocesan priesthood?

Before attempting an answer to this query it will prove useful to restate the religious superior's rights of presentation when

---

[98] Cans. 471 §1 and 1425, which allow the incorporation of a parish with a local branch of the religious institute (*domus religiosa*, can. 488 5°), confirm this view of the local superior's potential capacity in the matter of presentation. Religious superiors who act with a delegated power as the heads of strictly filial houses are not to be classified as local superiors (S. C. de Rel., die 1 Feb. 1924—*AAS*, XVI [1924], 95). But, directors of schools, hospitals, and other pious institutes, who are at the same time the superiors of religious placed under them for the guidance of their religious discipline, can come under this classification (Pont. Com. Int., die 2-3 Junii 1918, ad II—*AAS*, X [1918], 344).

[99] Cf. cans. 4, 18, 20, 29, 30, 1508, 1509, 1511 §2. See also Gommaire, "De vi actuali Consuetudinum praeter Codicem ante Codicis Promulgationem vigentium," *Jus Pont.*, IV (1924), 175-82, especially pp. 180-81; *NRT*, L (1923), 196.

[100] Cans. 456, 1425 §§1-2, 1427 §5, 1432 §1, 1438, 1442-1447.

the local ordinary fills the vacancies in the pastoral offices of parishes entrusted to a religious community. A correct understanding of the superior's rights in this regard will enable one to obtain a clearer insight into the analogous rules that determine his kindred rights in the presentation of adjutants.

When the parish is incorporated with a religious house or community *quoad temporalia tantum,* then the parochial benefice retains its secular status. In consequence of canon 1442 the presentee for the parochial incumbency must be chosen from the ranks of the secular or diocesan clergy.[101] The right of making this selection is vested in the superior of the religious house with which this partial incorporation has been effected.[102] However, when the parish is incorporated *pleno iure,* then the religious superior enjoys the distinct and exclusive right of selecting the prospective parochial incumbent in office from the membership of his own religious house or community with which the parish has been fully incorporated. In other words, full incorporation makes of the parish a religious benefice and accords the superior the consequent capacity (together with the obligation) of nominating a member of the respective religious house or community over which he is the superior.[103] In both

---

101 The word "*diocesan*" is of course used synonymously here with that of "*secular*" as defined by canon 1411 2°. It is related of Cardinal Mercier that on the occasion of one of his retreats conducted for his priests he began a sentence thus: "Secular priests—oh, what a villanous word to apply to priests!" For this quotation along with an added discussion on the advisability of substituting the term "*diocesan*" for "*secular*" see *AER*, LXXXI (1929), 620-21.

102 Can. 1425 §1. Cf. Pistocchi, *De Re Beneficiali*, p. 100 ss.

103 Cans. 456 and 471 §2 use the word "*praesentare*" to indicate the same right that can. 1425 §2 indicates with the term "*nominare*." The two expressions are obviously employed in a convertible and reciprocative sense with regard to the superior's preliminary act in the constitution of a canonical appointment. The term "*praesentare*" is practically constant and invariable when there is question of the right of patronage or advowson. Cf. cans. 1451 §1, 1455 1°, 1457-64, 1471. Only one canon (1450 §2 2°) offers a variant terminology by employing the term "*designare*," which implies the restricted privilege of one single act of presentation, namely, when the benefice is conferred for the first time. See Godfrey, *The Right of Patronage according to the Code of Canon Law*, p. 52; Hilling, *Das Sachenrecht*, p. 241, footnote 1: "Die Ausdrücke nominatio und praesentatio werden auch promiscue gebraucht."

cases the definite approval and ultimate institution in office are reserved to the local ordinary.[104]

In view of canons 456, 471 §2, and 1442, which leave no other option than the appointment of a *religious* priest to a *religious* parochial benefice as its pastoral incumbent in office, there is implied a prerequisite *duty* on the part of the religious superior to select his presentee from the clerical membership of his own religious house or community. On the other hand, canon 1425 §2 indicates precisely the same religious status of a parochial benefice as that contemplated by the aforesaid canons; nevertheless, it employs the following wording: *"Superior* POTEST *sacerdotem a sua religione ad curam animarum exercendam nominare."* If, then, there be an *obligation* to present a religious priest, how is one to reconcile with it the *apparently contrary option* conceded by canon 1425 §2?

The rule of correct interpretation demands that not only the text, but also the context, of the canon in question be considered.[105] Now, the first paragraph of canon 1425 treats of secular, whilst the second deals with religious parishes. In the first instance the religious superior enjoys the right of presentation but *must* make his selection of the presentee from the members of a diocesan clergy. In the second case he enjoys not only a right of presentation, but also the necessary right of choosing the prospective appointee from the clerical membership of his own community. Consequently, the correlated progression of thought in the second paragraph of canon 1425 is quite naturally and correctly expressed when the legislator makes use of the word *"potest"* in order to indicate a particular right which is not enjoyed by the religious superior in the case mentioned in the preceding paragraph of the same canon. The option implied centers about the idea of a qualitative applica-

---

[104] Cf. can. 148 §1. In this canon the rights of the religious superior, relative to both fully and partially incorporated parishes, are covered by the term *"nominatio."* The patron's right is termed one of *"praesentatio."* The particle *"aut"* seems to make the legal differentiation of these two terms complete and mutually exclusive. Yet, since the execution of the right is identical whether it derives its motivation from a religious superior or from a lay or clerical patron, little, if any, confusion of thought becomes imminent from a looser use of the term *"praesentatio."*

[105] Cf. can. 18.

tion of right, abscinding altogether from any consideration of the *necessary manner* in which it is to be executed in its use.

The canon simply foregoes any mention as to whether the use of this right is optative or imperative. It leaves this consideration to other canons where the specification on this point is sufficiently clear and unmistakable.[106]

Finally, when a parish is committed to the care of religious by a mere concession in trust, revocable at the behest of the diocesan ordinary, its incumbent must be appointed with the consent of the religious superior.[107] In effect, this stipulation of previous consent on the part of the religious superior, when his subjects are called upon by the diocesan ordinary to assume the actual charge of secular parishes, is tantamount to his presentation of them for their ultimate assignment to the parishes by the ordinary of the diocese. Hence, also in this case one may speak of "*paroeciae religiosis concreditae*" with the result that the religious superior enjoys a right equivalent to that of presenting candidates chosen from the members of his own community for filling the pastoral offices entrusted thereto.[108]

A parochial benefice thus committed to the care of religious does not cease to retain its secular status.[109] Now, according to the general rule of the Code as expressed in canon 1442, abstracting from the singular circumstances attendant upon the

---

[106] Cans. 456 and 471 §2 treat of religious parochial benefices in particular; can. 1442 treats of all religious benefices in general. Cf. Pistocchi, *De Re Beneficiali*, pp. 103-04, where attention is called to the fact that a religious superior may be qualified for presenting a candidate selected from the diocesan priesthood in virtue of a legitimate privilege or custom. The excepted case of canon 471 §2 is, therefore, not one of exclusion, but rather one of concurrence with the normal mode of procedure. Hence, whenever a legitimate privilege or custom exists which permits of the appointment of a diocesan priest to a religious parochial benefice, the religious superior is free either to use his privilege or to follow the common law. In this light the various canons become perfectly unified in their concordant signification.

[107] Cf. footnote 84 of this chapter.

[108] Cf. Melo, *De Exemptione Regularium*, p. 86: "Quae hucusque dicta sunt de vicariis actualibus valent etiam respectu parochorum regularium, quando paroecia illis concreditur, quin incorporetur pleno vel minus pleno iure conventui regulari; . . . ."

[109] Can. 1425 §2 sanctions only one way in which parochial benefices can acquire the status of a religious parish, namely, by full and complete incorporation with the religious house or institute.

case of a temporary concession in trust to religious, the superior would be under obligation to select a presentee from the ranks of the diocesan clergy. But, since the unusual situation here contemplated is conditioned upon an exception to the law for its very origin and continued existence, it becomes patent that its further regulation will also cease to be subject to the normal and usual ruling of the law. Hence, whilst the parish thus entrusted retains a secular status, it nevertheless calls for the appointment of a religious priest for supplying its pastoral office. If, however, no religious priest may assume a pastoral charge without the previous expressed consent of his religious superior,[110] then his appointment follows in equivalent effect as a result of the latter's presentation for office.[111]

Correlative with the religious superior's right to present a candidate for the office of parish priest, parish vicar, or temporary supply pastor under the threefold conditions just indicated, is his right of presenting a prospective appointee in the capacity of adjutant vicar under the like circumstances. The important question connected with the exercise of this right is whether the religious superior must in all instances select the prospective adjutant presentee from his own religious subjects.

If one were justified in assuming that an adjutant's station in a parish constituted him the holder of a benefice, the answer would be easy. The same norm of procedure would then obtain in the manner of his presentation as for that of a parish priest, parish vicar, or temporary supply pastor.[112] Since, however, his parochial ministry does not possess the status of an

---

[110] Cf. can. 630 §1.

[111] Cf. Leo XIII, const. "*Romanos Pontifices*," die 8 Maii 1881—*Fontes*, III, n. 582, pp. 171-86. This papal constitution, first issued for England and Scotland, was later extended to the United States of America on September 25, 1885—Conc. Plen. Balt. III, *Acta et Decreta*, p. cv. The regulations were incorporated in the *Acta et Decreta*, nn. 20 and 86-91. If at the present time a similar special mode of provision becomes imperative in our country, the diocesan ordinaries will apply to the Apostolic Delegate who, in virtue of the special faculties granted him, can empower them with the necessary authority for this extraordinary mode of pastoral provision in their dioceses. See text of faculty as reproduced in footnote 84 above.

[112] Cf. cans. 456, 471 §2, 1425, 1442, and the special ruling which results from a use of the faculties previously cited.

ecclesiastical benefice,[113] the fact of presentation by the religious superior does not of itself entail the strict necessity of a selection from the membership of the religious house or institute to which the parish is entrusted. Unlike canons 456, 471 §2 and 1425, which indicate both the fact and the manner of the presentation by the religious superior, the limits within which it is to be exercised do not receive any particular and explicit specification. No direct mention is made as to whether the passive subject of presentation is a member of the diocesan or the religious clergy, or under what conditions he will exclusively be the one or the other.

Relative to the presentation of a prospective adjutant, the religious superior appears to enjoy the same degree of freedom as that possessed by a local diocesan ordinary when appointing an administrator in a vacant parish. The analogous correlation of canon 472 1° and 475 §1 seems to be fully reciprocal. Hence, a more detailed comparative study of these two canons is in order.

In virtue of canon 472 1° the local diocesan ordinary has the right of designating an administrator for any kind of parish whatsoever.[114] Whether the appointment of its titular beneficiary be reserved to the Holy See for any one or several of the causes mentioned in the law,[115] whether it must follow upon an act of presentation by a patron,[116] or whether it is consequent upon an act of presentation or nomination by a religious superior,[117] regardless altogether of the religious or secular status of the parish—under all of these conditions the local ordinary of the diocese remains the sole and exclusive authority for the appointment of an administrator in a vacant parish. The construction of canon 472 1° is so general that it reserves no cases in which he is not competent. Hence, he is also free to appoint a religious priest as administrator in a secular parish,

[113] Can. 1412 3°: "Licet aliquam cum beneficiis similitudinem praeseferant, in iure tamen beneficii nomine non veniunt coadiutoriae cum vel sine futura successione."

[114] The wording of the canon is such as not to allow of any exception. The phrase "*vacante paroecia*" simply includes all cases of parochial vacancies.

[115] Can. 1435 §1.

[116] Cans. 149, 1455 1°, 1465 §1, 1466 §§1 and 3.

[117] Cans. 465, 471 §2, 1425 §§1-2.

provided he has the prerequisite consent from the proper religious superior in whose competency it will remain to judge whether such an appointment may be conceded without infringement upon the rules and constitutions of the institute.[118]

In a similar manner, whenever a religious superior enjoys the right of presenting an adjutant, the Code defines no limitation in canon 475 §1 with regard to the religious or secular status of the person presented.[119] But, since there is only one specified case in which the religious superior is definitely instructed to select his presentee from the ranks of the diocesan clergy, namely, when a pastoral incumbent is to be appointed in a parish *quoad temporalia tantum* incorporated with a religious house, it would seem imperative that in all other cases when the religious superior selects a presentee from the ranks of the diocesan clergy—hence also when there is question of the presentation of an adjutant—he would require the previous consent of the local ordinary for the valid exercise of such a liberal option.

The reasons which necessitate this previous alternate consent from the respective authority to which the appointee or presentee is subject arise from the following considerations. A religious priest owes obedience primarily to his religious superior because of the bond of his vow.[120] A diocesan priest is directly subject to the obedience of his local ordinary in virtue of his incardination in the diocese.[121] That the religious superior has no direct authority over diocesan priests is obvious from the fact that he is not a local ordinary.[122] That the ordinary of the diocese has no absolute authority over religious priests, even though they be resident in his diocese, is equally clear from the very nature of the religious life.[123] In all events, a duality of complete and equal authority over the same individual is canonically inadmissible. The alternate exercise of a dual authority over one and the same subject indicates the very limit in which unity of

118 Cans. 472 1°, 608 §§1-2, 630 §1.

119 ". . . Ordinarius loci det vicarium adiutorem, praesentatum a Superiore, si de paroecia agatur religiosis concredita, ..."

120 Can. 608 §1, 630 §1.

121 Cans. 111 §1, 127.

122 Can. 198 §2.

123 Can. 501 §1.

government may be modified without resultant disorganization.[124]

Admitting that neither an administrator nor an adjutant becomes a beneficiary incumbent by appointment,[125] there is nothing contrary to canon 1442 in the selection of a religious priest by the diocesan ordinary for appointment to either of these two non-beneficed parochial ministries, nor in the selection of a secular priest by a religious superior when presenting a prospective appointee under like circumstances. Hence, the sole direct prohibition against such a course of action would find its motivation in the possibility of a conflict between the respective authorities. But, since neither of the two authorities can effectively proceed without the previous consent of the other, the slightest legal possibility of such a conflict is precluded. Therefore, neither the local ordinary in his act of appointment, nor yet the religious superior in his act of presentation, exceeds the strictly legal bounds of his competency when he proceeds in accord with these principles.

Canonical equity is the principal consideration that can be adversely invoked against this latitude of action aside from the principle of obediential solidarity inherent in the very nature of the religious and diocesan priesthood. The observance that *must* be accorded the law is indeed not legally violated when the interpretation of canons 472 1° and 475 §1 is pressed to its widest limits. But, since the Code has established a necessary procedural norm for the presentation and appointment of *beneficed* incumbents in churches entrusted to the care of religious, one may plausibly infer that, in as much as there is need of regulating the facts of presentation for, and appointment of, *non-beneficed* parochial ministries—concerning which no closer specification has been made directly available—, the adoption of a similar norm for their execution is not only not alien to, but also quite in agreement with, the manifest spirit of the law.

The lack of canon 475 §1 to specify that the religious superior must, in the act of presenting an adjutant, select him from

---

[124] Cf. e.g., cans. 44 §§1-2, 80, 204 §§1-2, 454 §5, 477 §1, 519, 874, 1050, 1553 §2, 1562 §1, 1569 §1, 2245 §2, 2252, 2253 3°, 2254 §1, 2290 §1, *et passim*.

[125] Cf. cans. 477 §1, 1406 §1 7°, 1412 1°, 1412 3°, 1443 ss.

the members of his own religious community, does not in itself compel the inference that the Code wished to deny any specific obligation in this matter. Nor does canon 1442, which speaks of benefices only, imply thereby that its ruling could not obtain for the presentation of adjutants whose ministry does not invest them with a benefice.[126] Whilst the silence of canons 472 1° and 475 §1 may indeed appear to leave room for a loose interpretation in view of the reasons indicated above, yet it is by no means of such a significance as positively to exclude an application of the norm that is followed when there is question of presentation for and appointment to parochial benefices. Rather, precisely because of the law's indefinite ruling on this point, one is justified to look to similar conditions and analogous circumstances wherein the law is plainly specified. The Code itself sanctions this mode of interpretation and canonizes it as a norm to be followed in seeking to gain a practical understanding of those matters in which a definite and unmistakable prescription of law be wanting.[127]

Now, the circumstances surrounding the presentation and the appointment of a pastoral incumbent are similar to those which attend the presentation and the appointment of an adjutant or an administrator. In both situations the same essential elements concur whether we consider the status of the parish, the person of the superior, the motive for action, or ultimately, the execution of the acts to be placed. Hence, it seems equitable to urge also the same norm of procedure.[128]

Finally, for the same reason that the local ordinary feels impelled by a sense of propriety, fairness and equity to select for administrator a diocesan priest in a secular parish, and a religious priest in a parish entrusted to religious, unless there be need of deviating from this plan for securing the better pas-

---

[126] Cf. can. 1412 3°; De Meester, *Iuris Canonici et Iuris Canonico-civilis Compendium*, III, P. I, n. 1396, p. 325; Vermeersch-Creusen, *Epitome Iuris Canonici*, II, n. 745, p. 464.

[127] Cans. 18 and 20.

[128] Cf. cans. 456, 471 §2, 1425 §§1-2; 472 1°, 475 §1; Melo, *De Exemptione Regularium*, pp. 90-91: "Quod autem spectat ad praesentationem, subjectionem atque amotionem vicarii *oeconomi* vel *substituti* vel *adjutoris* seu *regentis* vel etiam *cooperatoris*, qui apud Hispanos *coadjutor* appellatur, in dictis paroeciis eadem ferme praescripta inveniuntur in Codice, ac pro vicariis actualibus et parochis statuuntur."

toration of the parish, so also will the religious superior feel constrained by the same laudable impulses to select candidates from his own religious community in the presentation of adjutants whenever the particular needs of the parish can thus be properly consulted. There is only one instance in which the religious superior is directly told to select a candidate from the ranks of the diocesan clergy. This case, mentioned in canon 1425 §1, obtains in the parishes that are but partially incorporated with the religious institute. If under these conditions the superior uses his alternative freedom to present also a diocesan priest as adjutant for the disabled diocesan parish priest, his action is surely sustained by the latitude which the Code allows in this matter. In fact, such a course of action by the superior would seem to correspond more dutifully with the norm of canonical equity,[129] and the principle of obediential solidarity. Whilst this is not directly deducible from canon 1425 §1 which has exclusive reference to the priest who fills the parochial office in such a parish, it seems to follow from canon 472 2° through the mediation of the principle of the *leges latae in similibus.*[130]

The situation contemplated in canon 472 2° is one in which the actual pastoral incumbent of the parish is a religious. Resident with him are some other clerical members of the same religious order or congregation, forming a branch of their institute under the immediate authority of a locally constituted superior distinct from the person of the actual pastor. At the demise of the pastoral incumbent this local superior assumes the temporary government of the parish for the interim until the diocesan ordinary has appointed an administrator. The one appointed, when he is a religious, will be constituted for the interregnum with the consent of the religious superior.

In all probability the canon has here in mind only a strictly religious parish when it uses the general phrase "*si tandem agatur de paroecia religiosis concredita.*" The fact, namely, that the possibility of a parish given in temporary charge to reli-

[129] Cf. *Apollinaris,* I (1928), 363-83, for an illuminative discussion of the question of canonical equity. Of particular interest for the present consideration is the author's clear-cut differentiation between natural and canonical equity (pp. 370 ss.).

[130] Cf. can. 20.

gious is not excluded, would not alter the outcome, since one cannot even conceive of this situation as existent without at the same time presupposing the unavoidable need and consequent necessity of the appointment of a religious to supply the pastoral office. If, then, by the disposition of the Code itself, the one who is called upon to assume the government of the parish for the interim is to be a religious, by force of legal sequence one must conclude that he who will be called upon to assume the pastoral charge for the interregnum should also be a religious. This definite provision is specified by the law even though there is no question at all of conferring a religious benefice for which a religious incumbent would have to be assumed, since neither of the two temporary ministries constitutes an ecclesiastical benefice.

The converse of the foregoing case is had when a diocesan priest is instituted as the pastoral incumbent of a parish which is only partially incorporated with a religious house or institute. The parochial benefice thus incorporated retains its full secular status and for this reason demands the presentation and subsequent appointment of a diocesan priest for the pastoral office. Canon 1425 §1, since it treats of parochial *benefices* only, lays down no ruling concerning the religious or diocesan status of the *non-beneficed* adjutant who will have to be presented and subsequently appointed in the event of this pastor's permanent disability. Nor does canon 475 §1 offer any specific rule. But, in the absence of a particular norm for this particular situation, it becomes equitable with the sanction of canon 20 to adopt the legislation enacted for an analogous case in which the prescription of the law is certain. Hence, the definite ruling of canon 472 2° with regard to the assumption of a religious priest for a *non-beneficed* parochial ministry when the parish is a religious benefice seems to be matched by an implied legal counterpart in canon 475 §1 relative to the assumption of a diocesan priest for a like *non-beneficed* parochial ministry in a parish which remains a secular benefice.

Finally, the principle of obediential solidarity may be invoked in order to specify the passive subject of presentation when there is need of an adjutant in a parish belonging to the class mentioned by canon 1425 §1. In view of his status as a religious, a religious parish priest, parish vicar, or supply pastor is not to live alone and detached from the community life of his religious institute. The same premise of the law applies also to an adjutant who is a religious. But, if the latter were appointed to integrate a pastoral activity in a parish which is under the immediate government of a secular incumbent, this ideal of the religious life would suffer frustration in his case. Now, since his appointment can follow only upon the presentation, and consequently also upon the full consent, of his religious superior, the latter would under such circumstances actually endorse a procedure alien to the promotion of the very ideals cherished by the religious institute with which both he and the adjutant are identified. Hence, the more equitable, if not legally imperative, mode of procedure will be that the religious superior in this instance exercise his right of presentation in favor of an adjutant selected from the diocesan clergy.

The foregoing discussion on whether the religious superior must use his right of presentation in favor of the members of his own religious institute, or whether he is free to present candidates selected from the ranks of the diocesan clergy, may be summarized as follows: First, the Code does not strictly demand that the adjutant presentee be selected from the ranks of the religious clergy of the respective institute. Secondly, this latitude of action allowed by the Code makes possible a better adaptation of the peculiar needs in a parish that call for the appointment of an adjutant. Thirdly, the equitable method of consulting these needs under the usual circumstances will be best realized by presenting an adjutant whose personal status as a diocesan or religious priest corresponds with that of the actual incumbent in office. Lastly, a deviation from this implied rule of canonical equity and clerical solidarity is not only justified, but will even become imperative, whenever the welfare of souls outweighs all other attendant considerations.

§III. Limits of the Exercise of Presentation

Once it is certain which religious superior enjoys the right of presentation and which persons may come as passive subjects under the exercise of this right, it only remains to establish the radius of its competence. Canon 475 §1 states in a very general way that this right is enjoyed by the religious superior whenever the parish is entrusted to religious. Now, in accord with what has been previously stated, the Code seems to leave room in its expression of "*paroecia religiosis concredita*" for the inclusion of all parishes that have been committed for their administration or care to a religious house or community, whether the commitment be one of full incorporation, of partial union, or of mere concession in trust. To make the phrase "*paroecia religiosis concredita*" synonymous with the term "*paroecia religiosa*" would appear to be either an unwarranted restriction of the first or an undue extension of the second.[131]

The term "*paroecia religiosa*" can have but one meaning. This exclusive meaning is constituted for it by the Code itself which declares that religious parishes are such as are fully incorporated *(pleno iure unitae)* with some religious house by an indult of the Holy See,[132] and thus become religious parochial benefices whose parish vicars must be appointed from the ranks of the religious community or house to which the benefice belongs.[133]

To interpret the phrase "*paroecia religiosis concredita*" in this exclusive sense would imply that religious superiors have the right of presentation for the filling of parochial offices only then when the parishes are by full right, in matters both spiritual and temporal, incorporated with religious houses or institutes. But, canon 1425 §1 plainly grants this same right to them when parishes are only partially incorporated. Furthermore, parishes only partially incorporated do not cease to remain secular parochial benefices. This, too, is evident from the same canon, since the religious superior is there instructed to present a candidate selected from the numbers of a diocesan clergy.

---

[131] Cf. Wernz-Vidal, *Ius Canonicum*, II, *De Personis*, n. 743, II, where this very confusion is imminent because of the somewhat loose terminology that is used. But in n. 154, II (*op. cit.*), where the subject of benefices is treated specifically, the wording employed is clear and unmistakable.

[132] Cf. can. 1425 §2.

[133] Cf. can. 1442; Pistocchi, *De Re Beneficiali*, pp. 103-05 and pp. 218-20.

If partial incorporation had the effect of converting a parish into a religious parochial benefice, then the appointee for this parish would have to be selected from the members of the religious house or institute with which it was thus united. But, the Code plainly prescribes that in this case not a religious, but a diocesan priest, is to be appointed by the ordinary of the diocese upon the superior's act of presentation. Now, if even the partial incorporation *(quoad temporalia tantum)* cannot convert a secular parochial benefice into a religious parish, then much less is it possible for a mere concession in trust—whether it be committed with or without the definition of a time limit—to effect a change of canonical status in the nature of the parochial benefice thus entrusted to the care of religious. In consequence, it becomes evident that the phrase "*paroecia religiosis concredita*" may not be pared down to the degree of becoming synonymous with the term "*paroecia religiosa,*" nor may the latter be amplified in its interpretation to the extent of embracing the former.[134]

The differentiation between a *parish entrusted to religious* and a *religious parish* is that the former denotes a genus whilst the latter forms one of its species. The former is in contraposition with a *parish entrusted to diocesans;* the latter finds its parallel opposition in a *secular parish,* or what is more commonly called a *secular parochial benefice.* The actual incumbent of a parish entrusted to religious may, under given conditions, be a member of the diocesan clergy; the actual incumbent of a religious parish must always by rule be a member of the religious clergy. On the other hand, the actual parochial minister in a parish entrusted to diocesans may, under certain circumstances, be a member of the religious clergy; the actual titular in a secular parish must always by rule be a member of the diocesan clergy. Not only when the parish is a religious benefice, but also when it is in any way entrusted to religious, will the religious superior be competent for the presentation (or approval) of an adjutant in aid of the disabled pastor or parish vicar.

---

[134] Cf. Prümmer, *Manuale Iuris Canonici,* Q. 250, pp. 337-38; Q. 427, pp. 511-12; Schäfer, *De Religiosis,* nn. 498-99, pp. 533-35; Vermeersch-Creusen, *Epitome Iuris Canonici,* II, nn. 753-54, pp. 468-71; De Meester, *Juris Canonici et Canonico-civilis Compendium,* III, P. I, n. 1402, p. 330.

ART. VII. THE QUESTION OF FUTURE SUCCESSION IN OFFICE

The final consideration in this chapter will turn about the point whether a parochial adjutant may be appointed to his parochial ministry with the right of succeeding to the parochial office as its titular incumbent. In answer to this question the Code does not offer any canon sufficiently expressive in its regulation to indicate an altogether unmistakable norm. Neither canon 475 §1 which specifically deals with the appointment of parochial adjutants, nor canon 1433 which generically treats of the constitution of coadjutors,[135] affords us a direct answer. This contention is borne out by the very circumstance that different authors adopt variant interpretations concerning this question.

Augusine,[136] Prümmer,[137] Vermeersch-Creusen,[138] Schäfer[139] and Stutz[140] leave the question an open one. D'Angelo[141] and Fanfani[142] concede to the local ordinary the power of appointing an adjutant vicar with the right of future succession to the pastoral office. Cocchi,[143] Pistocchi,[144] De Meester,[145] Eichmann[146] and Hilling[147] completely deny him this right. The two latter authors are very explicit in their statement on this point. Koeniger, while stating the simple fact that an adjutant is not infrequently accorded the right of future succession to his pastor's office, does not clearly indicate this fact as arising

[135] The word *coadjutor* must here be taken in the sense of canon 1412 3°. In this passage of the canon all classes of coadjutorship, whether episcopal or non-episcopal in rank, are embraced. Cf. Prümmer, *Manuale Iuris Canonici*, Q. 423, p. 508.

[136] *A Commentary on Canon Law*, VI, 517.

[137] *Manuale Iuris Canonici*, Q. 430, Nota 3, p. 516.

[138] *Epitome Iuris Canonici*, II, n. 765, p. 477.

[139] *Die Kirchenämter*, II Band, *Pfarrer und Pfarrvikare*, p. 99.

[140] *Der Geist des Codex iuris canonici*, p. 245, footnote 4.

[141] *Parroco e Parrocchia*, p. 37.

[142] *De Iure Parochorum*, n. 440, p. 376.

[143] *Commentarium in Codicem Iuris Canonici*, lib. II, P. I, n. 364, p. 441, but see also n. 113, p. 246.

[144] *De Re Beneficiali*, pp. 178-79.

[145] *Juris Canonici et Juris Canonico-civilis Compendium*, II, n. 872, p. 336, footnote 2.

[146] *Lehrbuch des Kirchenrechts*, §46, 3, p. 106, and §197, I, 2, p. 485.

[147] *Das Sachenrecht des Codex Juris Canonici*, §40, p. 252.

from a grant inherent in the local ordinary's intrinsic powers of office.[148]

§I. THE INTERPRETATION OF CANONS 475 AND 476

Canon 475 §1 is altogether silent about the possibility of future succession as a potential right for the adjutant. Nor does it even intimate that his adjutancy is normally to continue for the entire period of time during which the permanently disabled parish priest retains the title to his parochial incumbency. On the contrary, canon 477 §1 speaks of the adjutant's assignment as being revocable (similarly as that of other non-beneficed parochial vicars mentioned in canons 472-76) at the will and behest of the bishop, of the vicar capitular, or even of the vicar general when empowered by a special mandate for this act of diocesan administration.

If a local ordinary were to appoint an adjutant with the right to future succession in the pastoral office, or even if he were to assign him with the right of continuance in his ministry until the parochial benefice became vacant for any of the reasons stipulated in canon 183 §1, he would thereby forfeit the ready aptitude of prompt procedure and the available facility of opportune administration that the Code wishes him to enjoy for the suitable provision necessary in the parish under these unusual circumstances. By its lack of indicating any excepted cases, canon 477 §1 implies that the adjutant's removal shall depend, not upon the local ordinary's act of predetermination in the past, but upon his actual will for the present. Now, be it that the appointment is permanent in relation to the parochial benefice itself, or be it that the assignment perdure in respect to the parochial incumbent, in either case the local ordinary would pre-establish a somewhat fixed condition of his will. His will ought rather to be entirely free from all self-imposed legal limitations. It should remain perfectly adaptable to the special demands that may arise. In this manner alone will an

[148] "Der Pfarrverweser (auch Provisor, Koadjutor; vicarius adiutor), der bei dauernder Inhabilität des Pfarreiinhabers diesem vom Ordinarius, nötigenfalls auf Grund vorausgegangener Präsentation durch den Klosterobern, beigegeben, manchmal sogar mit dem Recht der Nachfolge versehen wird; . . ." —*Katholisches Kirchenrecht*, §41, 4, p. 237.

immediate and suitable provision in the case be safeguarded. The tenor of this argument has, of course, a merely negative value, but it is not without its cogency in defense of the contention that adjutants are to be appointed in a temporary manner only. The continuance in their ministry should be made dependent upon the concurrent prudent judgment and consequent will of the ordinary.

The law of the Code seems nowhere to grant an explicit and specified right to local ordinaries whereby they are empowered to concede future succession in office to adjutants. It is indeed true that canon 1433 sets canons 475 and 476 aside from the rule in virtue of which the appointment and constitution of all coadjutors—whether with or without the right of succession, regardless also of the consistorial or non-consistorial nature of the benefice—is reserved to the Apostolic See. But, to assume that this dissociation means to indicate for local ordinaries the same unrestricted powers, when appointing adjutants and assistants, that canon 1433 accords to the Apostolic See for all other cases of coadjutors, is but a begging of the question. The faculty extended by this canon by no means takes for granted that adjutancies and assistancies allow of an appointment with the right of succession; it merely points to canons 475 and 476 as in themselves indicating a norm in accordance with which the local ordinary may and should proceed.[149]

§II. The Interpretation of Canon 1433

It must be recalled that canon 1433 does not employ a phraseology equivalent in meaning to "*exceptis tamen casibus in can. 475, 476 statutis,*" but uses a wording quite diverse in its conceptual import, namely, "*salvo tamen praescripto can.*

[149] Cf. Pistocchi, *De Re Beneficiali,* pp. 178-79: "Non est, haec, vera exceptio, cum non agatur de *coadiutore* in sensu canonis (1433), id est, *perpetuo* saltem ad vitam coadiuti vel eius discessum a beneficio; est facultas non adempta Ordinario providendi, prout ei in Domino placuerit, ne vita paroecialis detrimentum capiat . . . Pro vera coadiutoria, cum vel sine futura successione, quae, praeter concessa Ordinario, videretur vere necessario instituenda, adeundus est Antistes supremus, de quo scripta sunt haec verba: 'Qui secundum plenitudinem potestatis de iure possumus supra ius dispensare.' " (c. 4, X, *de concessione praebendae et ecclesiae non vacantis,* III, 8)."

475, 476." Consequently, the phrase just cited provides no objective basis for the contention that canon 1433 reserves to the local ordinary the same faculty in the appointment of adjutants and assistants which in all other cases it reserves to the Holy See alone; rather, this phrase remains the basic objective and the pivotal point of the whole discussion. It is to be admitted, however, that this argument also, like the foregoing one, borrows its potency from merely negative factors rather than any positive canonical regulations.

A. Analogous Legislation

Still, the Code does present an argument which if not because of identical, then at least for analogical reasons, limits the local ordinary's competency in the manner of appointing adjutants and assistants within a narrower scope than that accorded by canon 1433 to the Holy See for all cases in general. In canon 150 the present law sets up a general prohibitive norm concerning appointments to offices. This general prohibition presents a twofold aspect under which every appointment to an ecclesiastical office is invalidly conferred. If the appointment is actually executed at a time when the office is not legally vacant, the action is invalid for the present and remains invalid for the future.[150] If the appointment is merely promissory but intimated under the like circumstances of a *de iure* non-vacant office, its provision begets no juridical efficacy, regardless of the person by whom it is undertaken, and irrespective of the time when it is to be actualized.[151]

---

[150] Cf. cans. 150 §1, 2146 §3, 2395; De Meester, *Juris Canonici et Juris Canonico-civilis Compendium*, I, n. 397, p. 283; Maroto, *Institutiones Iuris Canonici*, I, n. 593, p. 702. An office is *de iure* vacant when it has no titular incumbent; *de facto* when it has no possessory incumbent; *de iure et de facto* when it has neither a titular nor a possessory incumbent.

[151] The Roman Pontiff is, of course, not subject to this ruling. His exemption from this law is unmistakably insinuated by cans. 350 §1, 1431 and 1433. Moreover, as the supreme lawgiver in the Church, he is not circumscribed in his action by any of her merely disciplinary enactments. Consequently, he is free to proceed at the dictation of his own prudential judgment. Cf. cans. 218, 1518, 1556, 1557 §3; Maroto, *op. cit., loc. cit.*: "Huiusmodi prohibitio et irritatio respicit imprimis provisiones factas a quolibet infra Romanum Pontificem provisore, qui nequit agere contra ius, ac proinde nullitas provisionis habetur ex defectu potestatis."

In canon 150 §1 the Code considers the attempt of an *actual* appointment whose obvious import is to confer an *immediate* incumbency in office. In canon 150 §2 the law contemplates a *promissory* appointment whose sole intent is to provide a *future* incumbency. Now, it must be conceded, indeed, that neither of these two cases *directly* and *explicitly* includes that of the coadjutor who in his appointment is accorded the right of future succession in office. He is appointed neither as the immediate actual incumbent, nor yet as a mere promisee upon whom the office is to devolve when it becomes vacant. The lack of the element of possessory incumbency excludes him from the sphere of §1; the accession of the element of coadjutorship places him outside the realm of §2. In reality, his status occupies an intermediate stage between these two contingencies of canon 150. But, it is equally true that the additional circumstance of his coadjutorship does not neutralize his status as a promisee; rather, it becomes accentuated in virtue of the continued palpable evidence furnished by his very station and ministry. In view of this, the conclusion drawn from canon 150 by Maroto,[152] to the effect that the appointment of a coadjutor for any office with the right of future incumbency is reserved to the Roman Pontiff, appears fully justified because of the implied ruling there contained.[153]

B. Former Legislation

On the other hand, if any or all of the above arguments are rejected on the score that they presuppose the legislation to be certain, whilst actually it is only in doubtful agreement with the discipline of the past, the obvious answer is that the Code itself directs that no departure from the traditional interpretation is to be made as long as it remains doubtful whether a canon in the present codification differs from the law of the past.[154]

---

[152] *Ibid.* See also Cocchi, *Commentarium in Codicem Iuris Canonici*, lib. II, P. I, n. 65, p. 152; Wernz-Vidal, *Ius Canonicum*, II, *De Personis*, n. 212, p. 229; Prümmer, *Manuale Iuris Canonici*, Q. 74, n. 2, p. 104.

[153] Can. 11 leaves room for the invalidation of an act by an *equivalent* statement of its nullity.

[154] Can. 6 4°.

In this connection it is worthy of note that in the edition of the Code prepared by Cardinal Gasparri the footnotes to canons 150 §2, 350 §1 and 1433 incorporate the same extracts from the disciplinary regulations of the council of Trent as a common source for the laws expressed in these canons.[155] Upon this basis it would seem permissible to conclude that the reasons prompting the enactment of these two distinct but kindred laws were identical in motive and consequently eventuated in an identity of regulation with regard to both contingencies. In both cases the Roman Pontiff alone could proceed independently of all prohibitions in view of his supreme authority which was not subjected to the disciplinary enactments of the Council.[156]

In accordance with these regulations the pre-Code authors uniformly taught that the local ordinary enjoyed no competency for the appointment of coadjutors with the right of future succession to any office. Where help was needed in the pastoration of the parochial churches he was to proceed according to the special norms elsewhere prescribed by the Council.[157] In these regulations there was not contained any mention of a right enjoyed by the bishop for the appointment of adjutants or the approval of assistants with a claim upon future succession. Because of this significant silence, the existence of such a faculty was consistently disclaimed by the authors.[158] It will

[155] Cf. Sessio XXIV, *de ref.*, c. 19, which abolishes the practice of provisory mandates and expectative grants in the filling of ecclesiastical offices; sessio XXV, *de ref.*, c. 7, which similarly prohibits the concession of coadjutorships for any ecclesiastical offices whatsoever, except in the more important cases of urgent need or evident utility. Any provision that might be made was to fall under the personal supervision of the Roman Pontiff—*Canones et Decreta*, pp. 201, 230; S. C. C. *in Albiganen. Parochialium*, die 1 Sept. 1663—Pallottini, *Collectio omnium Conclusionum et Resolutionum*, XIV, p. 517, n. 24.

[156] Sessio XXV, *de ref.*, c. 21: "Postremo sancta Synodus, omnia, et singula, sub quibuscumque clausulis et verbis, quae de morum reformatione, atque ecclesiastica disciplina, . . . in hoc sacro Concilio statuta sunt, declarat, ita decreta fuisse, ut in his salva semper auctoritas Sedis apostolicae et sit, et esse intelligatur."—*Canones et Decreta*, p. 244. Cf. Benedictus XIV, *De Synodo Dioecesana*, lib. XIII, cap. 10, n. 29.

[157] Cf. sessio XXI, *de ref.*, cc. 4, 6—*op. cit.*, pp. 127-29.

[158] Cf. Ferraris, *Bibliotheca*, v. *Coadjutor*, n. 6: "Coadjutoria temporalis *sine* futura successione in Ecclesiis et beneficiis Episcopatui inferioribus, potest concedi a proprio Praelato." Joannes Andreae and Abbas are cited by this compiler of canonical lore in substantiation of his own teaching on this point.

also be seen that whilst Pope Benedict XIV strongly favored the appointment of parochial adjutants with the right of future succession whenever parochial needs were similar to those which under like circumstances warranted the appointment of coadjutors with the right of succession in cathedral churches and monasteries, yet, like all the other authors, he concedes the right to make such an appointment to the Roman Pontiff alone.[159]

C. Present Legislation

In the Code there is nowhere found any canon which *expressly* grants local ordinaries the faculty of appointing parochial adjutants and assistants in such a manner as to bestow upon them the right of future succession to the office supplied or integrated by them. Nor does canon 1433 offer any likelihood that such a faculty is enjoyed in virtue of a right implicitly or equivalently granted. Canons 475 and 476 do not present cases which constitute full-fledged exceptions to the ruling of canon 1433 in *all* of its constituent elements. When these two cases are considered as exceptions to the general rule, one must regard them as such only in a relative or restricted measure. They are simply mentioned as dissociated instances in which the local diocesan ordinary shares the otherwise universally exclusive competence of the Holy See in relation to the simple fact of appointment, but entirely unrelated with the dual mode

---

Zitelli, *Apparatus Iuris Ecclesiastici*, p. 186; Berardi, *De Parocho Compendium*, n. 882, p. 277; Hinschius, *System des katholischen Kirchenrechts*, II, pp. 84-85, 324-25; Bouix, *Tractatus de Parocho*, pp. 423-25: "Hinc fit quod talis coadjutoria cum futura successione nequeat concedi neque a Cardinali Legato seu Nuntio." Wernz, *Ius Decretalium*, II, n. 315, p. 81, and n. 839, p. 691: "Quodsi *in casu raro* parocho coadiutor perpetuus cum iure successionis *concedatur*, . . ." and again: "Deputatio coadiutoris temporanei ex causis canonicis spectat ad Episcopum etiam invito parocho; coadiutor vero perpetuus *cum iure successionis* a solo Romano Pontifice potest concedi." Lämmer, *Kirchenrecht*, pp. 258 and 283-84 with appended footnotes.

[159] *De Synodo Dioecesana*, lib. XIII, cap. 10, nn. 26-28. ". . . arbitramur, neque potuisse, neque voluisse Tridentinos Patres vinculum injicere Romanis Pontificibus, ne, justis, ac validis urgentibus causis, coadjutores cum futura successione inferioribus beneficiis valerent constituere; sed tantum voluisse monitum quoddam iis relinquere, ne suam hisce coadjutoribus praestent auctoritatem, nisi cum re ipsa debitae circumstantiae id expostulent."—*Ibid.*, n. 28.

of its execution.[160] The modified factor of the law is bound up with the question of exclusiveness in the faculty or the right for the act of appointment. It has no point of contact with the consideration of modality in the execution of that act.[161]

If someone were still to contend that the right of appointment with future succession is not clearly denied to the local ordinary, and that he can therefore proceed to the exercise of this probable right in virtue of canon 15, the evident answer will be that such an interpretation would render meaningless the prescription of canon 6 4°, which plainly stipulates that in a case of doubt the revocation of a pre-existing law is not presumed. In such a juridical emergency the later laws are rather to be compared with the previous laws, and, as far as possible, harmonized with them. The law of continuity in the legislation of the Church is a legal presumption which yields only in the face of an express abrogation, a contrary enactment, or a complete re-ordering of the content of the law.[162]

In consideration of the various negative indications in the Code, moreover, in view of its analogous positive illustrations, and finally, in pursuance of the legal necessity of harmonizing the law of the Code with the past legislation as long as the revocation is not certain beyond reasonable doubt, it would seem that the opinion proposed by Fanfani [163] and D'Angelo,[164] which presupposes the ordinary's right of appointing parochial adjutants and assistants, must be relinquished as untenable. Precisely because of its solid juridical basis, both in the light of

---

[160] Can. 19: "Leges quae . . . exceptionem a lege continent strictae subsunt interpretationi."

[161] Cf. Hilling, *Das Sachenrecht des Codex Juris Canonici*, p. 252: "Nach dem heutigen Recht können Koadjutoren mit oder ohne Nachfolge nur vom Apostolischen Stuhle bestellt werden . . . . Jedoch findet diese Bestimmung keine Anwendung auf die Vicarii coadjutores und die Vicarii cooperatores der Pfarrer, *die aber kein Recht auf Nachfolge haben*, can. 475 und 476."

[162] Cf. can. 22; see also Augustine, *A Commentary on Canon Law*, I, pp. 102-04.

[163] *De Iure Parochorum*, n. 440, p. 376: ". . . si fiat [institutio adiutoris cum iure ad futuram successionem] ab Episcopo, et paroecia per concursum sit conferenda, etiam pro institutione coadiutoris cum futura successione *concursus* habendus sit."

[164] *Parroco e Parrocchia*, p. 37: "La prassi è che il Vescovo conferisca una tale coadiutoria (nempe, cum iure successionis) dietro regolare concorso a norma della *'Cum Illud'*."

the present and the past legislation, the opinion proposed by the other above mentioned authors [165] appears to offer the correct interpretation of the question dealing with the *terminus ad quem* of an adjutant's or assistant's appointment.

ART. VIII. RECAPITULATION

The present chapter has treated in particular, of the manner of appointment for *adjutants*. Attention was drawn to the respective modifications of the law resulting from the variation of parochial status and personal relation. In addition to this, discussion was offered regarding the religious superior's and local ordinary's rights entering into the integration of the act of appointment. Furthermore, consideration was given to the act of appointment in its relation to the threefold conditions of occupancy, vacancy, and quasi-vacancy of the episcopal or vicarial see. The specification of canon 430 §2 relative to the conferment of ecclesiastical offices and benefices occasioned a joint treatment of the law as applicable to both adjutants and assistants. Finally, cognizance was taken of the special canonical question of future succession in office. Here, too, the intimate connection between canons 475 and 476, as suggested by canon 1433, called for a concurrent illustration of the point in regard to both adjutants and assistants.

The following chapter will treat, in particular, of the manner of appointing *assistants*. Since many of the details surrounding the two contingencies of *personal* and of *real* need in the pastoration of the parochial ministry run parallel to one another, whatever has been adverted to in this chapter will not recur for observation in the next. Thus, for example, a restatement of the religious superior's and local ordinary's rights inherent in the act of appointment will be of negligible interest, because of the almost uniform disposition of the law in canons 475 §1 and 476 §§3-4 relative to the personal sources of this authoritative act. An item of interest is indeed contained in the legal fact that the Code has selected a closer, more personal, and strictly obediential bond within which to circumscribe the religious superior's faculty in the presentation of a

---

[165] See footnotes 139-43 preceding.

prospective assistant vicar. The chief concern, however, will center in the distinctive feature of the *auditio parochi*. Nevertheless, whenever an indication of the divergencies or analogies existing between the stipulations of canons 475 and 476 relative to the act of appointment will serve the purpose of a clearer illustration of some specific point under consideration, an effort will be made to utilize this additional aid in achieving a clarified interpretation.

CHAPTER VII

THE MANNER OF APPOINTING ASSISTANTS

CANON 476

§1. Si parochus propter populi multitudinem aliasve causas nequeat, iudicio Ordinarii, solus convenientem curam gerere paroeciae, eidem detur unus vel plures cooperatores, quibus congrua remuneratio assignetur.

§3. Non ad parochum, sed ad loci Ordinarium, audito parocho, competit ius nominandi vicarios cooperatores e clero saeculari.

§4. Vicarios cooperatores religiosos Superior cui id ex constitutionibus competit, audito parocho, praesentat Ordinario, cuius est eosdem approbare.

ART. I. POINTS OF COMPARISON BETWEEN CANONS 475 §1 AND 476 §§3-4

The disposition of the law in canon 476 §§3-4 runs parallel to the legislation of canon 475 §1 in a major number of the points involved in the act of appointment. The same local ordinary who is competent in the act of assigning an adjutant vicar is also endowed with competency in the act of appointing an assistant vicar. The same norm indicated by canon 1433 concerning the duration of an adjutant's assignment is intimated also for the term of an assistant's ministry. The same remedy of law against the decree of the local ordinary obtains for the one case as for the other.[1]

[1] Can. 2146 §1: "A definitivo decreto unicum datur iuris remedium, idest recursus ad Sedem Apostolicam." Cf. S. C. C. *Romana et aliarum*, die 12 Jan. 1924—*AAS*, XVI (1924), 165, in which the available time-limit for instituting such recourse is indicated as ten days; the time is to be computed according to cans. 34 §3 3° and 35; see also Vermeersch-Creusen, *Epitome Iuris Canonici*, III, n. 346, pp. 162-63; Wernz-Vidal, *Ius Canonicum*, VI, *De Processibus*, n. 746, pp. 707-08.

In either instance the decree of the local ordinary is sustained in its dispositive efficacy whilst the recourse is pending for the ultimate ratification or rejection of its claim. It follows logically that from the decree of the ordinary no recourse is admitted to the Roman Rota, since all actions of recourse are exclusively referred to the respective Sacred Congregations.[2] Furthermore, the law itself establishes the legal presumption that the local ordinary is accredited as possessing a basic priority of right and claim in all matters appertaining to the administration of his diocese.[3] Finally, presentation of the adjutant by the religious superior for a parish entrusted to religious has its counterpart in the presentation by the superior of an assistant who belongs to his religious institute.

There are notable points of difference, however, which may not be left disregarded. They account not only for a modification in the act of appointment, but also for an altered basis in the right of presentation. The first of these rests on the prerequisite of the *auditio parochi;* the second clings more closely to the idea of a personal relation. Because of their far-reaching implications both of these marks of differentiation demand a more intimate study.

ART. II. THE *Auditio Parochi*

The Church is habitually loath to the institution of radical innovations in her positive legislation. This historical fact is so universally acknowledged that at times, through a lack of genuine insight or sympathetic understanding, men brand her public polity as one of ultra-conservatism. A fuller knowledge would reveal to them the excellent advisability of her traditional caution in the enactment of new legislation, since it would

---

[2] Can. 1601; see also cans. 1569 §2 and 246-57; Camp, *Die organisatorische Trennung der Gewalten in der römischen Kurie,* §11 (*Die Kompetenz der Kongregationen*), pp. 99-113; Oietti, *De Romana Curia,* §III (*De discrimine inter res ordinis judicialis et administrativi*), pp. 18-26.

[3] Cf. Leo XIII, const. *Romanos Pontifices,* die 8 Maii 1881—*Fontes,* III, n. 582, p. 178: ". . . praesertim vero quod, ut doctorum fert adagium, Episcopus intentionem habet in iure fundatam in rebus omnibus, quae ad dioecesim suam administrandam attinent." Relative to the conferring of parochial benefices the Code appropriates the same legal axiom in can. 1432 §1.

also lead them to a recognition of her equally traditional respect for the legal potentiality of reasonably established customs.

The Church has unequivocally sanctioned the utility and the force of custom in the formation of consuetudinary law.[4] A community capable of being made the recipient of ecclesiastical law is also able to form a custom which obtains the force of law, as long as there accedes to it the consent—express, tacit, or legal—of the competent ecclesiastical superior.[5] A reasonable custom can legitimately prescribe an ecclesiastical law by an unbroken continuance of forty full years. If this custom perdures for a period of a hundred full years, it has the power of prescribing an ecclesiastical law which even prohibits the formation of future contrary customs. Only such customs which are expressly reprobated in the law, or which militate against divine-natural or divine-positive law, lack any power of legal prescription.[6] Safeguarding the ruling of canon 5, any custom which runs counter to law, or which is operative outside of its sphere, is recalled by contrary custom or contrary law; but, unless express mention of them is made, the law does not revoke centenary or immemorial customs, nor does a general law recall particular customs.[7] Such, in short, is the Church's outlook upon the future relative to the potentiality of custom in obtaining the force of law.

As to the past, all reprobated general and particular contrary customs are once for all abolished; suppressed also are all contrary customs which lack the sanction of a centenary or immemorial usage, unless the Code expressly retains them; but, all contrary customs of a hundred years' standing or of immemorial usage will be maintained within the realm of tolerance

---

[4] Reg. 45, R. J., in VI°: "Inspicimus in obscuris quod est verisimilius, vel quod plerumque fieri consuevit." Cf. cc. 3-4, D. XII; c. 6, D. VIII; cc. 1-11, X, *de consuetudine*, I, 4; cc. 1-2, *de consuetudine*, I, 4, in VI°; Leo XIII, litt. ap. "*Apostolicae Curae*," die 13 Sept. 1896, §6—*Fontes*, III, n. 631, p. 498.

[5] Reg. 43, R. J., in VI°; cans. 25 and 26; cf. Chelodi, *Ius de Personis*, n. 71, p. 126; Hilling, *Die allgemeinen Normen des Codex Juris Canonici*, §20, pp. 43-46.

[6] Can. 27 §§1-2.

[7] Can. 30.

by the Church, if ordinaries, in the light of local and personal circumstances, deem it an imprudent policy to displace them.[8]

This restatement of the Church's acknowledgment of the legal efficacy of custom in the domain of ecclesiastical law together with the consideration of her abiding predilection for retaining, whenever feasible, the traditions of her own positive legislation [9] furnishes the keynote for the present law on the appointment of assistant vicars as expressed in canon 476 §§3-4. In these two paragraphs a dual element is discernible: 1) The overruling force of an acknowledged custom which ran counter to the law of the council of Trent;[10] 2) the tempering influence of the Church's lingering legislative tradition on the assertiveness of contrary custom.[11]

Formerly the parish priest or rector selected for his assistant a priest approved by the bishop for the performance of the parochial ministries. To the bishop's power and exclusive right of approval for the prospective assistant custom gradually added the faculty of selection and appointment.[12] The present law retains this faculty for the local ordinary, but conditions its rightful exercise upon a preparatory act of consultation with the actual pastor to whose parish the prospective assistant is to be appointed.

Concerning the *auditio parochi* three queries may be raised: 1) Is the *auditio* prescribed merely for the initial appointment

---

[8] Can. 5.

[9] Cans. 6 2°—4°, 20, 22, 23. Cf. Reg. 15, R. J., in VI°; c. 29, *de electione et electi potestate*, I, 6, in VI°; Koeniger, *Katholisches Kirchenrecht*, §12 (*Die Rechtsauslegung*), pp. 86-88; Eichmann, *Lehrbuch des Kirchenrechts*, §§15-16, pp. 41-45.

[10] Sessio XXI, *de ref.*, c. 4: "Episcopi, etiam tamquam apostolicae Sedis delegati, . . . cogant rectores, . . . sibi tot sacerdotes ad hoc munus *adiungere*, quot sufficiant ad sacramenta exhibenda, et cultum divinum celebrandum."—*Canones et Decreta*, pp. 127-28.

[11] Cf. Rettenbacher, "*Der Kooperator nach dem Codex Juris*," *LQS*, LXXII (1919), 337-48. See also Wernz, *Ius Decretalium*, II, n. 838, II, p. 688; Scherer, *Handbuch des Kirchenrechtes*, I, 648.

[12] Cf. Chaillot, "Traité des Vicaires Paroissiaux," *Anal. Jur. Pont.*, V (1861), (*Nomination*), 855-77; S. C. C. die 14 Aug. 1863, ad V—*Revue des Sciences Ecclėstiastiques*, XI (1865), 273-74, and *NRT*, XXIV (1892), 603; Kohn, "De Cooperatoribus," *AkKR*, XXXIX (1878), 3-35, especially pp. 9 ff.: Zimmermann, "Über die amtliche und rechtliche Stellung der Pfarrkapläne besonders in der Diözese Mainz," *AkKR*, XLII (1879), 410-22, especially p. 413.

of an assistant to a parish, or does the law demand its repetition at each appointment thereafter? 2) Does the law of the Code require the *auditio* as a prerequisite for valid appointment? 3) Does the ruling of canon 476 §§3-4 admit of a contrary observance in virtue of canon 5?

§I. Requirement of the *Auditio* for Each Individual Appointment

In regard to the first query Augustine [13] writes as follows:

> Something of the old rights of parish priests remains, for the bishop is obliged to ask the opinion of the pastor concerning the necessity of appointing an assistant. But if the Ordinary is convinced of the necessity, he may appoint an assistant even against the will of the pastor.
>
> If the parish belongs to a religious community, the assistant to be appointed must be presented by the competent superior. This competency, as said above, is determined by the constitutions of the respective community. But in the case of religious, too, the pastor should be heard as to the necessity, *not the person*, of the assistant.[14]

A. Scope of the *Auditio*

The wording of canon 476 §3 is terse and direct: "Not to the parish priest, but to the local ordinary, upon granting a hearing to the pastor, belongs the right of nominating assistant vicars taken from the body of the diocesan (secular) clergy." It may readily be conceded that the local ordinary ought not to proceed to the initial appointment of an assistant in any parish without previous consultation with the pastor regarding the need of appointment. Still, such an appointment does not call

[13] *A Commentary on Canon Law*, II, 574.

[14] In later works the author does not stress this earlier restrictive opinion. Cf. *Rights and Duties of Ordinaries*, pp. 182-83; *The Pastor according to the New Code of Canon Law*, p. 46; *Canonical and Civil Status of Catholic Parishes*, pp. 240-41. In this later work (*loc. cit.*) the author's words—"Such considerations ought to render Ordinaries very careful in appointing assistants or curates to pastors, not to speak of the natural courtesy they owe to their own helpers,"—might even admit of the more comprehensive interpretation commonly given by canonists.

for as serious a consideration of its need, importance, or utility as is demanded from the local ordinary when proceeding to the union, transfer, division or dismemberment of parishes.[15] For these latter acts of administration the law prescribes the hearing of the diocesan chapter or body of diocesan consultors besides such other persons, especially the rectors of the churches, as have a direct interest in the case (can. 1428 §1). Nevertheless, if a just and canonical cause be present, the ordinary is authorized to proceed even without the consent of the parochial rectors or the parishioners (can. 1427 §1).

In these instances the legal act of consultation is rooted in the desire of the Church that nothing of far-reaching import in the government of his diocese be undertaken by the local ordinary without the aid of counsel, either from his official body of counsellors (the diocesan chapter or consultors),[16] or from specially constituted or selected advisers,[17] or, again, from persons vested with a direct interest in the case.[18] In very important matters the local ordinary can act only after obtaining the consent of the episcopal senate or council, which consists of the diocesan chapter or body of consultors.[19]

If, then, the law requires that no additional church be erected, that no new parochial benefice be created, that no parishes be united, transferred, divided or reapportioned, and that no pledges, mortgages or debts be contracted on ecclesiastical properties until the persons concerned in these transactions have been granted a hearing,[20] it would also appear entirely practicable on the part of the local ordinary to consult his parish priests before determining upon the initial appointment of an assistant in their parishes. But, it is to be remembered that the principle of conformed practice is to be invoked only after it is evident

---

[15] Cf. cans. 1427 and 1428.

[16] Cf. cans., 302, 303, 386, 388, 391 §1, 394 §1, 394 §3, 400 §1, 403, 406 §1, 411, 426 §3, 428, 454 §3, 895, 1234 §1, 1292, 1359 §2, 1428 §1, 1520 §1, 2292.

[17] Cf. e.g., cans. 1164 §1, 1234 §1, 1280, 1520 §3, 1521 §§1-2, 2145, 2148, 2152-54, 2159, 2165, 2171, 2174, 2183.

[18] Cf. e.g., cans. 476 §§3-4, 1162 §3 with 1676, 1416, 1428 §1, 1538 §1.

[19] Cf. e.g., cans. 391 §1, 394 §2, 426 §5, 459 §3 3°, 712 §2, 958, 1532 §3 with 1653 §1, 1541 §2.

[20] Cf. cans. 1532 §2, 1533, 1538 §1.

that an express prescript of law is not available for the particular act of administration in hand.[21]

When canon 476 §1 treats of the causes which demand an added help for the suitable pastoration of the parochial flock, it exclusively points to the judgment of the ordinary as being the qualified legal medium through which a decision on the matter is to be effected. The passage leaves altogether unmentioned the need of any previous consultation by the ordinary with the parochial beneficiary or pastoral incumbent. This silence of the canon is significant. It can mean nothing else than that the ordinary is recognized solely and alone to possess the full right of determining, even apart from any consultation with the pastor, when and under what conditions there is need of the appointment of an assistant in the parish.

On the other hand, canon 476 §§3-4 enunciates a general ruling with regard to the appointment of *all* assistant vicars. Whether they belong to the body of the diocesan clergy, or whether they be members of some religious institute or order, in both cases their act of appointment follows only after an act of consultation with the *actual* pastor or incumbent of the parish. Whether they be appointed to a parish which has *never* had the services of an assistant, or whether they be assigned in a parish which has *always* demanded his ministries, the law remains uniform: the pastor is to be consulted before the appointment of an assistant takes place. It is precisely the question of the assistant's person, and not the question of his necessity in the parish that forms the content of the required consultation.

The local ordinary enjoys the complete and unhampered right of deciding on the need of additional pastoral agencies in a parish through the appointment of one or more assistants whenever conditions warrant it. His capacity in this regard is as ample now as it was when the ruling of the Council of Trent still obtained. At most, there can be question of a modal difference only. The council of Trent enabled him to act either in his own native right, namely, as the bishop of his diocese, or in consequence of sharing a superadded right, namely, as a delegate of the Apostolic See.[22] In the latter event recourse was

---

[21] Can. 20.

[22] Cf. Sessio XXI, *de ref.*, c. 4—*Canones et Decreta*, pp. 127-28.

open only to the Holy See. In virtue of his office the local ordinary now always acts with a power that is ordinary.[23] Since his act is one of administration, there can be question of recourse only.[24] But, the legal procedure of recourse is so constituted now that there likewise remains no intermediate authority between the ordinary and the Holy See for the settlement of a question which has been carried beyond the scope of the ordinary's final action. Whilst the mode of legal redress emanates from an altered application of the law, yet, the extent of the ordinary's power is sustained as long as the Holy See has not patently disavowed it.[25]

In determining the need of an assistant in the parish the local ordinary is fortified by the law to proceed without the aid of a judgment other than his own. But, for appointing a certain priest to a certain parish in the capacity of an assistant the Ordinary's final provisionary act follows only upon a previous act of consultation with the actual pastor. If the prospective assistant belongs to the diocesan clergy, the consultation will devolve upon the diocesan ordinary; if the new curate belongs to a religious institute or order, the consultation will be made by the religious superior who is competent for his presentation. In the latter case the act of appointment is not one of free collation, but rather of ultimate approval by the ordinary of the diocese.[26]

B. Reasons for the *Auditio*

There are both negative and positive reasons in view of which the diocesan ordinary in the act of appointment as also the religious superior in the act of presentation are asked to consult

[23] Can. 334 §1: "Episcopi residentiales sunt ordinarii et immediati pastores in dioecesibus sibi commissis." Can. 335 §1: "Ius ipsis et officium est gubernandi dioecesim tum in spiritualibus tum in temporalibus cum potestate legislativa, iudiciaria, coactiva ad normam sacrorum canonum exercenda." Cf. can. 455 §2 1° and §3; further, cans. 1432 §1 and 1435 §2.

[24] Can. 1601.

[25] Cf. can. 1428 §3: "Adversus decretum Ordinarii, unientis, transferentis, dividentis aut dismembrantis beneficia, datur *in devolutivo tantum* recursus ad Sanctam Sedem." The ruling of this canon is made applicable for the case in hand by the principles of cans. 18 and 20. See also Reg. 35, R. J., in VI°.

[26] Can. 148 §1.

the pastor before a definite assignment of a new assistant be made. Every appointment should furnish a solid hope of successful collaboration with the pastor in the parochial ministry.[27]

Moreover, aside from the admission that all pastors have an intimate interest in the proper selection of a suitable co-worker, it must be acknowledged that amid a generous variety of circumstances their consulted information can be of supreme helpfulness for their bishop in enhancing the efficacy of his conscientious task of appointment.

1. Negative Reasons

Quite apart from all personal motives in the mutual relationship between pastor, assistant, and people, there may exist reasons which would annoy, embarrass, or even nullify the efficacy of a certain curate's service when enlisted in some particular parish. If these reasons are unknown to the ordinary, even his best efforts cannot crystallize in a model of administrative efficiency for the good of the several parishes throughout the diocese.

He might assign a young assistant to a parish in which the latter has spent a considerable portion of his time at school. The lingering memories of school days are not infrequently questionable factors in the heightening of an assistant's priestly regard or esteem for the people of his childhood acquaintance. Similarly, they can readily offer a serious handicap for the people in the cultivation of a reverent and confidential respect for him who has thus been placed in a new relationship toward them. The familiarity may not exhibit such positive notes in its noxious results as to breed the proverbial contempt, but it may operate rather unfavorably even when it becomes no more than an occasion for apathy and indifference where otherwise a spontaneous effort of innate reverence and respect would emanate from the people. If the ordinary can be notified of this possible hazard by the timely intervention of the pastor, not only the pastor and his people, but especially the young priest also, can be spared the experience of a vexing situation. Again, there may be living in the parish a group or family of relatives

[27] "Salus animarum suprema lex."—S. C. Consist. decr. *Maxima Cura*, die 20 Aug. 1910—*AAS*, II (1910), 636.

of the prospective assistant. Their repute in the parish or the community may not be above suspicion. To appoint as assistant in such a parish a relative of theirs might cast unpleasant, if not blighting, shadows upon the fair reverence of his priestly name.

On the other hand, the temperament and character of a given pastor and his prospective curate may be cast in such deep lines of contrariety or unadaptableness that the hope of a harmonious co-operation in the parish ministry will remain extremely unpromising. It would be improvident not to requisition a pastor's information regarding this circumstance when it is so available for guarding against an act of unhappy administration on the part of the diocesan ordinary.

Finally, some actual memory on the part of the people of a misdemeanor in the assistant's earlier life, or even some ill-founded suspicion in their minds concerning his irreproachable integrity and uprightness of conduct could make the fact of his appointment in their midst a trying situation in the lives of all concerned. It is but too true that even the sacred character of his priestly person together with the manifestation of a blameless life will not always succeed in sealing up the eruptive fountains from which popular suspicions, derogatory innuendos and perverse insinuations pour forth to blight a priest's pastoral efficiency.

Normally, no one is better qualified to be in cognizant touch with the local mentality of a people than a pastor amongst his parishioners. His competent suggestions, when taken under advisement by the bishop, can help most beneficially in offsetting needless and avoidable inequalities, or even guiltless, but none the less real, blunders in the administration of parochial appointments.

The mention of a few typical cases such as these may serve to indicate that the success of an assistant's work in a parish will hinge, in no small measure, upon the prudence exercised in making due allowance for the factors which, because of merely incidental circumstances, might jeopardize his desired effectiveness. In this matter as in other important parochial concerns [28] the requisition of previous counsel by the ordinary is well-

[28] Cf. canons cited in footnotes 17 and 18 of this chapter.

advised and therefore made a requirement by the law of the Code.[29]

2. Positive Reasons

There are also positive reasons which suggest that the appointment of an assistant in a parish should not be made without previous consultation with the pastor. Schäfer [30] lists a comprehensive number of the objective agencies which may demand the assignment of added pastoral help to a parish through the appointment of one or more curates. Different parishes have different needs and, in consequence, necessitate different positive qualifications in the ones enlisted to second the pastor's efforts in meeting them successfully. For example, parish A will require of its parish and assistant priests a special competence in the sacred art of preaching; parish B will invite a ministry which demands a thorough and sympathetic understanding of sociological principles and their effective application; parish C will offer special opportunities to priests who are trained and practiced in the apostolate of convert-making; parish D will call for a more than ordinary aptitude in linguistic accomplishments; and so on. Each of these separate needs presupposes a distinctive ability or capacity in the one appointed to help the pastor in relieving and satisfying them.

Since parish priests are the immediate shepherds of their flocks,[31] their knowledge of the particular needs and specific agencies of their pastoration will also be more intimate and comprehensive than that of any other person. To disregard this consideration would be tantamount to the courting of inefficient methods in the administration of parochial appointments. If the ordinary is directed by the Code to avail him-

[29] Cf. Haring, "Die Bestellung des pfarrlichen Hilfspriesters," *LQS*, LXXVII (1924), 337.

[30] *Die Kirchenämter*, II Band, *Pfarrer und Pfarrvikare*, p. 100.

[31] Cf. can. 460 §2; S. C. C. *in Nicien.*, die 7 Oct. 1604—Richter, *Canones et Decreta Concilii Tridentini*, p. 39, n. 19; S. C. C. *in Grossetana*, die 16 Sept. 1645—Pallottini, *Collectio omnium Conclusionum et Resolutionum*, XIV, 513, n. 2; S. C. C. *in Sabinen. Jurium Parochialium*, die 10 Mart. 1742—*op. cit.*, XIV, 628, n. 13: Ad V: "An parochus praesens et non impeditus, nec in aliis exercitiis parochialibus occupatus, debeat per se ipsum exercere munia parochialia? R. Affirmative."

self of the advice of his diocesan consultors in many of the matters that touch the welfare of the diocese at large, it is little less imperative that he should be instructed by the Code to consult his parish priests in the appointment of assistants who constitute "a mobile force at the service of the diocese for which they were ordained." [32] It is the *special* qualifications of assistants that furnish the hope of achieving the *desired* success for the good of the parish. The combined spiritual welfare of the individual members of the parish eventuates in the common welfare of the parish itself. The welfare of the individual parochial units will, in turn, result in the corporate good of the diocese. Ultimately, a beneficial parochial administration prospers the weal of the Church.

It is evident from these considerations that the requirement of the *auditio parochi* is buttressed by both negative and positive reasons. The reasons here mentioned by way of exemplification have been adduced not as if they in themselves—without the sanction of a positive law to confirm them—were sufficient to establish the requirement of a consultation with the pastor, but rather to indicate the foundation they furnish for the structure of the law itself. Even if in isolated instances the law does not borrow its *raison d'être* from the verification of these or equivalent reasons, nevertheless the law continues to assert its universal sway. All laws whose intent is to caution against a general hazard maintain their binding force even then when the common element of danger has lapsed entirely from the environments of particular cases. Hence, the requirement of the *auditio parochi* is inseparably associated with every appointive act that terminates in a parochial assistancy.[33]

---

[32] Cf. *AER*, LXXVII (1927), 307; Augustine, *Canonical and Civil Status of Catholic Parishes*, p. 242: "The former practice [of removal] exposed the assistants to arbitrary treatment on the part of the pastors, while now they are raised to the sphere of public law and interest."

[33] Cf. e.g., 133 §1, 727 §2, 897, 1022, 1396, 1398 §1, as instances in which the legal continuum of can. 21 is fully vindicated. Vermeersch-Creusen, *Epitome Iuris Canonici*, I, n. 102, p. 93; Cicognani, *Commentarium ad Librum I Codicis*, pp. 140-41; "Cessante fine legis *adaequate sed negative* tantum in casu particulari, . . . tunc lex non cessat." Hilling, *Die allgemeinen Normen des Codex Juris Canonici*, §23, III, p. 51: "Mit der inneren Zweckursache darf der äussere Anlass nicht verwechselt werden. Bezeichnet man diesen als ratio, so gilt der Satz: Cessante ratione legis, non cessat lex ipsa."

C.' MODE OF EXECUTING THE *Auditio*

One may inquire after what fashion the local ordinary is to proceed in consulting the pastor. 1) May the consultation precede or is it to follow the proposal of the name of the tentative appointee? 2) Is the ordinary required to invite a hearing from the pastor by some positive written or oral communication, or has he fulfilled the requirement of the law when he has received an expression of the mind of the pastor even without the latter's invitation to speak? 3) If the ordinary withholds from the knowledge of the pastor the name of the prospective appointee and merely allows him to voice his preference of candidate, is his action in agreement with what is required by law? 4) Is the pastor accorded the necessary consultation if the local ordinary *definitely* appoints an assistant and only thereafter shows himself ready to entertain a reasonable protest from the pastor?

In answer to these questions it is indeed permissible to retain the aim and the purpose of the law as a juridical background, but it is fundamental to remember that the most primary of all methods of law interpretation consists in gaining an understanding of its import from the proper and native signification of the words as employed in text and context.[34] To appeal to the aim of the law or to opine the intention of the legislator for the sake of interpreting the meaning of a law is warranted only when a lack of clarity in the wording itself, or a dearth of parallel passages make necessary a recourse to these

[34] There are many legal axioms which stress the aim of the law or the intention of the lawgiver as a norm of interpretation. They may be culled from the domain of civil and ecclesiastical law alike. But, their value is relative, not absolute. Cf. e.g., Reg. 88, R. J., in VI°: "Certum est, quod is committit in legem, qui, legis verba complectens, contra legis nititur voluntatem." D. I, 3, 17: "Scire leges non hoc est verba earum tenere, sed vim ac potestatem." "Concorda tempora, et concordabis iura." "Ratio legis est anima legis." "Verba sunt intelligenda, non secundum quod sonant, sed secundum mentem proferentis." See also Reiffenstuel, *Ius Canonicum Universum*, I, ("Proëmium") n. 96 ss.; Chelodi, *Ius de Personis*, n. 67, pp. 117-20; De Meester, *Juris Canonici et Juris Canonico-civilis Compendium*, I, n. 273, pp. 182-84; Maroto, *Institutiones Iuris Canonici*, I, n. 240, pp. 253-55; Cicognani, *op. cit.*, pp. 125-30; Hilling, *op. cit.*, p. 51.

subsidiary and supplementary standards.[35] There is, above all, a juridic presumption which in its universal assumption and comprehensive application overshadows all norms of interpretation. It is expressed in the following formulary: *"Legislator, quod voluit, expressit."* [36]

1. The Circumstance of Time

Canon 476 §§3-4 is most indefinite in its indication of the time and the manner in which the *auditio* is to take place. The sole requirement is that the consultation of the pastor shall have taken place before the appointment has been definitely sealed. No specification is made that the tentative appointment *must* precede the consultation. Nor is it directly stated anywhere in the Code that the hearing of the pastor must embrace the double opportunity of declaring his prudent objection to the proposed appointment and of voicing his hopeful suggestion for a definite candidate in the ensuing appointment. The phrase *audito parocho* harbors only one essential connotation. In the point of time it must exist previous to the definite appointment.[37]

2. The Circumstance of Manner

a. Positive Consultation

Is the ordinary bound to invite or facilitate an expression of mind from the pastor by some positive written or oral communication, or may he passively abide word from the latter once the proposed appointment has been intimated? Here again one must not urge an interpretation that would amplify the strict requirement of the condition. Laws which impose a re-

---

[35] Can. 18.

[36] Related to this legal postulate are the following: "Verum est quod finis non est lex; cum in verbis nulla ambiguitas est, non debet admitti voluntatis quaestio." Cf. D. XXXII, 25 and the passages of the authors indicated in footnote 34 above.

[37] Although can. 105 states that it is enough for the superior to hear or consult the persons, yet, its own use of the ablative absolute in formulating the condition of the *auditio,* as also the phrase *audito parocho* in can. 476 §§3-4, plainly indicates the temporal precedence of the consultation.

striction upon the free and discretionary exercise of rights are set within the limits of a strict and close interpretation.[38] The axiom *"Generali per speciem derogatur"* [39] does indeed come into play here since the consuetudinary law which previously exempted the ordinary's act of appointment from all requisites external to his own prudential will has been modified. The Code now requires the hearing of the pastor as an antecedent condition which, when fulfilled, opens the way to the ultimate realization of a definite appointment. But, even a changed law will have to be interpreted in the light of its former existence except in the measure by which a difference has been positively introduced through its altered wording.[40]

This altered wording consists in the introduction of the phrase *audito parocho*. According to canon 105 1° nothing more is required by this condition than the positing of a mere fact. Hence, one may certainly conclude that once this fact has been placed, the local ordinary and the religious superior may immediately proceed to execute their acts of appointment and presentation respectively. An invitation granted to the pastor in such a manner that he may enjoy the facility of expressing both his inclinations and disinclinations in the matter of the pending appointment would, beyond all doubt, correspond with the minutest indications traceable in the spirit of the law. Such exactitude, however, on the part of the local ordinary or religious superior is by no means strictly demanded.

The pastor is aware of his right of being heard. That right becomes operative as soon as he has received official intimation regarding the prospective appointment or presentation. His opportunity to manifest his mind is at hand. Whether or no he be encouraged by authority to do so, his observations are intended by the legislator as a contribution to the administrative prudence with which every act of appointive provision in parishes should be invested. It is as much a duty as a privilege for him to co-operate with authority in effecting a suitable

---

38 Cf. can. 19.

39 Reg. 34, R. J., in VI°.

40 Cf. can. 6 3°. In perfect agreement with the ruling of this canon is the axiom of the jurists: "Non censetur plus de priori lege mutatum, quam est expressum in posteriori." See also Chelodi, *Ius de Personis*, n. 59, p. 100 ss.

provision. If he holds his silence when he was able to make utterance, his passiveness will rightly be construed as one of tacit approval. *"Is qui tacet, non fatetur, sed nec utique negare videtur,"* or, even more positively, *"qui tacet, consentire videtur."* [41]

b. INDEFINITE CONSULTATION

If the local ordinary or the religious superior allows the pastor or actual incumbent of the parish an expression of preference regarding a number of available candidates, even though he definitely withholds the name of the prospective appointee or presentee, he seems not to transgress against the strict requirement of the *auditio parochi*. This follows logically from the view already expressed, namely, that a pastor is sufficiently consulted when he is allowed to make known his positive preferences in the prospective appointment. The fuller and deeper purpose of the law seems to suffer somewhat, however, in as far as this method does not as readily permit of a comprehensive consideration of all the negative reasons in view of which a given appointment might be diverted into other and more useful channels of parochial efficiency.

c. NEGATIVE CONSULTATION

Finally, is the mere readiness on the part of authority to leave room for a possible re-appointment or re-presentation whenever the pastor reasonably offers his protestation an adequate insurance of the latter's right of being consulted? The answer here is plainly a negative one. Neither the spirit nor the letter of the law would be observed by such a method of procedure.[42]

As a consequence of such action conditions could easily result which would place the authority of the local ordinary in a compromising situation. If he gives heed to the protest by a quick change of appointment, he will soon invite inevitable spec-

[41] Reg. 44 and 43, R. J., in VI°.

[42] Cf. Haring, "Die Bestellung des pfarrlichen Hilfspriesters," *LQS*, LXXVII (1924), 337: "Die Umwandlung der Befragung in ein nachträgliches Einspruchsrecht gegen vollendete Tatsachen entspricht kaum dem Gesetzeswortlaut, würde aber auch, insofern bereits eine Publikation der Anstellung erfolgt ist, sich noch odioser gestalten."

ulations concerning the stability and intelligence of his administrative methods; if he disregards the protest by sustaining his original appointment, he will soon occasion a lack of spontaneous co-operation among the pastoral agencies of his diocese in this important matter of parochial provision. In a relative sphere, the religious superior who follows similar methods of imperious approach to the gaining of a personal aim in the approval of a predetermined candidate presented by him would adopt a course of action unsustained by the law and thus invite the risk of untoward consequences.

The situation arising from this method of appointment to parochial assistancies might prove equally unfortunate for the pastor and his newly appointed assistant. Any man's efforts at reconciling himself with a disagreeable fact or situation become all the more taxing when its presence seems to be brought upon him through a manifest lack of positive endeavor on the part of authority to avert it. Identical facts and situations always lose much of their distressing nature when the person involved in them is at the same time convinced that they cannot be prudently altered in view of existing circumstances.

A parish priest will ever remember that his individual parish has not an unconditional and exclusive claim upon the best pastoral agencies available in the diocese.[43] The individual good of the parish will ever remain subservient to the corporate welfare of the diocese. It is simply unavoidable that cases will arise in which some particular parish will have to sacrifice what the diocese will gain in return.

Similarly, an assistant will constantly recall that in the title of his ordination his services were enlisted directly for the diocese and only mediately for any particular parish.[44] It is true

---

[43] Cf. cans. 153 §2 and 459 §§1-2. Although canon 476 does not specify a similar norm of procedure in the appointment of assistants, yet, the consultation with the pastor previous to an assistant's canonical appointment is obviously meant to help achieve approximate results in the determination of his fitness for the parochial ministry to which he is to be assigned.

[44] Cf. cans. 969, 974 §1 7°, 979 §1 as supplemented by can. 981 §1; S. C. Consist., die 24 Nov. 1908; die 6 Aug. 1909—*AAS*, I (1909), 148 ss.; 678 ss. See also Ayrinhac, *Legislation on the Sacraments in the New Code*, nn. 302-03, pp. 353-56; Augustine, *A Commentary on Canon Law*, IV, 471-73.

that his service in the parish constitutes a medium through which his service for the diocese becomes actual. Even more; his diocesan service presupposes his parochial ministry as an essential condition for its realization precisely because the canonical status of a parochial assistant cannot be conceived without a parochial ministry for its objective. Still, his ministry is basically specified by the pledge of his diocesan service and derives its ultimate and decisive merit from the measure of good it accomplishes for the diocese. His parochial ministrations are but so many agencies with the aid of which the pledge of his title of ordination is to achieve its fulfillment. In the prudent knowledge of his diocesan ordinary it may be foreseen that an assistant will be serving the interests of his diocese best even when his ministry must be localized in apparently unfavorable conditions.

3. A Possible Mode of Procedure

In concluding this discussion on the necessity of consultation in connection with each separate act of appointment, the writer may be permitted to outline what he considers to be a mode of procedure which will not only correspond most fully with the demand of the law, but also lend itself as a practicable rule for ensuring its fulfillment. An advance printed formulary could be prepared in the diocesan curia. When a number of assignments to parochial assistancies are to be made, the names of the tentative appointees can be filled in and the signed documents forwarded to the respective pastors. In each document the pastor is *confidentially* notified whom the ordinary would wish to appoint. He is at the same time encouraged in all candor to make known if he anticipates any serious objective reasons in view of which an execution of the tentative appointment might seem dissuaded and to state these negative reasons in full.[45]

In order to allow the pastor also a positive expression of his prudent suggestions, there can be appended to the document a list of the names of the remaining appointive candidates from whose number the pastor will indicate whom he considers above

---

[45] Cf. *LQS*, LXXVII (1924), 337.

all the rest as best fitted for the particular exigencies of his parish. In connection with this designation, he will be asked to manifest the characteristic needs of his parish and to indicate his reasons for the preference expressed.[46]

For the sake of ordering the entire procedure with reasonable expedition, the document will fix a sufficiently liberal time-limit within which the pastor is given the opportunity of a reply. His failure to make one will be interpreted as an attitude of acquiescence in the appointment as proposed.

Even in a numerically large or territorially extended diocese the cases in which this method of procedure would jeopardize efficiency or clog the execution of a well-ordered administrative programme must remain comparatively few. Whilst the Sacred Congregation of the Council did not insist on any particular method, still it was at a loss how to account for a sufficient reason to exempt the Archbishop of Agram (Zagreb) from the ruling of canon 476 §3.[47] It must be admitted that this decision had only a particular force since it settled the difficulties of a mere individual case. But withal, it surely indicates in unequivocal terms the mind of the Congregation concerning the requirement of the *auditio parochi* as demanded by canon 476 §§3-4 and its appreciation of the general possibility of its observance.

---

[46] Cf. can. 105 3°: "Omnes de consensu vel consilio requisiti, debent ea qua par est reverentia, fide ac sinceritate sententiam suam aperire."

[47] In the archdiocese of Agram it was a centenary custom for the local ordinary to appoint assistants *inaudito parocho*. This custom had become current on account of the existing scarcity of priests in the locality and the consequent need of a more efficient administration. "Quaeritur utrum huiusmodi consuetudo possit servari. R. Standum dispositioni Codicis c. 476 §3." —S. C. C. *in Zagabrien. Nominationis Vic. Cooperatorum*, die 13 Nov. 1920 (*AAS*, XIII [1921], 43-46). In the *Animadversiones ex officio* are contained the following reflections: "At vero, dum in casu Episcopus dubitet num consuetudo possit servari, *palam profitetur nullum dubium superesse quin illa possit servari. Nec* reversa, si objectum removendae consuetudinis attendatur, *facile quis exponere valeat*, quid incommodum suboriturum sit, si, de persona nominandi *coadiutoris*, prius coadjuvandus interpellatur, nulla statuta obligatione illius sententiam sequendi (c. 105 1°). Quae cum ita sint, profecto nullum subest impedimentum quominus Codex, *datus praecipue ad uniformitatem legis et disciplinae ecclesiasticae inducendam*, hunc suum effectum in casu sortiri possit." Italics in above passage are indicated by the present writer.

II. REQUIREMENT OF THE *Auditio* FOR THE VALIDITY OF THE APPOINTMENT

Canon 105 1° establishes the following rule:

Cum ius statuit Superiorem ad agendum indigere consensu vel consilio aliquarum personarum: Si consensus exigatur, Superior contra earundem votum invalide agit; si consilium tantum, ex. gr.: de consilio consultorum, *vel* audito Capitulo, parocho, *etc., satis est ad valide agendum ut Superior illas personas audiat; quamvis autem nulla obligatione teneatur ad eorum votum, etsi concors, accedendi, multum tamen, si plures audiendae sint personae, concordibus earundem suffragiis deferat, nec ab eisdem, sine praevalenti ratione, suo iudicio aestimanda, discedat.*

A. CONSIDERATION OF THE DIFFICULTIES PROPOSED

Rettenbacher [48] labels as traditional the opinion amongst the older canonists which admitted for the wording now employed by canon 105 1° a requirement *ad validitatem*. Although he does not dissociate himself from their number, yet he readily concedes the possibility of difficulties standing in the way of its enforcement in populous dioceses. Where the clergy are so numerous the pastor will in all likelihood have a very limited acquaintance with the younger priests in the diocese and hence he will be little qualified for an informed opinion concerning their special fitness for his specific parochial needs. Likewise, his meager acquaintance will little capacitate him to urge a well-founded objection under any given occasions. The author further sees a great loss of time involved if an effort should have to be made to abide by the ruling of canon 476 §§3-4 in instances where the appointment of a large band of assistants would simultaneously imply the change or transfer of a considerable number of them from one parish to another. The thoughtful weighing of these reasons induces him to come to the conclusion that in ordinary circumstances where the needs of the parish

[48] "Der Kooperator nach dem Codex Juris," *LQS*, LXXII (1919), 337 ff.

are not of an especial nature the pastor might be expected to forego his right of being consulted before the appointment.[49]

A much more decided stand is taken by Vermeersch,[50] Boudinhon [51] and Creusen.[52] These three authors are the principal proponents of the view that canon 105 1° does not mean to establish a condition without the positing of which the subsequent act of the superior will be invalid whenever there is mere question of the obtaining of previous counsel. They base their contentions chiefly on the following considerations:

1. The wording of the text in canon 105 1°;
2. The correlation of this text with canons 11 and 1680;
3. The addition of some other word as a suppletive term in connection with the word *satis* when the test of invalidity is invoked;
4. The addition of such phrases as *ut valide agat* and *ne invalide agat* in connection with the clauses *auditis iisdem examinatoribus* and *auditis duobus parochis consultoribus;*
5. The negative element of the *auditio;*
6. The canons wherein the obtaining of advice is made optional;
7. The intent of the law in canon 105 1°;
8. The teaching of older canonists;
9. The momentous consequences of invalid acts resulting from a neglect to seek counsel.

---

[49] Cf. *ibid.*, p. 340: "Es dürfte wohl die Ansicht Berechtigung haben, dass der Pfarrer sein Recht, gehört zu werden, nur beanspruche, wenn besondere Gründe vorliegen, und dass es daher der Diözesanregierung erlaubt sein muss, Kooperatoren anzustellen auch 'non audito parocho,' wenn in dringenden Fällen das Interesse der Diözese es so erheischt." For the diocese of Linz he quotes the following statute: "Wie bisher, kann auch fernerhin der Pfarrer bei der Admittierung eines Kooperatoren Einwände dagegen erheben: werden sie nicht als wesentlich und begründet erkannt, bleibt die Admittierung aufrecht."—Linzer Diözenstatuten, 1918, (Appendix) p. 4*.

[50] *Epitome Iuris Canonici,* I, n. 197 bis, pp. 151-52; *Periodica,* XII (1923), (6)-(9).

[51] "An nullus semper sit actus Superioris non petito consilio," *Jus Pont.,* VIII (1928), 29-35.

[52] "L'effet juridique des consultations," *NRT,* LV (1928), 100-116.

Most of the arguments under the above headings are used by all three authors; it is in the minor details of their presentation of them that any difference really appears.[53]

1. The Meaning of the Text in Canon 105 1°

Vermeersch points to the lack of clearness in the wording. He contends that the meaning of the clause "*satis est ad valide agendum ut Superior illas personas audiat*" is not identical with stating that the superior would act invalidly unless he sought counsel. If validity be in question then the use of the word *necessarium* would be needed to identify that concept, since even in popular usage the word *satis* seems not to be equivalent in force to the word *necessarium*. Hence the wording of the phrase in canon 105 1° remains indifferent in meaning. It is neither one of apodictic affirmation nor yet one of conclusive negation of the necessity of taking counsel for valid action.

Boudinhon admits the primary and direct sense of the phrase to be the following: If the superior hears the counsel (altogether apart from any consequence of his submission to or departure from it) the subsequent act is valid. But, he does not admit that the wording, *satis est ad valide agendum*, is perfectly convertible with the more definite statement, *satis est ne invalide agat*. He feels convinced that if the legislator accords validity to an act of the superior after the latter has heard, yet not followed the counsel, the lawgiver does not simultaneously contemplate the hypothesis in which the superior does not take counsel before acting. In a word, the author thinks it would be presumptive to maintain that the legislator wished to establish a nullifying sanction of law by means of an indirect mode of speech.

---

[53] No strict effort need be made in all the instances to cite the exact pages or passages in which their individual arguments appear. Footnotes 50-52 preceding indicate the relatively small compass in which they are produced. Vermeersch's arguments are concentrated in the space of a single page in his *Epitome Iuris Canonici;* Boudinhon offers a defense of his opinion in six pages of the *Jus Pontificium;* Creusen, the latest to write in support of the same doctrine, consumes less than 17 pages in the *Nouvelle Revue Théologique*. He divides his matter into three parts: The law prior to the Code; pp. 101-05; the legislation of the Code, pp. 105-11; the argument from authority, pp. 111-16.

Creusen likewise refers to the undecisiveness of the wording of the clause. Canon 105 1°, because of its very nature and import, calls for a strict interpretation. *"Contra eum, qui legem dicere potest apertius, est interpretatio facienda."* [54]

Against these views Oietti contends most vigorously.[55] In his mind the legislator's mode of speech does not allow of a repudiation of the effect implied by an equivalent negative form of statement. Moreover, he sees in the word *indigere,* which is used at the beginning of the canon, a necessary requirement for the previous hearing of counsel in order to constitute the ensuing act as valid. If that were not the meaning, he continues, then the canon would take on the following signification: When for a *valid* action the hearing of counsel is required, the superior, whether he grants a hearing or not, will nevertheless act validly as long as his act does not clash with the specifications of canon 11. Thus constructed, the second alternative of canon 105 1° would not only be useless, but even illogical, since it would utterly destroy the force of its own statement in the opening words of the canon.[56]

In answer to this objection by Oietti his opponents significantly point to the omission of the word *valide* in the opening clause of canon 105, where it could so easily have been joined with the *"ad agendum"* if an unmistakable designation of the requirement for validity were intended. Moreover, they insist, if the word *indigere* there employed were meant clearly to express a necessary means for valid action, would not the same canon become tautological when it continues, *"si consensus exigatur, superior contra earundem [personarum] votum invalide agit?"* To them it does not seem objectively incorrect to translate the antecedent clause in the following manner: "Whenever the law states that for his act (be it for validity, or be it for liceity) the superior must get the consent, or obtain the counsel of the persons in question," and the subsequent one thus: "The validity of the act requires, in the first case, that the

[54] Reg. 57, R. J., in VI°.

[55] *Jus Pont.,* VII (1927), 13-25. See also Oietti, *Commentarium in Codicem Iuris Canonici,* II, 180-85, and 186-202, which latter section is but a reprint of his former article in the *Jus Pontificium.*

[56] *Jus Pont.,* VII (1927), 17; *Commentarium in Codicem Iuris Canonici,* II, 191.

superior abide by their consent, whilst it suffices, in the second, that he bespeak their counsel." [57]

In counter reply it will be necessary to remark, however, that the discussion does not hinge on the word *indigere*, but on the question of whether the statement "*satis est ad valide agendum*" implies with sufficient clarity the force of an equivalent negative formulation of its import. Now, in order to formulate an equivalent negative statement it is not allowable to transpose *all* the positive, predicating terms of the original proposition into as many negative terms for its attempted negative expression of the same concept. By so doing one will simply arrive at a direct contradictory statement.

The proposition under question is the following: The superior acts validly when he has sought the required counsel. If one negates *all* the predicative terms of this proposition, the following intricate form of contradiction will result: The superior does *not* act *invalidly* when he has *not* sought the required counsel. But, since the two first negatives in this statement readily coalesce into a simple affirmative, one may express the proposition in the following equivalent form: The superior acts validly when he has *not* sought the required counsel. Obviously, when reduced to this simplified form, the negated proposition must be acknowledged as eventuating in a *simple* contradictory statement; by no means can it be considered as a restatement of the original proposition in negative form.

When one wishes to effect an equivalent negative statement, the dual concept of validity and invalidity of act must be preassumed as a starting point from which to proceed in formulating a negative expression of the original meaning of the proposition. If the *hearing* of the counsel gives expression to the *validity* of an act, then the *non-hearing* of the counsel necessarily expresses its *invalidity*. It is by the use of a *double* contradiction, namely, by a successive contradiction of the truth previously contradicted, that one must arrive at the formulation of a statement which in negative terms reproduces what has originally been stated in positive terms.

---

[57] Cf. *NRT*, LV (1928), 113. But see *Jus Pont.*, VIII (1928), 44, where Toso incisively takes issue with this view of Creusen.

It is a postulate of logic that the truth of any positive statement may be reproduced in negative terms by employing the principle of *double* contradiction. So absolute is this principle that without its peremptory force the Church could not undertake to formulate solemn definitions on matters of faith and morals. Her condemnation of an heretical doctrine is equivalent to her affirmation of a Catholic one, and vice versa. Correspondingly, if the supreme legislator of the Church has stated in a positive manner that the presence of certain conditions is adequate for the constitution of valid acts, then his statement that the absence of these same conditions is inadequate for the same effect is equivalently indicated by the logical principle of *double* contradiction.

According to canon 11 even an equivalent statement of nullity suffices for establishing the nullifying force of any law. Therefore, canon 105 1° appears to fill every requirement of definitely indicating the invalidity of acts placed by the superior *non petito consilio.*

2. The Correlation of Canon 105 1° With Canons 11 and 1680

In the light of canons 11 and 1680 §1 Boudinhon finds additional evidence for maintaining that an act placed by the superior, *non petito consilio,* does not become invalid through the mere circumstance of a neglect to hear the counsel. If the superior's act is to be acknowledged as null inasmuch as he has neglected to hear the counsel of others, its nullity will result from a lack of those elements which essentially combine in the constitution of a valid act according to canon 1680 §1. Since the superior is free not to follow the advice received, the counsel itself cannot be regarded as an intrinsic and necessary element in the forming of the legal act. But, if the counsel itself is not a constitutive element, then, *a fortiori,* also the seeking of the counsel or the hearing of the persons cannot be such. Hence, the nullity would have to be sought rather in the defect of the solemnities or the lack of the conditions which are required by the sacred canons under pain of nullifying sanction. In the case, however, no other solemnity or condition can be conceived than the seeking or hearing of the counsel. But, in order that the fulfillment of this condition may be regarded as a requirement for validity, it is necessary that it be demanded in express or equivalent words according to the ruling of canon 11. That express words are wanting no one can deny. That equivalent terms are lacking is highly probable. Therefore the author concludes that canon 105 1° does not unmistakably specify the seeking or the hearing of counsel as a *conditio sine qua non* for the valid constitution of the superior's act. If the obligation is not unmistakable, then it can at most be doubtful. And, if it is doubtful, canon 15 tells us, it cannot be urged as binding.[58]

In answer to this argument one might say that its value and efficacy can be certified only if it can be shown that canon 1680 §1 actually exerts any legal force outside of the domain of trials, suits, and court actions with which it seems exclusively concerned. The validity and the invalidity of all administrative acts can be sufficiently discerned from their agreement and disagreement respectively with canons 11, 15 and 105. Canon 1680 §1 sets up a norm for determining when a suit may be filed in order to obtain redress against a court decision which was invalid because of the juridical nullity of one or the other of its essentially constitutive acts. Moreover, if the strict interpretation of canon 11 renders the requirement relative to validity in connection with canon 105 1° nugatory only in so far as it can be linked with the import of canon 1680 §1, then it is equally certain that canon 11 exerts no such force when it is made to stand alone. On the other hand, canon 105 1° offers a wording which in its implicit equivalent force ably measures up to the legal potency of canon 11 which equips a law with an invalidating sanction whenever that sanction is equivalently expressed.[59]

3. The Limited Meaning of the Word *Satis*

The addition of some suppletive term in connection with the word *satis*, or its equivalent, when the Code wishes to invoke a

---

[58] *Jus Pont.*, VIII (1928), 30 ss.

[59] Cf. Chelodi, *Ius de Personis*, n. 66, p. 115; n. 102, p. 180.

sanction of nullity, is indicated by Vermeersch, Boudinhon and Creusen in a considerable number of canons.[60] But, Oietti[61] places a number of canons in contraposition to those cited by his opponents to show that necessary means and conditions for the validity of acts are expressed in the Code by the use of simpler forms, and in a number of instances by the use of the word *sufficit* or *satis* alone.[62] It seems perfectly admissible, then, to conclude with Oietti that the Code does not limit itself to the use of stereotyped legal forms or phrases when it gives expression to necessary or essential conditions, the previous fulfillment of which becomes a *conditio sine qua non* for the validity of the subsequent act.

4. The Use of Superadded Explicit Sanctions

For anyone who regards the clauses "*auditis examinatoribus,*" "*auditis parochis consultoribus,*" or their equivalents as sufficiently indicative of conditions whose fulfillment is required for valid actions, it may be somewhat arresting to find certain canons in which these clauses seem not to have this desired efficacy. Canons 2152 §1, 2153 §1, 2159 and 2165 add such expressions as "*ut valide agat,*" "*ne invalide agat,*" and "*ut valide procedat*" when stigmatizing the ordinary's act as invalid if he promulgates his decree without requisitioning the counsel of two diocesan examiners or parish priest consultors in the case. Certain other canons[63] in intimate connection with these are without this superadded and express indication of a nullifying sanction. Are we to conclude with Boudinhon[64] and Creusen[65] that when the ordinary's consultation with the two diocesan examiners or parish priest consultors is prescribed without the addition of the explicit sanction as contained in the

[60] "*Necesse et satis est*" in can. 556 §2; "*necesse est et sufficit*" in can. 692; "*requiritur et sufficit*" in cans. 534 §1, 1228 §2, 1470 §3; etc.

[61] *Jus Pont.*, VII (1927), 18; *Commentarium in Codicem Iuris Canonici*, II, 192.

[62] E.g., "*requiritur*" in cans. 572 §2, 723, 1133 §§1-2, 1453 §2, 1546 §1: "*oportet*" in can. 573; "*necesse est*" in can. 1136 §3; "*sufficit*" in cans. 708, 1727; "*satis est*" in cans. 752 §2, 1135 §§2-3, 1136 §2.

[63] Cans. 2148 §1, 2154, 2160, 2166, 2171, 2172, 2175, 2178 and 2179.

[64] *Jus Pont.*, VIII (1928), 32-33.

[65] *NRT*, LV (1928), 106-07.

four canons above enumerated, his acts will nevertheless be valid despite his neglect to seek or obtain the required counsel?

In the light of the Decree *"Maxima Cura,"* which was issued by the Sacred Congregation of the Consistory on August 20, 1910,[66] and which offered the primary source for the present legislation of the Code contained in the III Part of its IV Book, rather a negative answer would be expected. The law contained in this decree was enacted precisely for safeguarding the more securely the supreme demand of the welfare of souls [67] by making possible a more expeditious procedure in the removal or transfer of parish priests.[68] Yet, in all the articles of this decree, save one,[69] the ordinary executed his act validly only upon the requisition of consent. His valid action in this isolated instance of more urgent need was conditioned upon a mere procuring of advice.[70]

---

66 Cf. *AAS*, II (1910), 636-48.

67 "Salus animarum suprema lex.—. . . parochi ministerium fuit in Ecclesia institutum, non in commodum eius cui committitur, sed in eorum salutem pro quibus confertur.—Quod si, vi canonici iuris, criminali judicio ac poenali destitutioni non sit locus, parochus autem hac illave causa, etiam culpa semota, utile ministerium in paroecia non gerat, vel gerere nequeat, aut forte sua ibi praesentia noxius evadat; alia suppetunt remedia ad animarum salutem consulendum."—*Ibid.*, p. 636.

68 Cf. Sebastianelli, "Inamovibilitas Parochi." *Anal. Eccl.*, IV (1896), 43-45, for a comprehensive and concise outline of the law prior to the new decree.

69 Can. 15 §4—*AAS*, II (1910), 642. In cans. 9 §2, 12 §1, 15 §3, 19 §§1-2, 21, 22 §2, 23, 25 §1—*ibid.*, pp. 641-45—there is constant mention of the consent of either the examiners or the parish priest consultors.

70 This appears evident from the specifications of canons 6 and 3 of the decree. According to can. 6 §1 the ordinary and the two examiners (or the two parish priest consultors on occasion) take a secret vote. It requires two concurrent votes to decide the issue. According to can. 6 §2, when the ordinary proceeds *de consilio*, ". . . *satis est ut eos audiat, nec ulla obligatione tenetur ad eorum votum, quamvis concors, accedendi.*" But, according to can. 3 §§1-2, whether it be question of consent or merely counsel, ". . . *Ordinarius, ut legitime agat, non potest ipse solus procedere.*" It cannot be denied that, when consent is required, the phrase *ut legitime agat* involves the validity of the ordinary's act, since his exclusive way in reaching a decision is through a majority vote of the three secret ballots. Since the same clause is made to apply, in the same connection and without any change of meaning, also to the cases in which only counsel is required, the obtaining of the counsel is likewise made a necessary prerequisite for the ordinary's valid action. Concerning the older discipline cf. Conc. Tridentinum, sessio XXIV, *de ref.*, c. 18—*Canones et Decreta*, pp. 199-200.

It would seem to imply an uncalled for departure from the Church's traditional method of framing her laws to insist that in the Code the expressions *auditis duobus examinatoribus* and *auditis duobus parochis consultoribus* take on a meaning different from the one they possessed antecedently.[71] To say the least, no legal presumption favors such a view. Rather, there must be at hand positive proof to overthrow the contrary presumption.[72] The explicit insertions in canons 2152 §1, 2153 §1, 2159 and 2165 can be shown to imply an added sanction only after there is proof that this sanction does not preexist without them. To say that the clauses *ut valide agat, ut valide procedat,* and *ne invalide agat* demonstrate the absence of such a sanction is to assume the very point that calls for proof. The point is precisely this: The clauses *auditis duobus examinatoribus* and *auditis duobus parochis consultoribus* possess no nullifying sanction in themselves. They require the additional clauses *ut valide agat, ut valide procedat,* and *ne invalide agat* for the sake of investing the obligation implied by them with the sanction of invalidity. Now, is it not a begging of the question to maintain that these additions were made to induce a sanction where none existed, when the legal proof of its nonexistence forms the very core of the argument? Moreover, why would it be unreasonable to explain the addition of these confirmatory clauses through the circumstance that the lawgiver, sensitive to the graver importance of the situation, simply adumbrated the letter of the law with a heightened expression of the gravity of his mind? [73]

---

[71] The full force of the decree "*Maxima Cura*" becomes evident, by way of negative demonstration, through the partial exemption from it granted to the United States by the Sacred Consistorial Congregation on June 28, 1915: "Utrum in Foederatis Americae Statibus rectores paroeciarum seu missionum, qui inter inamovibiles iuxta Conc. Balt. III non recensentur, sed adhuc amovibiles nuncupantur, vi decreti "*Maxima Cura*" et praesertim canonis XXX eiusdem decreti, *solummodo* amoveri seu transferri possint servato ordine processus in memorato decreto statuti? R. Negative; sed amoveri posse ad nutum Episcopi, firmo tamen monito Concilii Baltimorensis II, ne Episcopi hoc iure suo, nisi graves ob causas et habita ratione meritorum, uti velint."—*AAS*, VII (1915), 380. The reasons assigned for this decision are contained on pp. 380-82.

[72] Cf. cans. 6 3° and 23.

[73] Cf. *Jus Pont.*, VIII (1928), 44, where Toso offers a rebuttal to Creusen on this very head.

5. The Negative Element of the *Auditio*

The circumstance of the mere negative force of the *auditio* is also pressed by these authors to indicate its inability to invalidate an act when the required counsel is neither sought nor obtained. Vermeersch [74] formulates the argument very succinctly. He uses it as a mode of proof *a priori*. When there is question merely of seeking counsel from which the superior is nevertheless free to recede, then the entire efficacy of the act inheres in the will of the superior. But, *per se*, the validity of acts necessarily depends on *causal* elements only. Therefore, since the acquired counsel does not furnish any decisive or causal element, it also may not be regarded as an essential for the act.

First of all, it is imperative to remember that there exists a clear cut distinction between causal elements constitutive of an act and necessary conditions preliminary to an act. If the perfection of the act depends merely upon the accumulation of causal elements, then the consideration of its essential conditions must indeed be stressed. But, whilst it is very true that every act must derive its existence from a cause, or a combination of causes, legal acts may also demand a concurrent verification of specified conditions before they are accredited with a legal existence. These conditions may be of a positive or of a negative nature relative to their influence upon the outcome of the act. This variation in the nature of the conditions in no way detracts from the essence of their requirement. Whether positive or negative, once they have been established by ecclesiastical authority as essential conditions preliminary to the ensuing act, they become as indispensable for the constitution of the act as are the causal elements which actually produce the act.[75]

Moreover, the right and capacity of the lawgiver to formulate such conditions for the validity of acts is beyond dispute. It is not a question of law as to what can be done. It is entirely a point of fact as to what has been done. One need but ask if the law has posited such conditions. If it has, then all discussion is closed.

---

[74] *Epitome Iuris Canonici*, I, 197 bis, 1, d, p. 152; see also *Jus Pont.*, VIII (1928), 30 ss.; *NRT*, LV (1928), 108.

[75] The list of matrimonial impediments established by merely ecclesiastical law serves as an excellent illustration.

6. THE QUESTION OF THE OPTIONAL *Auditio*

Again, it is maintained by Boudinhon [76] that if the legislator has established a generic and all-inclusive nullity for the facts of a superior in which the procurement of advice has been pretermitted, it would be hard to understand why the same legislator should consider it necessary in certain canons [77] to be so explicit, whilst in other canons [78] he should deem it feasible to leave the *petitio consilii* entirely discretionary *(facultativa)*, without at the same time revoking the nullity that inherently attaches to its omission.

An effort was made under number 4 of this section to answer the first objection. A word is here in place regarding the second.

The author seems to hold that, in cases where the *auditio* is plainly discretional or optional, nothing is done by the legislator expressly to relax the nullifying sanction which is claimed to be inherent in the stereotyped phrases of canon 105 1°. In other words, by the use of such phrases the law would first establish an obligation from which there is no escape except at the price of nullified action, and then, despite the absence of an express derogation to or revocation of that obligation, acknowledge its nature as entirely discretionary.

In the author's mind, the very possibility of connecting the rightful use and exercise of a discretionary option with such a clause as *audito capitulo* or *de consilio* shows in a most positive way that the respective clause or phrase cannot actually imply an obligation which is binding under pain of nullity, similarly as the addition of such forms as *ut valide agat, ut valide procedat*, and *ne invalide agat* demonstrate, in a clearly negative way, the absence of the same obligation. To admit the simultaneous existence of a legal bond of obligation together with a legal option of discretion in one and the same passage of the law would be identical with an admission that the law can be contrary to itself. In order to avoid such a crisis he prefers to

---

[76] *Jus Pont.*, VIII (1928), 33-34.

[77] E.g., cans. 388, 428, 2152 §1, 2153 §1, 2159, 2165.

[78] E.g., cans. 1164 §1, 1234 §1, 1428 §1, 1520 §1, 1532 §2. These canons are not all cited by the author. Still, they may serve to indicate the examples he has in mind.

interpret the phrases of canon 105 1° in a manner that will efficaciously obviate the inevitableness of such a clash. This can be accomplished on the sole condition that one is ready to concede the non-inherence of any legal sanction of nullity in the wording of canon 105 1° relative to the requirement of the *auditio*.

But, if the author is ready to admit that canon 105 1° implies at least a simple obligation, that is to say, one which has no sanction of nullity attached, then he must also concede the possible conversion of this simple obligation into one of discretionary option in all the cases where its need of being fulfilled is made to depend on the prudent judgment of the ordinary or the superior. To do so is but to acknowledge the force and application of canon 18 which furnishes the primary norms for any individual's interpretation of the law.

Moreover, no law, however useful it may be under general conditions, means to bind under such individual circumstances where its stipulation would frustrate its ultimate proper aim.[79] It is only such laws which intend to safeguard against a common danger that retain their obligatory force even though in particular cases no safeguard is necessary because no danger exists.[80] The observance of this kind of general law by particular individuals or in particular cases can under no conditions become a frustration of its proper aim. Since its intent is an altogether negative one, namely, the avoidance of a danger, the aim of the law will remain fulfilled by its observance, whether the danger against which the safeguard is invoked be present or absent. If in the absence of all danger a relaxation of the law will promise the achievement of some positive good, then the need of individual exemptions can always be properly consulted through the medium of a dispensation.

On the other hand, when the aim of the law is a positive one, namely, the achievement of some particular good or benefit, and when the employment of its means to that end is based upon a general presumption of the helpfulness of certain condi-

[79] Reg. 37, R. J., in VI°: "Utile non debet per inutile vitiari." See also Hilling, *Die allgemeinen Normen des Codex Iuris Canonici*, §23, p. 51.

[80] Can. 21. The general ruling of this canon is exemplified, for instance, by the cases mentioned in cans. 1020 §1, 1022, 1060, 1071, 1396, 1398 §1.

tions or facts, then the lack of verification in this factual presumption can readily effect a lapse of the legal prescript.[81] It is precisely for such cases that the Code has provided in the particular canons which leave the requisition of counsel at the discretion and judgment of the ordinary.[82]

If, then, these principles are applicable for the extinction of a law that enjoys no other than a mere obediential sanction, by what process do they become irrelevant when they come in contact with a law that enjoys even a nullifying sanction? If, for instance, canon 1141 states absolutely that a *sanatio in radice* can be granted only by the Apostolic See, does not the very wording of this canon imply a nullifying sanction for a *sanatio* granted by any other authority? And yet, the special faculties accorded not only to Nuntios, Internuntios and Apostolic Delegates,[83] but also to local ordinaries, whether they govern a diocese [84] or whether they rule over a mission territory,[85] surely qualify the unconditional statement of canon 1141 without detracting from the import of its general nullifying sanction. In a similar manner other canons [86] grant powers of dispensation which normally are reserved to higher authorities. Do these exemptions from the observance of a general invalidating law set up a general contradiction by the fact of their being granted? If, despite the text of the law, a dispensation can be granted by him to whom the faculty of dispensing has been committed either by a particular stipulation of the law itself,[87] or by a later special authorization, what is there to prevent an ordinary or a superior from placing a valid act, the performance of which, invalid in the light of general principles, nevertheless becomes valid through the medium of a special derogation affect-

---

[81] Cf. Chelodi, *Ius de Personis*, n. 69, p. 122, footnote 6; Hilling, *loc. cit.*: "Cessante ratione legis, cessat lex ipsa. Unter ratio ist das Rechtsverhältnis oder die Grundursache, der innere Zweck, zu verstehen."

[82] See the canons mentioned in footnote 78 above.

[83] Cf. "Index Facultatum. . . ."—Vermeersch-Creusen, *Epitome Iuris Canonici*, I, 526 (Appendix I, cap. III, n. 31).

[84] Cf. *op. cit.*, 536-37 (Appendix III).

[85] Cf. *op. cit.*, 531 (Appendix II, nn. 22* and 23*).

[86] E.g., cans. 81-84, 459 §3 3°, 1043-45, 1048 in connection with 204 §2, 1050, *et passim*.

[87] Cf. can. 80.

ing the general import of the law? *"Generali per speciem derogatur."* [88]

Many laws of the Code are merely conditional laws since their fulfillment depends either on the verification of extraneous circumstances or the prudent judgment of the ordinary.[89] After a like manner, canons which employ the wording of canon 105 1° *(audito Capitulo,* etc.) may yet leave the obligation of seeking or obtaining counsel a conditional one. Still, this potential difference remains: If, *in the prudence* of the superior, the seeking of the counsel may be dispensed with, his action is valid without it; if, *in his discretion,* the need of seeking counsel exists, he remains obliged to seek it, not only for the sake of fulfilling a duty of conscience, but also for the purpose of safeguarding the validity of his act.

Should someone contend that interior acts of prudence or discretion may not be invoked as norms whereby the consequent validity of acts is to be judged, it will suffice to point to canons 2166 and 2167 §§1-2, where the local ordinary's sense of prudence and discretion is made the final deciding factor in the transfer of a parish priest from one parish to another.[90] Furthermore, canon 5 lends legal sanction to this same principle in regard to the toleration of contrary centenary customs not reprobated by the law. And, again, it may be asked: Does not the very possibility of a legal recourse against decrees of the ordinary postulate the premise that a misuse of his discretionary powers may jeopardize the validity of his act?

7. The Intent of the Law in Canon 105 1°

In interpreting the intent of the law in canon 105 1°, Vermeersch [91] states that the aim is to define whether or not a superior may recede from the counsel of the persons whom he

---

[88] Reg. 34, R. J., in VI°.

[89] E.g., cans. 120 §1, 122, 134, 136-37, 139 §3, 356 §2, 358 §2, 360, 366 §1, 373 §§1-3, 379 §4, etc.

[90] Cf. c. 5, X, *de rerum permutatione*, III, 19: "Si autem episcopus causam inspexerit necessariam, licite poterit de uno loco ad alium, transferre personas, ut quae uni loco minus sunt utiles, alibi se valeant utilius exercere." —If licitly, then surely also validly.

[91] *Epitome Iuris Canonici*, I, n. 197 bis, 1, f, p. 152.

is instructed by law to ask. Gillet [92] attaches a like signification to the clause in question. Creusen [93] is of the same mind, and Boudinhon [94] maintains that if the legislator grants validity to an act of the superior who has heard, even though he has not followed the counsel, one is not justified in assuming that the legislator really contemplates the hypothesis in which the superior has not sought the advice.

But, an inspection of the natural literary structure of the canon will hardly bear out these strong statements. The consent that must be asked, needs at the same time to be followed before the superior can perfect a valid act. Now, just as the consent is intermediate to the act, so also its requisition is intermediate to the consent itself. Both the one and the other are equally necessary for the ensuing valid act. Proceeding to the next member, the canon deals with counsel. The counsel that *must be asked needs not* at the same time *to be followed* for the positing of a valid act.

The parity between consent and counsel patently continues relative to their need of being sought; the discrepancy, or rather the antithesis between them becomes evident only then when the canon states that counsel, unlike consent, needs not to be followed. In other words, the stipulation of consent bespeaks two requirements for validity, the specification of counsel only one. This one is precisely the procurement of the *auditio*. Where this falls by the way, the requirement for validity is not satisfied. If the hearing of the counsel is in itself sufficient, then, *vi sensus contrarii*, its omission becomes insufficient for the desired validity of the act.[95]

8. The Teaching of the Older Canonists

Creusen [96] recapitulates the teaching of the older canonists. He finds from a representative collating of their passages on this question that the more common opinion among them was to

[92] *La Personnalité juridique en Droit ecclésiastique*, p. 263.

[93] *NRT*, LV (1928), 108.

[94] *Jus Pont.*, VIII (1928), 30.

[95] Cf. Toso, in a review of Creusen's article, "L'effet juridique des consultations," (*NRT*, LV [1928], 100-16)—*Jus Pont.*, VIII (1928), 44.

[96] *Loc. cit.*, pp. 101-05.

the effect that the hearing of the chapter was *ad validitatem*, but that none of them seem to cite examples where the seeking of counsel from one or more individual persons was a requirement for validity except Passerini. His examples, however, were cases borrowed from the civil law. Moreover, in regard to this latter case, he shows that authors were not wanting who disclaimed the *auditio* as a *conditio sine qua non* for valid action. Lastly, he regards the lack of any indication of sources in the footnotes to canon 105 1°—when it would have been so easy to appeal to the Decretals upon which the older canonists based their assertion of the nullity of acts placed without the consultation of the diocesan chapter—as a negative evidence of the change induced in the present law relative to the strict requirement of counsel.[97]

Concerning the first argument little need be said. One may readily admit with the author that the cases in which consultation had to be sought from one or more individuals were so extremely rare, that their treatment by the canonists was most sparing. Furthermore, whilst the III Book of the Decretals contains two titles which treat of the acts to be executed by prelates either in view of or apart from the *consent of the diocesan chapter*,[98] it offers no special heading that would indicate a like requirement with regard to the *consultation of individual persons*.

Regarding the second statement, which adduces the authority of the authors who contended for the validity of acts undertaken without the seeking of counsel from individual persons, the following reply seems in order. The trend of the former law shows a preponderance of consideration for the diocesan chapter to the relative exclusion of individuals when there was question of the obtaining of consent or counsel. The tendency of the present law is to prefer the advice of such persons who are most directly concerned with the project in hand and hence are likely to be the best fitted in the suggestion of advice.[99] Furthermore, the appreciable reduction of the number of cases

---

[97] *Ibid.*, pp. 110-11.

[98] X., *de his quae fiunt a Praelatis sine consensu Capituli*, III, 10; X, *de his quae fiunt a maiore parte Capituli*, III, 11.

[99] Cf. footnotes 17 and 18 of this chapter.

in which consent from the diocesan chapter had been required opens the way to a more expeditious administrative policy on the part of the ordinary who, not without the helpful counsel of others, will be enabled to bring a well-ordered plan to a speedier conclusion.[100]

Relative to the opinion that a lack of citation from the Decretals under canon 105 1° points to an attenuation of the former strict requirement of consultation, the following observations may be made. It appears to be universally observed throughout the annotated edition of the Code that when source citations are produced for canons which consist, not of paragraphs, but of numbers, the footnote will be indicated, not at the end of each separate number, but at the end of the concluding member of the canon. This mode of citation by no means argues that only the last member of the canon is taken into account. Generally the annotations bear references to the entire canon in all its numerical portions.[101] Moreover, although the single annotation appears at the end of the canon, it may, even primarily, bear reference to one of the earlier numerical portions of that canon. This is verified in the case of canon 105.

The annotated reference to canon 6 §§1-2 of the decree "*Maxima Cura*" seems to show that the wording of canon 105 1° was inspired by the wording contained in this source. The law there contained was in the following form: " . . . *satis est ut eos audiat, nec ulla obligatione tenetur ad eorum votum, quamvis concors, accedendi.*" [102] Canon 15 of this decree presents the isolated case in which counsel alone was required. But, canon 3 plainly makes its requisition a condition for valid action.[103]

---

[100] Cf. "An nullus semper sit actus Superioris non petito consilio," *Jus Pont.*, VIII (1928), 32, where Boudinhon adverts to this altered discipline by stating that the cases in which consent is still required have been reduced in an approximate ratio of 10 to 1.

[101] For instances of this see cans. 14, 34, 101 §1, 106, 188, 223, 267, 349, 358, 415, 420-21, 459 §3, 542, 600, 723, 765-66, 825, 974, 984-85, 987, 1031 §§1-2, 1092, 1184, 1186, 1553 §1, 1603, §1, 1968-69, 2031, 2106, 2109, 2147, 2253, 2265, 2275, 2298, 2343 §§1-2, 2412. Every book and section of the Code offers examples.

[102] *AAS*, II (1910), 640.

[103] *Ibid.*, 642, 639. See also footnote 70 of this chapter.

The law now contained in canon 105 1° employs the following form: " . . . *satis est ad valide agendum ut Superior illas personas audiat; quamvis autem nulla obligatione teneatur ad eorum votum, etsi concors, accedendi.*"

In the writer's mind the near-identity of the wording in these two passages seems unequivocally to call for the application of canon 6 2° to the case in hand. Even if a doubt remained, the revocation of the preexisting law is not to be presumed; the law of the Code is rather to be brought into conciliation with its legal forbear.[104]

If the annotation to canon 105 carries no mention of the Decretals, this negative fact can be explained readily enough. It was the ruling of the decree "*Maxima Cura*" that provided the immediate basis for the formulation of this canon. References to the Decretals are found under a number of canons where the phrases *audito Capitulo* and *de consilio Capituli* are employed; especially is this the case whenever the legal traditions of the Decretals were not completely supplanted by such later legislation as that of the council of Trent, of the Papal Constitutions, or of the General Decrees of the Roman Congregations.[105]

9. The Momentous Consequences of the Strict Interpretation

Finally, the momentous consequences of invalid acts resulting from the neglect of seeking counsel are adduced as a reason for the more liberal interpretation.[106]

Creusen surmises that this very practical consideration suggests the reason for the delay by the Pontifical Commission for the Authentic Interpretation of the Canons of the Code in giving a reply to the difficulty which has actually been proposed. But, if the legislator intended that the wording of canon 105 1° is not to be considered as binding under pain of nullity, were it not better, in the words of Oietti,[107] to effect an author-

[104] Cf. can. 6 4°.

[105] Cf. e.g., cans. 391 §1, 394 §§1 and 3, 1234 §1, 1428 §1, 2292, and their appended annotations.

[106] Vermeersch-Creusen, *Epitome Iuris Canonici*, I, n. 197 bis, 1, e, p. 152; *Periodica*, XII (1923), (8); *Jus Pont.*, VIII (1928), 31-32; *NRT*, LV (1928), 109, 116.

[107] *Commentarium in Codicem Iuris Canonici*, II, 202.

itative abrogation of the legal disposition of canon 105 1°, or, at least, to seek through the intervention of the Commission an interpretation that will restrict its meaning in unequivocal terms, than to overreach the law by artificializing its wording, thus converting into a contrary agency what has been most wisely instituted by the law as a helpful medium, namely, that superiors will safeguard their acts against imprudence by not relying independently on their own unaided judgment?

Besides regarding the declaration of the Sacred Congregation of the Council on November 13, 1920, as confirmatory of his interpretation,[108] Oietti also states that, in the light of information received by him, this Sacred Congregation seems altogether to adhere to this same interpretation in its practice.[109]

B. Enumeration of the Opinions Expressed

Unmistakably in agreement with Oietti on the question of the strict interpretation of canon 105 1° are the following authors: Chelodi,[110] De Meester,[111] Arregui,[112] Cocchi,[113] Ferreres,[114] Maroto,[115] Muñiz,[116] Blat,[117] Toso,[118] Coronata,[119] Eich-

---

108 *Op. cit.*, 199, footnote 37. See also footnote 47 of this chapter. An examination of the import of this declaration of the Council will be made a little later in connection with the discussion of the force of custom regarding the ruling of canon 105 1°.

109 *Ibid.*, 202.

110 *Ius de Personis*, nn. 102, 231b, footnote 3, pp. 180, 383-84.

111 *Juris Canonici et Juris Canonico-civilis Compendium*, II, n. 879, p. 339; but see also *op. cit.*, I, n. 333, p. 225, where the author does little more than repeat the words of can. 105 1°.

112 *Summarium Theologiae Moralis*, n. 494, p. 302, footnote 1.

113 *Commentarium in Codicem Iuris Canonici*, lib. II, P. I, Sectio II, n. 11, p. 39.

114 *Institutiones Canonicae*, I, nn. 229, 771, II, pp. 91, 338.

115 *Institutiones Iuris Canonici*, I, n. 471, p. 555.

116 *Derecho Parroquial*, II, n. 496.

117 *Commentarium Textus Codicis Iuris Canonici*, lib. II, *De Personis*, nn. 36, 526, pp. 45, 516.

118 *Commentaria Minora*, lib. II, P. I, tit. I, p. 54; also *Jus Pont.*, VIII (1928), 44.

119 *Institutiones Iuris Canonici*, I, n. 153, c, p. 172, footnote 8. The author, however, admits the opposite opinion as probable.

mann,[120] Schäfer,[121] Koeniger,[122] Leitner,[123] Hilling,[124] Haring,[125] Sägmüller,[126] Ayrinhac[127] and Stutz.[128]

On the other hand Prümmer,[129] Woywod,[130] Bargilliat,[131] Bouuaert-Simenon,[132] Fanfani,[133] Rettenbacher[134] and Augus-

---

[120] *Lehrbuch des Kirchenrechts,* §38, p. 84.

[121] *Die Kirchenämter,* II Band, *Pfarrer und Pfarrvikare,* p. 101.

[122] *Katholisches Kirchenrecht,* §14, p. 97.

[123] *Handbuch des katholischen Kirchenrechts,* I, §12, 77.

[124] "Ich trete deshalb Ojetti durchaus bei, wenn er in einem schönen Exkurse auf S. 186 ff. (*Commentarium,* II) den Nachweis zu erbringen sucht, dass die in can. 105 erwähnte Einholung des Rates *unbedingt* für die Gültigkeit der in Frage stehenden Rechtshandlung in Betracht kommt. Denn der Ausdruck 'satis est ad valide agendum' ist so klar und deutlich, dass er keiner Auslegung, sondern nur einer Anwendung bedarf."—*AkKR,* CIX (1929), 294-95.

The same author is of the opinion that when the Bishops' Conference of the ecclesiastical Province of Cologne on February 19-20, 1918, determined that the custom of not consulting the parish priest before the appointment of an assistant to him would be retained, their action was not compatible with the law.—*AkKR,* CI (1921), 51-52.

[125] "Die Bestellung des pfarrlichen Hilfspriesters," *LQS,* LXXVI (1923), 335-37.

[126] *Lehrbuch des katholischen Kirchenrechts,* I, §60, p. 316, footnote 1: "Die Auffassung dass die betreffende Handlung doch gültig sei, wenn auch der Rat, wie vorgeschrieben, nicht eingehalten wurde . . ., ist sicher nicht stichhaltig."

[127] *Constitution of the Church in the New Code of Canon Law,* n. 302, p. 361; *General Legislation in the New Code of Canon Law,* n. 225, p. 225.

[128] *Der Geist des Codex iuris canonici,* p. 225, footnote 4, and p. 292, footnote 3.

[129] *Manuale Iuris Canonici,* Q. 56 3c, p. 76; Q. 144, II, IIb, p. 198; Q. 165 1, p. 224.

[130] *A Practical Commentary on the Code of Canon Law,* I, nn. 81, 353, pp. 46, 173.

[131] *Praelectiones Iuris Canonici,* II, n. 1173b, p. 199.

[132] *Manuale Iuris Canonici,* n. 585, p. 303. But see Oietti, *Commentarium in Codicem Iuris Canonici,* II, 200, where these authors are cited as positive witnesses to the strict interpretation.

[133] *De Iure Parochorum,* n. 452, pp. 380-81. Oietti (*Commentarium,* II, 200, footnote 42) cites this author in positive support of his own opinion. Fanfani, however, leaves ample room for the application of canon 5 despite the decision of the Sacred Congregation of the Council on November 13, 1920. Hence, this modification must be borne in mind.

[134] "Der Kooperator nach dem Codex Juris," *LQS,* LXXII (1919), 340.

tine [135] either content themselves with a bare restatement of the wording of canon 105 1° or adopt one or the other kind of modification in their interpretation.

Directly opposed to the opinion of Oietti are Vermeersch,[136] Creusen,[137] Boudinhon,[138] Wernz-Vidal,[139] Vromant,[140] Gillet,[141] the *Revue Ecclésiastique de Metz* [142] and the faculty at the University of Louvain.[143] The opinion of *L'Ami du Clergé*,[144] after apparently admitting that the interpretation of canon 105 1° involved a *dubium iuris*, nevertheless, in the end, supported the view of the strict requirement for validity. Similarly, Coronata [145] strongly inclines to the strict interpretation; but he also leaves room for the lesser probability of the opposite opinion.

---

135 *A Commentary on Canon Law*, II, 35. This author (*op. cit.*, 574) confuses the issue when he says that the bishop and religious superior are obliged to ask the opinion of the pastor, not about the person, but concerning the necessity of the assistant's appointment. But, see also footnote 14 of this chapter where other passages are indicated in his works which at least mitigate, if they do not also correct, his former view.

136 *Epitome Iuris Canonici*, I, n. 197 bis, 152; *Periodica*, XII (1923), (6)-(9).

137 *NRT*, LV (1928), 100-16.

138 *Jus Pont.*, VIII (1928), 29-35. Oietti's reference in his *Commentarium* (II, 201, footnote 46) to page 99 of this same volume reveals nothing in connection with the present question.

139 *Ius Canonicum*, II, *De Personis*, n. 33, p. 35, footnote 3. The question is not discussed in connection with the commentary on can. 476 §§3-4. Cf. *ibid.*, n. 744, II, p. 803.

140 *De Bonis Ecclesiae Temporalibus*, n. 40; *Ius Missionarium*, II, *De Personis*, n. 356, p. 314: "*Consulendum videtur* ut ad mentem can. 476, §3, titularis stationis praevie a Superioribus audiatur."

141 *La Personnalité juridique en Droit ecclésiastique*, pp. 262-63.

142 Vol. XXIX (1922), 153, footnote 1, as cited by Creusen—*NRT*, LV (1928), 115.

143 This information is furnished by Creusen—*ibid.*, p. 116.

144 Vol. XLIII (1926), 504-10, quoted by Creusen—*ibid.*, p. 115.

145 *Institutiones Iuris Canonici*, I, n. 153, p. 172, footnote 8: "Communis doctrina quae consilii requisitionem ad valorem requirit, probabilior videtur et litterae Codicis conformior." But, in n. 492, p. 577, footnote 7, he has the following: "Deputatio facta, non audito parocho, est irrita, et nulla potestas ordinaria vicarii hoc modo electi c. 105, n. 1; Santamaria (*Comentarios*), II, 215; contradicit tamen, non sine fundamento, Vermeersch, *Epitome*, I², 194, pag. 127."

C. Statement of the Interpretation Adopted

Amid such a variation of opinion among the authors, what practical conclusion is to be drawn? Must it be admitted that the arguments adduced by the group representing the liberal interpretation are of sufficient cogency to establish a *dubium iuris* with regard to the meaning of canon 105 1°, so that this canon would involve the ruling of canon 476 §§3-4 in its own uncertainty? Or, is it still permissible to brand with nullity any act undertaken by the superior who has not complied with the stipulation contained in the clause *audito parocho,* despite the opinion of these weighty authors?

To the writer it would seem that the discussion of this question has reached a stage where any private person might reasonably hesitate in giving an apodictical answer. There is satisfaction in knowing that the difficulty has been proposed for an authentic solution.[146] Until such time when an official reply will be given, it seems indicated to acknowledge the extrinsic probability of the less common opinion, and hence, not to be disturbed about the consequences of acts which superiors might execute in violation of the demand of canon 105 1°. Yet, whilst the validity of the act might remain intact in view of the general principle of canon 11, which admits the potentiality of a recognized extrinsic probability in rendering a law doubtful, it is hardly conceivable that such a legal fiction of doubt with regard to the requirement *ad validitatem* should lend encouragement to the non-observance of a law which still continues imperative in its full obediential sanction, despite the cherished possibility of its lack of nullifying force.

§III. Requirement of the *Auditio* in the Light of Canon 5

A. The Recognized Force of Custom Prior to the Code

Perhaps even more incisive than the sole consideration of the presence or absence of an invalidating sanction in canon 105 1°

146 Vermeersch-Creusen, *Epitome Iuris Canonici,* I, n. 197 bis, p. 151; Coronata, *op. cit.,* n. 153, p. 172, footnote 8.

is the element to be sought in the part that centenary or immemorial custom may have in determining the actual binding power of canon 476 §§3-4. Before the Code it was the admitted teaching of canonists that custom had the power of abrogating a law with an invalidating sanction attached to it. This was true, irrespective of the law's prescription of some definite substantial form, or of its incapacitation of certain individuals for the placing of acknowledged legal acts, or the acquisition of canonically recognized rights, or the assumption of juridically binding obligations.[147]

Furthermore, it was held that a subsequent law, unless it expressly reprobated *all* previous customs, still left intact all opposed centenary or immemorial customs, despite its employment of such apparently all-inclusive clauses as *"non obstante consuetudine contraria,"* or even, *"non obstante quacumque consuetudine contraria."* It was commonly agreed that centenary or immemorial customs were abrogated by a contrary law only then when the opposition of the law to *all* customs was expressed in a clause equivalent to *"non obstante quacumque consuetudine, etiam immemoriali."* [148] If the law contained no clause specifically abrogative of contrary customs, then all particular customs, in as far as they were buttressed by a reasonable observance, remained in force.[149]

B. The Canonized Force of Custom Since the Code

The guiding principles *now in force* regarding the abrogation of past legal enactments and practices must be sought in the canons of the present codification of the Church's law. Rela-

---

[147] Cf. Bauduin, *De Consuetudine in Jure Canonico*, nn. 172, 304, pp. 94, 156; Biederlack, "Gewohnheiten gegen die Disciplinardekrete des Trienter Konzils," *Zeitschrift für katholische Theologie* (*ZkT*), VI (1882), 438-71, and 608-58.

[148] Cf. Bauduin, *op. cit.*, n. 214, p. 112.

[149] C. 1, *de consuetudine*, I, 2, in VI°: "Licet Romanus Pontifex, qui iura omnia in scrinio pectoris sui censetur habere, constitutionem condendo posteriorem priorem, quamvis de ipsa mentionem non facit, revocare noscatur; quia tamen locorum specialium et personarum singularium consuetudines et statuta, cum sint facti et in facto consistant, potest probabiliter ignorare, ipsis, dum tamen sint rationabiles, per constitutionem a se noviter editam, nisi expresse caveatur in ipsa, non intelligitur in aliquo derogare." Cf. Bauduin, *op. cit.*, n. 215, pp. 112-13.

tive to *preexisting laws* canons 6, 22 and 23 must be invoked. Relative to *previous customs* canons 5 and 30 must be accepted as providing a norm. Canon 5 deals with all previous customs, both general and particular, which are now opposed to the legislation of the Code. Canon 30, safeguarding the prescription of canon 5, states that a custom, whether contrary to law or outside of its scope, is recalled by a corresponding contrary custom or contrary law.[150]

The canon next proceeds to indicate the conditional limitation of the law in its abrogative effect upon customs *praeter legem* which are at the same time centenary or immemorial.[151] Finally, it specifies the conditional limitation of a *general* law relative to the abrogation of *particular customs praeter legem.*[152] The essential diversity of disposition relative to particular customs as expressed in canons 5 and 30 is the following: Canon 30 sanctions the retention of particular *praeter legem* customs

---

[150] On the supposition that a contrary law or a contrary custom supervene, this member of canon 30 obviously considers all customs, whether general or particular, whether *contra* or *praeter legem.* It thus serves to give a more comprehensive interpretation to canon 5 which does not explicitly, but only equivalently, include *praeter legem* customs which, through the enactment of a contrary law, acquire the status of customs *contra legem.*

[151] That only *praeter legem customs* are treated in this member of can. 30 becomes evident from the consideration that can. 5 offers a complete regulation with regard to all *contrary customs.*

[152] Canon 30 may not be understood as exemplifying an exception to the general ruling of can. 5: ". . . ceterae [consuetudines ordinariae] suppressae habeantur, *nisi expresse Codex aliud caveat.*" The regulation of can. 30 is itself one of general import. Its acceptance in the light of a derogation to can. 5 would, by converse relation, imply a similar derogation to itself. Thus considered, these two canons would reciprocally nullify the general efficacy that each of them asserts.

In a word, according to can. 30 all particular customs existing *outside the law* continue in force, unless the general law expressly recalls them (cf. e.g., cans. 1035 and 1041); according to can. 5 all particular customs existing *contrary to the law* continue in force only when the Code expressly retains them (cf. e.g., cans. 106 6° and 695, where particular customs are sustained by the general law as suppletive norms); cans. 1169 §4 and 1186 1°-3°, where particular customs are expressly sanctioned by the general law as alternate norms.

by way of general rule; canon 5 upholds the force of particular *contra legem* customs by way of specified exception.[153]

C. The Particular Application of Canon 5

Canon 476 §§ 3-4 requires that the appointment and the presentation of an assistant vicar be made *audito parocho*. The Council of Trent had ruled that his services were to be engaged at the selection of the pastor.[154] In the course of the intervening centuries this discipline changed so that the answer received by Bishop Louis M. O. Epivent from the Sacred Congregation of the Council under date of August 14, 1863, for the diocese of Aire in southwestern France, was but a reflection of the custom which had become all but universal.[155] Spain, Italy and Sardinia seem to be the only countries which in the beginning of the present century still retained the Tridentine legislation.[156]

---

153 Cf. S. C. C., die 10 Jan. 1920 (*AAS*, XII [1920], 43-46), which ruled tbat the clergy, now as before the Code, are forbidden the wearing of beards. Chelodi (*Jus de Personis*, n. 59, e, pp. 103-04, footnote 8) and Bremer (*LQS*, LXXII [1919], 224-34, 573-78) contend that general customs *praeter ius* are according to can. 6 6° abrogated similarly as general laws *praeter ius*; on the other hand, Plöszl (*TQS*, LXXII [1919], 571-73), Gommaire (*Jus Pont.*, IV [1924], 175-82) and Cicognani (*Commentarium ad Librum I Codicis*, II, 34-36) maintain that all customs *praeter Codicem*, whether of a general or a particular nature, are still in force according to can. 30, unless some contrary specification has expressly abolished them. The latter opinion is surely in fuller accord with the principles underlying the above mentioned official decision.

154 Sessio XXI, *de ref.*, c. 4—*Canones et Decreta*, pp. 127-28.

155 Ad V: "An nominatio vicariorum, a fortiore Capellanorum, prout res nunc se habent in Gallia, et eorum stipendia componuntur, exclusive pertinet ad parochum.

R. "De jure spectare ad parochum cum approbatione Episcopi; attentis vero peculiaribus circumstantiis, servandum esse usum in ceteris Galliarum dioecesibus obtinentem, usquedum aliter a S. Sede declaratum."—*RSE*, XI (1865), 274; *AkKR*, XXXIX (1878), 18; *NRT*, XXIV (1892), 603, 607; Bouix, *Tractatus de Parocho*, Appendix I, §V, pp. 643-44. The delayed publication of this decision of the Congregation by the Bishop of Aire on February 22, 1865, is perhaps to be explained by the intermediate submission of M. Molet, curé of Mont-de-Marson, at whose instance the Congregation had been addressed for a settlement of the difficulty. Cf. *NRT*, XXIV (1892), 601, footnote 1.

156 Cf. S. C. C. *in Zagabrien. Nominationis Vicariorum Cooperatorum*, die 13 Nov. 1920 (*AAS*, XIII [1921], 45), where I. Mori, Secretary of the Congregation, gives this information. But, with regard to Spain see also footnote 75 of Chapter III.

In our own country the practice of the free appointment of assistants by the bishops can be traced back to the First Provincial Council of Baltimore, held in 1829.[157]

The United States were missionary territory then and remained such until they were withdrawn from the Sacred Congregation for the Propagation of the Faith by the Apostolic Constitution *"Sapienti Consilio"* issued on June 29, 1908.[158] It is highly questionable whether this country, even for the time intervening between then and the promulgation of the present Code, became subject to the ruling of common law relative to the appointment of *all* assistant priests.[159] It would seem that to churches where irremovable rectors were not yet assigned assistants could still be appointed in technical accord with the law prevalent before 1908.

In practical effect, however, the course to be followed was the same for all the churches, regardless entirely of whether the rector belonged to the class of *"removables"* or *"irremovables."* In the first instance the bishops executed the free appointment of assistants according to the practice of a custom induced *praeter legem communem;* in the second they proceeded according to the discipline of a custom established *contra legem communem.* With the advent of the present codification these two customs, previously distinct from each other, were merged into one and became even technically identified, for, thenceforth neither of

---

[157] See canon 4 of this Council—*Coll. Lac.*, III, 25. This same canon also regulated that where more than one priest had been assigned to a certain mission territory, the first-appointed was to become the rector of the mission; the others were to remain his assistants until such time when the bishop might dispose otherwise.

[158] "Itaque a iurisdictione Congregationis de Propaganda Fide exemptas et ad ius commune deductas decernimus . . . in America—provincias ecclesiasticas dominii Canadensis, Terrae Novae (Newfoundland) et Foederatorum Civitatum, seu *Statuum Unitorum."—ASS*, XLI (1908), 431; *AAS*, I (1909), 12.

[159] In accord with the II Plenary Council of Baltimore (*Acta et Decreta*, n. 125) the bishops could continue to remove or transfer *ad nutum* all removable pastors, for, in these cases they were not bound to follow the administrative procedure outlined by the decree *"Maxima Cura."* Cf. S. C. Consist., *Statuum Foederatorum Americae Septentrionalis*, die 28 Junii 1915—*AAS*, VII (1915), 378-82. The original decree is contained in *AAS*, II (1910), 636-48. See also *AAS*, II (1910), 854-55, where a number of doubts concerning the appointment of the examiners and consultors are answered by the Congregation under date of October 3, 1910.

them could continue its existence without running counter to the prescription of the *auditio parochi*. Hence, the legal requirement of the *auditio* must now be judged from an identical standpoint, regardless of whether the centenary or immemorial custom covered its own span of existence in the capacity of a custom *contra legem, praeter legem,* or *partim praeter* and *partim contra legem.*[160]

Once a custom, which has endured for a sufficient length of time to merit its classification as centenary or immemorial,[161] begins to conflict with the present, positive, general law of the Church, its erstwhile relation of contrariety, concomitance, or conformity to an earlier law no longer affects its present or its future status. Its *present* condition of contrariety, modified by the term of its past duration, constitutes the sole pivotal determinant of its ultimate retention or rejection in practice.

Every custom endowed with centenary or immemorial usage is vested with a unique legal force. Its efficacy is not *absolutely* nullified when a contrary general law supervenes. Its toleration is not confined within the strait and narrow domain of mere theoretical contingencies or technical possibilities. It is permitted entrance into the wider realm of imperative action

160 Cf. can. 5: "Vigentes *in praesens* contra horum statuta canonum consuetudines sive universales sive particulares, si quidem ipsis canonibus expresse *reprobentur,* tamquam iuris corruptelae corrigantur, licet sint immemorabiles, neve sinantur in posterum reviviscere; aliae, quae quidem centenariae sint et immemorabiles, tolerari poterunt, si Ordinarii pro locorum ac personarum adiunctis existiment eas prudenter submoveri non posse; ceterae suppressae habeantur, nisi expresse Codex aliud caveat." See also Maroto, *Institutiones Iuris Canonici,* I, n. 170, p. 161; Oietti, *Commentarium in Codicem Iuris Canonici,* I, 62.

161 Cf. Benedictus XIV, const. *"Inter Multa,"* die 4 Aprilis 1747, § Atque: "Quum sit de essentia immemorabilis consuetudinis, ut nihil contra eam auditum unquam, vel dictum, aut factum fuerit. . . ."—*Fontes,* II, n. 379, p. 107; Bauduin, *De Consuetudine in Jure Canonico,* n. 187 II, p. 101: "De essentia autem consuetudinis immemorialis non est, ut nulla quidem historica investigatione consuetudinis initium determinari possit. Quam ob causam exhibetur ut consuetudo, cuius initii non exstat memoria, non vero cuius initii nulla datur cognitio, et propterea quoque omnes consuetudinem immemorialem sufficienter probatam habent, modo testes affirment neque seipsos, neque concives contrarium vidisse, aut audivisse." See also *ibid.,* n. 22, p. 12; Oietti, *op. cit.,* I, 63; Maroto, *op. cit.,* I, n. 250, p. 266; D'Annibale, *Summula Theologiae Moralis,* I, nn. 245-47; Vermeersch-Creusen, *Epitome Iuris Canonici,* I, n. 111, p. 101; Cicognani, *Commentarium ad Librum I Codicis,* II, 33.

and practical urgency to maintain its life. Wherever and whenever local conditions and personal circumstances solidly suggest that by adhering to the requirements of a contrary law the displacement of a centenary or an immemorial custom cannot be accomplished without imprudence, there and then its toleration by the ordinary is acknowledged in the law itself. That the lawgiver's enforcement of a positive law to the probable detriment of administrative discretion may, in such instances, prove more inexpedient than his connivance at its neglect to the likely safeguard of sagacity in ecclesiastical government, is the very presumption from which canon 5 borrows its legal force. Hence, the hallowed customs of centenary or immemorial age, though they impinge upon the authority of a contrary law, are nevertheless permitted, at the instance of prudence, to retain their honorable force, as long as legal reprobation has not dislodged them.[162]

The appointment and the presentation of assistants *inaudito parocho* were rooted in a centenary, or at least an immemorial custom prior to 1918. The law in canon 476 §§3-4 specifies that the appointment and the presentation be made *audito parocho*. Thus, the practice of the past is no longer upheld by the positive stipulation of the present law. Yet, the law of the Code on this point does not abolish the past custom with a reprobating clause. In consequence, this custom falls among that class whose continuance is made possible when the conditions of canon 5 are verified. The verification of these conditions rests with the prudent judgment of the ordinary. Therefore, whenever he deems it impossible prudently to set aside the past custom, he acts within the full concession of the law if he regulates the appointment and the presentation *inaudito parocho*.

1. The Action of the Sacred Congregation of the Council, November 13, 1920

To invoke in this connection a decision of the Sacred Congregation of the Council, rendered on November 13, 1920, for

[162] Cf. Pfatschbacher, "Römisches Recht und katholische Kirche," *Th Gl*, XXII (1930), 28-46. On page 44 the author adverts to the significant influence of custom in the legislation of the Church.

the Archbishop of Agram (Zagreb) in Jugoslavia,[163] in order to deny the force of the conclusion stated in the preceding paragraph is, upon closer inspection of the declaration itself, without logical effect. In the *Animadversiones ex officio* the Archbishop's mind is interpreted as signifying, not a doubt as to whether the circumstances in his archdiocese justified a contravention of the general law, but a doubt relative to the possibility of retaining a century-old custom when a general law in direct opposition to it had supervened.[164]

It must also be recalled that the ordinary cannot retain the old custom on the score of its constituting a *ius quaesitum*. This argument was advanced privately by the consultor of the case, but rejected by the Congregation as inadmissible. Furthermore, the administrative efficiency of the past discipline may not be regarded as automatically implying a hazard in the altered ruling for the present. Even in such dioceses, where the conditions prevalent in the past gave rise to the appointment or presentation *non petito consilio*, no inconsistency attaches to the new law, despite the unchanged status of these conditions in the present. The purpose of the law is not to subtract from the powers which the ordinary formerly possessed; its aim is rather to increase the efficiency of his continued free exercise of these powers through the helpful medium of previous consultation.

Nevertheless, in the face of all this it must still be admitted that the Congregation did not settle a juridical, but merely a practical doubt. The ruling of canon 476 §3 was confirmed simply because the Congregation did not detect in the case any verification of the suppositions posited in canon 5 in view of which centenary custom might continue, even in a conditioned manner, to assert its prevalence against the present law.[165]

---

163 Cf. *AAS*, XIII (1921), 43-46.

164 "At vero, dum in casu Episcopus dubitat num consuetudo possit servari, *palam profitetur nullum dubium superesse quin illa possit servari*. . . . Quae cum ita sint, profecto nullum subest impedimentum quominus Codex, datus praecipue ad uniformitatem legis et disciplinae ecclesiasticae inducendam, hunc suum effectum in casu sortiri possit."—*Ibid.*, p. 46. The italics in the passage are indicated by the present writer.

165 *Ibid.*, pp. 45-46.

2. The Action of the Sacred Congregation of the Council, June 8, 1927

In view of the legal setting in which the above mentioned case was presented, it seems admissible to take exception to the strictures of Hilling previously recounted.[166] The force of his then expressed opinion lapses all the more when one adverts to a recent communication by the Sacred Congregation of the Council (No. 2551) to the ordinariate of Seckau on June 8, 1927. In this official rescript the local ordinary of that diocese is accorded the right of appointing assistants *inaudito parocho.*[167]

Even if this communication should have been forwarded as a rescript of favor, in all likelihood its grant was determined by the existence of conditions which, if inadequate in themselves, yet closely approximated such suppositions as would have allowed the use of canon 5 in favor of the past custom. If one admits that canon 5 conditionally allows the toleration of centenary customs despite a supervening contrary law, then one must also concede the application of this principle relative to the appointment or presentation of parochial assistants in all the individual dioceses where the specified conditions exist.[168]

If, then, the ordinaries of individual dioceses or bishops of an ecclesiastical province determine to follow the old practice of appointing parochial assistants *inaudito parocho,* the compatibility of their joint action with the law of the Code is assured, provided only that the conditions in their dioceses are such as to justify the application of the principle contained in canon 5. It will be seen, therefore, that although canon 105 1° formulates the requirement of a previous consultation with the pastor in each separate case when an assistant vicar is to be presented or appointed, and, in all likelihood, even fortifies this requirement with the force of a most efficacious sanction, circumstances may nevertheless intervene concurrent with which the toleration of the old custom may be accorded a valid prece-

---

[166] See footnote 124 of this chapter.

[167] Cf. Haring, "Die Trauung durch einen 'inaudito parocho' bestellten Hilfspriester," *LQS*, LXXXII (1929), 126-27.

[168] Cf. Fanfani, *De Iure Parochorum*, n. 452, pp. 380-81; Chelodi, *Ius de Personis*, n. 59e, p. 103, footnote 6; Lindner, *Die Anstellung der Hilfspriester*, in the closing pages of his book.

dence over the present demand of the law. That the combination of such circumstances will be rare is, perhaps, beyond reasonable dispute, for the law is not essentially a restriction of the former administrative policy of free appointment, but obviously a stabilizing medium in securing greater efficiency in its continued application.[169]

ART. III. RIGHTS ENJOYED BY THE RELIGIOUS SUPERIOR

§I. THE RIGHT OF PRESENTATION

The right of presentation exercised by the religious superior in connection with the appointment of an adjutant is verified then when the appointment is to be made in a parish which is entrusted to religious.[170] The same right of presentation is accorded to the religious superior qualified therefor by the constitutions of his institute when one who is a member of that institute is to be appointed in the capacity of a parochial assistant.[171] One notes in these two separate regulations a difference of wording which at least technically seems to differentiate the sphere of competent action for the superior. Practically, however, these two regulations may and generally do eventuate not only in a uniform mode of procedure, but also in an identified extent of application.

In strict adherence to the wording of canon 475 §1 the religious superior must be acknowledged competent for the presentation of an adjutant vicar in a parish entrusted to his institute, even if that vicar were selected from the body of the diocesan clergy. According to canon 476 §4 a religious superior is competent for the presentation of an assistant vicar in a parish entrusted to his institute only when the prospective appointee is a religious and at the same time a member of the superior's own religious institute. That both adjutants and assistants who are not members of a religious institute can nevertheless be

169 "Nec revera, si objectum removendae consuetudinis attendatur, facile quis exponere valeat quid incommodi suboriturum sit, si, de persona nominandi coadiutoris, prius coadiuvandus interpellatur, nulla statuta obligatione illius sententiam sequendi (c. 105 1°)."—*AAS*, XIII (1921), 46.

170 Can. 475 §1.

171 Can. 476 §4.

appointed to parishes which are entrusted to religious, or even to parishes incorporated with a particular religious institute, seems not to be incompatible with the law on the score of canon 1442, provided one is ready to admit that the charges committed to adjutants and assistants do not constitute ecclesiastical benefices.[172]

Thus, for instance, the sudden decimation of the numbers of a religious institute through the ravages of a local epidemic might transiently call for the appointment of diocesan priests to its incorporated parochial churches in the capacity of adjutants and assistants. Since there is no general law in the Code to the contrary, it would also seem that canon 1442 leaves possible the adaptation of the need in the manner suggested, when it follows upon the mutual agreement of the superior and the local ordinary and provided, of course, that such manner of appointments do not militate against the specific regulations of the approved constitutions of the respective institute. Likewise, the paucity of diocesan priests might necessitate a similar appointment in secular parishes of adjutants and assistants who are members of some religious institute. Nuntios, Internuntios and Apostolic Delegates possess the faculty of granting to diocesan ordinaries a special concession in this regard.[173] Since by the use of this concession the religious who are appointed by the diocesan ordinary with the consent of their superior to preside over secular parishes do not become parish priests,[174] but merely acquire the status of temporary administrators, it seems, *a pari*, that the rule of appointment here specified for the assign-

---

[172] Can. 1442 excludes the optional appointment of seculars or of religious to parochial incumbencies and ministries only when these parochial charges constitute at the same time ecclesiastical benefices.

[173] ". . . Concedendi in casibus particularibus, vel ad tempus, Ordinariis dioecesanis facultatem praeficiendi paroeciis religiosos in defectu sacerdotum saecularium, de consensu tamen suorum Superiorum, et cum clausula ut saltem duo alii religiosi cum parocho cohabitent, servatisque in reliquis sacrorum canonum dispositionibus."—*Index facultatum* . . ., cap. V, n. 48. Cf. *Appendix* I, apud Vermeersch-Creusen, *Epitome Iuris Canonici*, I, n. 813, p. 527; *Appendix* III, apud Augustine, *A Commentary on Canon Law*, I, 277.

[174] Notwithstanding the use of the word *parochus* in the text of the faculty, these religious may be classed as parish priests only in the applied sense of can. 451 §2 2°.

ment of parochial administrators [175] might also, under like conditions of extraordinary need and in virtue of canons 68 and 50, become the norm of appointment relative to the assignment of parochial adjutants and assistants.

§II. The Right of Approval

On the other hand, whilst a religious superior must present a diocesan priest for institution in the pastoral incumbency of a parish only *semi-pleno iure* incorporated with the religious institute,[176] it would seem to be little in conformity with the spirit of the law for the superior to present a member of his own institute as a prospective adjutant or assistant in such a parish, even though the letter of the law offers no direct and immediate prescription against it.[177]

Furthermore, in contingencies where the diocesan ordinary is constrained to call upon the temporary services of religious for filling the pastoral ministries in secular parishes of the diocese, it is he who is instructed to make the necessary appointments, yet, in such a manner that they are executed through the medium

---

175 Precisely because of their status as administrators, the norm of appointment to be followed in the use of this special faculty by the diocesan ordinary is fashioned in perfect agreement with the ruling of can. 472 1° in which: "Vacante paroecia, *Ordinarius loci* in ea quamprimum *constituat* idoneum vicarium *oeconomum, de consensu Superioris, si de religioso* agatur." In the one case there is question of secular parishes exclusively; in the other both secular and religious parishes are included. The canon uses the clause "*vacante paroecia*" in a fully generic sense.

176 Can. 1425 §1.

177 Cans. 475, 476, 1425, 1433 and 1442, which treat *ex professo* about this question in its various aspects, contain no positive prohibition against the appointment of religious adjutants or assistants in secular parishes, or against the assignment of diocesan priests as adjutants or assistants in religious parishes. Furthermore, the analogous legislation of cans. 465 §§4-6, 472, 474 and 1923 §2 would rather seem to confirm the possibility of a liberal sphere of action. But, the deeper spirit of the law becomes evident from the passages of the law contained in cans. 578 2°, 593, 594 §1, 606 §2, 608 §1, 610 §1, 630 §§1-2, 679 §1, *et passim*. All of these passages suggest or delineate obligations the fulfillment of which would be precluded, or at least seriously handicapped, in the case where a religious parochial adjutant or assistant would be placed in the parochial ministry of a secular parish. From the very nature of the case it is obvious that his opportunities for the adequate cultivation of the principles of religious life would be notably impeded.

of approval from the competent religious superior.[178] This regulation is based on the necessary presumption that the religious superior has a corresponding duty to accede to the legitimate demands of the diocesan ordinary when the needs of the faithful occasion the latter's request. The *fact of approval* does not remain optional with the religious superior; however, the *individualization of its expression,* as centering in the several persons approved by him, continues to abide within the realm of his voluntary discretion.[179]

It will be noted that in cases of need when the diocesan ordinary becomes empowered by special faculty to requisition the services of religious priests in the parochial ministries of secular parishes in his diocese, there is no mention of previous presentation by the religious superior, but only of concomitant or subsequent approval or consent. This mode of procedure is, of course, outside of the normal method of administration. Normally, the religious superior presents the prospective appointee and the local ordinary approves him for the appointment. In both eventualities, however, the completed act of appointment is integrated by the coalescence of two wills in an ultimate term of mutual equation. And, in so far, one is justified in saying that in both cases the issue remains *practically* identical. Yet, juridically the two procedures remain differentiated in as far as the one begins with the presentation by the religious superior and is consummated by the subsequent approval of the local ordinary, whilst the other originates with the designation of the local ordinary and receives its complement in the action of approval or consent by the religious superior.

---

[178] Cf. footnote 173 above.

[179] Can. 608 §1: "Curent Superiores ut religiosi subditi, a se designati, praesertim in dioecesi in qua degunt, cum a locorum Ordinariis vel parochis eorum ministerium requiritur ad consulendum populi necessitati, tum intra tum extra proprias ecclesias aut oratoria publica, illud, salva religiosa disciplina, libenter praestent." Whilst this canon has in mind the more particular needs of missions, retreats, Forty Hours' Devotions, *tridua,* Sunday services, added opportunities for confession, and the like, it appears that the force of its application must, *a fortiori,* be acknowledged under circumstances when the needs become even more pronounced and notably extended.

§III. The Determinant Factor of the Religious Superior's Rights

When the religious superior presents the prospective *adjutant* vicar, his action receives its specification from local and real circumstances, that is to say, from the fact that an appointment is to be made at a parish entrusted to religious. On the other hand, the religious superior's right of presenting an *assistant* vicar is confined within the limits of a personal consideration, that is to say, in the fact that an appointment is to be made whose recipient is the member of a religious institute. The contraposition of these two regulations plainly reveals the more intimate note of obediential solidarity to inhere in the latter. Relative to the adjutant the superior's right of presentation may indirectly achieve its expression outside the limits of his direct personal jurisdiction. Regarding the assistant it is confined within more definitive limits since it cannot externate itself except in cases of personal jurisdiction. In the former instance the right of presentation originates from sources extraneous to the presentee; in the latter this right abstracts from all extraneous conditions and strictly inheres in the obediential relationship of subject and superior.

Vidal paraphrases canon 476 §4 in the following words: "*Quodsi agatur de paroecia religiosa, Superior religiosus, audito parocho vicarium Ordinario praesentat, Ordinarius approbat si idoneum repererit.*" [180] Prümmer reproduces it thus: "*In paroeciis domui religiosae concreditis vicarios cooperatores religiosos superior (cui id ex constitutionibus competit), audito parocho, praesentat Ordinario, cuius est eosdem approbare.*" [181]

The mention made by these two authors of religious parishes and of parishes entrusted to a religious house or institute as constituting a condition for the verification of the superior's right of presentation is indeed borne out under all normal or ordinary circumstances. But, when extraordinary contingencies intervene, their statements seem not to cover the cases in any precise way, simply because it is not any local or real condition, but an exclu-

---

[180] *Ius Canonicum*, II, *De Personis*, n. 744, p. 803.

[181] *Manuale Iuris Canonici*, Q. 165, p. 224.

sively personal note of consideration that actuates the superior's right. Two such sets of circumstances are easily conceivable.

There may be an unescapable need of, and a corresponding faculty for appointing a diocesan assistant priest to a religious parish or to a parish entrusted to some religious house. In this case the diocesan ordinary will surely not have to abide a previous act of presentation on the part of the religious superior. To grant the religious superior a right of presentation is an unwarranted extension of the limits indicated by canon 476 §4. Hence, for this case the authors' interpretation appears too liberal.

There may also be a reason for, and an actual appointment of a religious priest as an assistant in a secular parish. To deny the superior the right of previous presentation, or to disclaim a practically equivalent right of concomitant or subsequent approval and consent, is an undue limitation of the right accorded by canon 476 §4. Therefore, in this event the interpretation seems too restrictive.

In her indication of the superior's harmonized rights of presentation and approval with respect to parochial assistant vicars the Church strikes her keynote on the chords of personal relation between subject and superior.

BIBLIOGRAPHY

SOURCES

Acta Apostolicae Sedis, Commentarium Officiale, Romae, 1909-

Acta Sanctae Sedis, 41 vols., Romae, 1865-1908.

Acta et Decreta Concilii Plenarii Americae Latinae in Urbe Celebrati anno 1899, Romae, 1902.

Acta et Decreta Conciliorum Recentiorum (Collectio Lacensis), 7 vols., Friburgi Brisgoviae, 1870-1890.

Breviarium Romanum, Ratisbonae et Romae, 1916.

Bullarium Diplomatum et Privilegiorum Sanctorum Pontificum Taurinensis editio, auspicante Cardinali Francisco Gaude, 25 vols., Augustae Taurinorum, 1857-1872.

Canones et Decreta Sacrosancti Oecomenici Concilii Tridentini, Editio Novissima ad Fidem Optimorum Exemplarium castigate Impressa (XIX Reimpressio Stereotypa), Taurini, 1913.

Codex Iuris Canonici Pii X Pontificis Maximi iussu digestus Benedicti Papae XV auctoritate promulgatus, Praefatione, Fontium Annotatione et Indice Analytico-Alphabetico ab Emo Petro Card. Gasparri Auctus, Romae, 1918.

Codex Theodosianus, Ed. P. Krueger, Th. Mommsen, P. M. Meyer, 3 vols., Berolini, 1905.

Codicis Iuris Canonici Fontes, cura Emi Petri Card. Gasparri editi, 4 vols., Romae, 1925-1928.

Collectanea S. Congregationis de Propaganda Fide, 2 vols., Romae, 1907.

Concilia Salisburgensia Provincialia et Dioecesana, ed. F. Dalham, Augustae apud Vindelicos, 1788.

Concilii Plenarii Baltimorensis II (1866), Acta et Decreta, Baltimorae, 1868.

Concilii Plenarii Baltimorensis III (1884), Acta et Decreta, Baltimorae, 1886.

Concilii Plenarii Quebecensis I (1909), Acta et Decreta, Quebeci, 1912.

Corpus Iuris Canonici, Editio Lipsiensis II (Richter-Friedberg), 2 vols., Lipsiae, 1922.

Corpus Iuris Civilis, 3 vols., Berolini, 1928-1929.—Vol. I: *Institutiones* recognovit P. Krueger; *Digesta* recognovit Th. Mommsen, retractavit P. Krueger; Vol. II: *Codex Justinianus* recognovit et retractavit P. Krueger; Vol. III: *Novellas* recognovit R. Schoell, opus Schoelli morte interceptum absolvit G. Kroll.

Corpus Scriptorum Ecclesiasticorum Latinorum, Editum Consilio et Impensis Academiae Litterarum Caesariae Vindobonensis *(Corpus Vindobonense),* Vindobonae, 1866-

Hardouin, Jean, *Acta Conciliorum et Epistolae Decretales ac Constitutiones Summorum Pontificum*, 12 vols., Parisiis, 1715.

Hartzheim, Joseph, *Concilia Germaniae*, 12 tom., Coloniae Augustae Agrippinensium, 1759-1790.

Mansi, Joannes Dominicus, *Sacrorum Conciliorum Nova et Amplissima Collectio*, 53 vols., Paris-Arnhem-Leipzig, 1901-1927.

Sacrae Romanae Rotae Decisiones seu Sententiae, Vol. III (1911), Romae, 1915.

Thesaurus Resolutionum Sacrae Congregationis Concilii, 167 vols., Romae, 1718-1908.

Wilkins, David, *Concilia Magnae Britanniae et Hiberniae*, 4 vols., Londini, 1737.

WORKS OF REFERENCE

Anler, Louis, *The Pastoral Companion*, translated and adapted from the German by Fr. Honoratus Bonzelet, Chicago, 1929.

Arregui, Antonius M., *Summarium Theologiae Moralis*, 10. ed., Bilbao, 1927.

Artaud de Montor, A. F. Chevalier, *The Lives and Times of the Popes*, 10 vols., New York, 1911.

Ayrinhac, H. A., *General Legislation in the New Code of Canon Law*, New York, 1923.

Ayrinhac, H. A., *Constitution of the Church in the New Code of Canon Law*, New York, 1925.

Ayrinhac, H. A., *Legislation on the Sacraments in the New Code of Canon Law*, New York, 1928.

Ayrinhac, H. A., *Marriage Legislation in the New Code of Canon Law*, New York, 1918.

Ayrinhac, H. A., *Administrative Legislation in the New Code of Canon Law*, New York, 1930.

Ayrinhac, H. A., *Penal Legislation in the New Code of Canon Law*, New York, 1920.

[Bachofen], Charles Augustine, *The Canonical and Civil Status of Catholic Parishes in the United States*, St. Louis, 1926.

[Bachofen], Charles Augustine, *A Commentary on the New Code of Canon Law*, 8 vols., St. Louis, 1921-1925: Vol. I, 4. ed., 1921; Vol. II, 4. ed., 1923; Vol. III, 3. ed., 1922; Vol. IV, 3. ed., 1925; Vol. V, 3. ed., 1923; Vol. VI, 2. ed., 1923; Vol. VII, 2. ed., 1923; Vol. VIII, 2. ed., 1924.

[Bachofen], Charles Augustine, *The Pastor according to the New Code of Canon Law*, 3. ed., St. Louis, 1926.

[Bachofen], Charles Augustine, *Rights and Duties of Ordinaries according to the Code and Apostolic Faculties*, St. Louis, 1924.

Badii, Caesar, *Institutiones Iuris Canonici*, 3. ed., 2 vols., Florentiae, 1921-1922.

Barbosa, Agostino, *De Officio et Potestate Episcopi*, Lugduni, 1656.
Barbosa, Agostino, *Iuris Ecclesiastici Universi Libri Tres*, Lugduni, 1660.
Bargilliat, M., *Praelectiones Juris Canonici*, 37. ed., 2 vols., Parisiis, 1923.
Bauduin, G., *De Consuetudine in Jure Canonico*, Lovanii, 1888.
Benedictus XIV, *Institutiones Ecclesiasticae*, Prati, 1844.
Benedictus XIV, *De Synodo Dioecesana*, 2 vols., Romae, 1806.
Berardi, Aemilius, *De Parocho Compendium*, Faventiae, 1887.
Blat, Albertus, *Commentarium Textus Codicis Iuris Canonici*, 6 vols., Romae, 1921-1927.—*Normae Generales*, Romae, 1921—*De Personis*, 2. ed., Romae, 1921.
Bouix, D., *Tractatus de Parocho*, 2. ed., Parisiis-Bruxellis, 1867.
Bouuaert, F.—Simenon, G., *Manuale Juris Canonici*, 2. ed., Gandae et Leodii, 1926.
Camp, George, *Die organisatorische Trennung der Gewalten in der römischen Kurie*, Zürich, 1926.
Cappello, Felix M., *Tractatus Canonico-Moralis de Sacramentis*.—Vol. III, *De Matrimonio*, 2. ed., Romae, 1927.
Cappello, Felix M., *De Visitatione SS. Liminum et Dioeceseon*, 2 vols., Romae, 1913.
Catholic Encyclopedia, The, 17 vols., New York, 1907-1922.
Chelodi, Joannes, *Ius de Personis*, 2. ed., Tridenti, 1927.
Chelodi, Joannes, *Ius Matrimoniale*, 3. ed., Tridenti, 1921.
Cicognani, Hamletus I., *Ius Canonicum*, Romae, 1925.
Cicognani, Hamletus I., *Commentarium ad Librum I Codicis*, Romae, 1925.
Cimetier, F., *Pour étudier le Code de Droit Canonique*, 2. ed., Paris, 1927.
Coady, John Joseph, *The Appointment of Pastors*, Washington, 1929.
Cocchi, Guidus, *Commentarium in Codicem Iuris Canonici*, 7 vols., Taurinorum Augustae, 1925-1927.—Lib. I, *Normae Generales*, 3. ed., 1925; lib. II, *De Personis*, 2. ed., 1925-1926; lib. III, *De Rebus*, 2. ed., 1926-1927; lib. V, *De Delictis et Poenis*, 1925.
Coronata, Matthaeus Conte a, *Institutiones Iuris Canonici*, Vol. I, Taurini, 1928.
Coronata, Matthaeus a, *De Locis et Temporibus Sacris*, Augustae Taurinorum, 1922.
Creusen, J.-Van Eyen, F., *Tabulae Fontium Traditionis Christianae*, 2. ed., Lovanii, 1926.
Cronin, Charles J., *The New Matrimonial Legislation*, 2. ed., London, 1909.
D'Angelo, Sosius, *Parroco e Parrocchia*, Giarre (Sicilia), 1921.
D'Annibale, Josephus, *Summula Theologiae Moralis*, 2. ed., Mediolani, 1881.
De Meester, A., *Juris Canonici et Juris Canonico-Civilis Compendium*, 3 vols., Brugis, 1921-1928.
Deneubourg, J., *Étude canonique sur les vicaires paroissiaux*, Tournai, 1871.
Denzinger, H.-Bannwart, C., *Enchiridion Symbolorum Definitionum et Declarationum de Rebus Fidei et Morum*, 14. et 15. ed., Friburgi Brisgoviae, 1922.
De Smet, Aloysius, *Tractatus Theologico-Canonicus de Sponsalibus et Matrimonio*, 4. ed., Brugis, 1927.

Devoti, J., *Institutiones Canonicae*, Romae, 1830.

Doheny, William J., *Church Property: Modes of Acquisition*, Washington, 1927.

Dugan, Henry Francis, *The Judiciary Department of the Diocesan Curia*, Washington, 1925.

Engel, Ludovicus, *Collegium Universi Juris Canonici*, Beneventi-Venetiis, 1760.

Eichmann, Eduard, *Das Prozessrecht des Codex Iuris Canonici*, Paderborn, 1921.

Eichmann, Eduard, *Das Strafrecht des Codex Iuris Canonici*, Paderborn, 1920.

Eichmann, Eduard, *Lehrbuch des Kirchenrechts*, 2. ed., Paderborn, 1926.

Fagnanus, P., *Commentaria in Libros Decretalium*, 4 vols., Venetiis, 1696.

Fanfani, Ludovicus I., *De Iure Parochorum ad Normam Codicis Iuris Canonici*, Taurini-Romae, 1924.

Ferraris, F. Lucius, *Bibliotheca Canonica, Iuridica, Moralis, Theologica, necnon Ascetica, Polemica, Rubricistica, Historica*, 9 vols., Romae, 1885-1899.

Ferreres, Ioannes B., *Casus Conscientiae*, 5. ed. (2a post Codicem), 2 vols., Barcinone, 1926.

Ferreres, Ioannes B., *Institutiones Canonicae*, 2. ed., 2 vols., Barcinone, 1920.

Funk, F. X., *A Manual of Church History*, translated from the German by P. Perciballi; edited by W. H. Kent, 2 vols., London, 1914.

Funk, F. X., *Didascalia et Constitutiones Apostolorum*, 2 vols., Paderbornae, 1905.

Funk, F. X., *Patres Apostolici*, 2. ed., 2 vols., Tubingae, 1901.

Garcia, Nicolas, *Tractatus de Beneficiis Ecclesiasticis*, Coloniae Allobrogum, 1636.

Gillet, Pierre, *La Personnalité Juridique en Droit Ecclésiastique*, Malines, 1927.

Gillmann, Franz, *Das Institut der Chorbischöfe im Orient* (Münchener Studien zur historischen Theologie, II Reihe, 4 Heft), München, 1903.

Godfrey, John A., *The Right of Patronage according to the Code of Canon Law*, Washington, 1924.

Golden, Henry Francis, *Parochial Benefices in the New Code*, Washington, 1921.

Gottlob, Theodor, *Der abendländische Chorepiskopat*, Bonn, 1928.

Gross, Carl, *Lehrbuch des katholischen Kirchenrechts*, 4. ed., Wien, 1903.

Hefele-Hergenröther, *Conciliengeschichte*, 9 vols., Freiburg im Br., 1873-1890.—Bände I-VII (2. ed.) nach den Quellen bearbeitet von Carl Joseph von Hefele; Bände VIII-IX fortgesetzt von J. Cardinal Hergenröther.

Herders Kirchenlexicon, 12 vols., Freiburg im Breisgau, 1882-1903.

Hilling, Nicolaus, *Codicis Juris Canonici Interpretatio*, Friburgi Brisigovorum, 1925.

Hilling, Nicolaus, *Codicis Juris Canonici Supplementum*, Friburgi Brisigovorum, 1925.

Hilling, Nikolaus, *Die allgemeinen Normen des Codex Juris Canonici*, Freiburg i. Br., 1926.

Hilling, Nikolaus, *Das Personenrecht des Codex Iuris Canonici*, Paderborn, 1924.

Hilling, Nikolaus, *Das Sachenrecht des Codex Juris Canonici*, Freiburg i. Br., 1928.

Hinschius, P., *Das Kirchenrecht der Katholiken und Protestanten in Deutschland*, 6 vols., Berlin, 1869-1897.—Vols. I-IV, *System des katholischen Kirchenrechts*, Berlin, 1869-1888.

Hostiensis (Henricus Card. de Segusio), *Summa Aurea*, Lugduni, 1568.

Hulme, Edward Maslin, *The Middle Ages*, New York, 1929.

Journel, M. J. Rouet de, *Enchiridion Patristicum, Loci SS. Patrum, Doctorum, Scriptorum Ecclesiasticorum*, 4. et 5. ed., Friburgi Brisgoviae, 1922.

Kearney, Raymond A., *The Principles of Delegation*, Washington, 1929.

Kirch, C., *Enchiridion Fontium Historiae Ecclesiasticae Antiquae*, 4. ed., Friburgi Brisgoviae, 1923.

Knecht, August, *Handbuch des katholischen Eherechts*, Freiburg im Breisgau, 1928.

Koeniger, Albert M., *Katholisches Kirchenrecht mit Berücksichtigung des deutschen Staatskirchenrechts*, Freiburg im Breisgau, 1926.

Köstler, Rudolf, *Wörterbuch zum Codex Iuris Canonici*, München, 1927-1929.

Kümpel, P. Johs. Chrysostomus (Anton), *Begriff und Abstufung der iurisdictio ordinaria und delegata in ihrer kanonistischen Entwickelung*, Bonn, 1922.

Lämmer, Hugo, *Institutionen des katholischen Kirchenrechts*, 2. ed., Freiburg im Br., 1892.

Leitner, Martin, *Handbuch des katholischen Kirchenrechts*, 5 vols., München, 1921-1927.—Erste bis vierte Lieferung (2. ed.), 1921-1924; fünfte Lieferung, 1927.

Leurenius, P., *Forum beneficiale*, 2 vols., Augustae Vindelicorum, 1757.

Lindner, Dominikus, *Die Anstellung der Hilfspriester* (Münchener Studien zur historischen Theologie, 3 Heft), Kempten, 1924.

Lingen, C.-Reuss, P. A., *Causae Selectae in S. Cong. Cardinalium Conc. Trident. Interpretum Propositae*, Ratisbonae, 1871.

Lotterius, Melchior, *De Re Beneficiaria*, Patavii, 1700.

McNicholas, John T., *The New Marriage Legislation—Commentary on the Decree "Ne Temere,"* Philadelphia, 1908.

Maroto, Philippus, *Institutiones Iuris Canonici*, 2 vols., Romae, 1919-1921.—Vol. I (3. ed.), Romae, 1921; Vol. II, Matriti-Barcelonae-Romae, 1919.

Melo, Antonius, *De Exemptione Regularium*, Washingtonii, 1921.

Mercati, A., *Raccolta di concordati su materie ecclesiastiche fra la Santa Sede et le autorità civili (1098-1914)*, Romae, 1919.

Migne, Jacques Paul, *Patrologiae Cursus Completus—Series Graeca*, 161 vols., Parisiis, 1857-1866.

Migne, Jacques Paul, *Patrologiae Cursus Completus—Series Latina*, 221 vols., Parisiis, 1844-1855.

Monumenta Germaniae Historica, Epistolae, Tom. III: *Epistolae Merowingici et Karolini Aevi*, Ed. E. Dümmler, Berlin, 1895.

Monumenta Germaniae Historica, Epistolae Selectae, Tom. I: *S. Bonifatii et Lulli Epistolae*, Ed. M. Tangl, Berlin, 1916.

Monumenta Germaniae Historica, Legum Sectio, 2, Capitularia Regum Francorum, Tom. I, Ed. A. Boretius, Hannoverae, 1883; Tom. II, Edd. A. Boretius et V. Krause, Hannoverae, 1897.

Muñiz, T., *Derecho Parroquial*, 2. ed., 2 vols., Sevilla, 1923.

Munro, Dana Carleton—Sontag, Raymond James, *The Middle Ages*, 2. ed., New York—London, 1928.

Murga, Petrus de, *Tractatus de Beneficiis Ecclesiasticis*, Lugduni, 1684.

Nussi, Vincentius, *Conventiones de Rebus Ecclesiasticis inter S. Sedem et Civilem Potestatem*, Moguntiae, 1870.

Ojetti, B., *Commentarium in Codicem Iuris Canonici*, 2 vols., Romae, 1927-1928.

Ojetti, B., *De Romana Curia—Commentarium in Constitutionem Apostolicam "Sapienti Consilio" seu de Curiae Piana Reformatione*, Romae, 1910.

Pallottini, Salvator, *Collectio Omnium Conclusionum et Resolutionum quae in causis propositis apud S. Cong. Cardinalium S. Concilii Tridentini Interpretum prodierunt ab anno 1564 ad annum 1860*, 17 vols., Romae, 1868-1893.

Pistocchi, Marius, *De Re Beneficiali*, Taurini, 1928.

Pistocchi, Marius, *De Synodo Dioecesana*, Taurini, 1922.

Prümmer, Dominicus, *Manuale Iuris Canonici*, 4. et 5. ed., Friburgi Brisgoviae, 1927.

Reiffenstuel, Anacletus F., *Jus Canonicum Universum*, 4 vols., Romae, 1833.

Richter, A. L., *Canones et Decreta Concilii Tridentini*, Lipsiae, 1853.

Rosshirt, C. F., *Lehrbuch des Kirchenrechts*, 3. ed., Schaffhausen, 1858.

Sägmüller, Johannes Baptist, *Die Entwickelung des Archipresbyterats und Dekanats bis zum Ende des Karolingerreichs* (Tübinger Universitätsprogramm), Tübingen, 1898.

Sägmüller, Johannes Baptist, *Lehrbuch des katholischen Kirchenrechts*, 4. ed., Freiburg im Breisgau, 1925-1930.

Santi, Franciscus, *Praelectiones Iuris Canonici*, 2. ed., 2 vols., Ratisbonae, 1892.

Schäfer, Timotheus, *Die Kirchenämter*, Band II (*Pfarrer und Pfarrvikare*), 1. et 2. ed., Münster i. W., 1922.

Schäfer, Timotheus, *De Religiosis*, Münster i. W., 1927.

Shahan, Thomas J., *The Middle Ages*, New York, 1904.

Scherer, Rudolf Ritter von, *Handbuch des Kirchenrechtes*, 2 vols., Graz-Leipzig, 1886-1898.

Schmalzgrueber, Franciscus, *Jus Ecclesiasticum Universum*, 12 vols., Romae, 1843-1845.

Schoepf, J. A., *Handbuch des katholischen Kirchenrechts*, Vol. III, Schaffhausen, 1865.

Smith, A. L., *Church and State in the Middle Ages*, Oxford, 1913.

Smith, S. B., *Elements of Ecclesiastical Law*: Vol. I, *Ecclesiastical Persons*, 9. ed., New York, 1893.

Sohm, Rudolph, *Kirchenrecht* (Anastatischer Neudruck), München-Leipzig, 1923.—Band I, *Die geschichtlichen Grundlagen*; Band II, *Katholisches Kirchenrecht*.

Sorrentino, G., *I Vicarii parrocchiali nel dritto canonico e nelle leggi italiane ecclesiastiche*, Romae, 1910.

Stutz, Ulrich, *Der Geist des Codex iuris canonici*, Stuttgart, 1918.

Suarez, Franciscus, *Opera Omnia*, 26 vols., Parisiis, 1861.

Taylor, Henry Osborn, *The Mediæval Mind*, 2 vols., London, 1914.

Thomassinus, Ludovicus, *Vetus et Nova Ecclesiae Disciplina*, 3 vols., Venetiis, 1730.

Toso, Al., *Commentaria Minora ad Codicem Iuris Canonici*, lib. II, P. I, Romae, 1921.

Van den Berghe, *Institutiones Canonicae*.—Tractatus Autographus.

Van Espen, Z. B., *Jus Ecclesiasticum Universum*, 5 vols., Lovanii, 1753.

Vering, Friedrich H., *Lehrbuch des katholischen, orientalischen, und protestantischen Kirchenrechts*, 2. ed., Freiburg im Breisgau, 1881.

Vermeersch, A.-Creusen, J., *Epitome Iuris Canonici*, 3 vols., Mechlinae-Romae, 1925-1927.—Vols. I-II, 3. ed., 1927; Vol. III, 2. ed., 1925.

Vromant, G., *De Bonis Ecclesiae Temporalibus*, Lovanii, 1927.

Vromant, G., *Ius Missionarium*, Vol. II, Lovanii-Parisiis-Bruxellis, 1929.

Walsh, James J., *The Thirteenth, Greatest of Centuries*, New York, 1912.

Walter, Ferdinand, *Lehrbuch des Kirchenrechts aller christlichen Konfessionen*, 11 ed., Bonn, 1854.

Wernz, F. X., *Ius Decretalium*, Vol. II, 2. ed., Romae, 1906.

Wernz, F. X.-Vidal, Petrus, *Ius Canonicum*, 3 vols., Romae, 1925-1928. —Vol. II, 2. ed., 1928; Vol. V, 1925; Vol. VI, 1927-1928.

Woywod, Stanislaus, *A Practical Commentary on the Code of Canon Law*, 2 vols., New York, 1925.

Zitelli, Zephyrinus, *Apparatus seu Compendium Iuris Ecclesiastici*, Romae, 1886.

PERIODICALS

American Ecclesiastical Review, The, Philadelphia, 1889-

Analecta Ecclesiastica, Romae, 1893-1911.

Analecta Juris Pontificii, Romae, 1855-1868; Parisiis, 1869-1890.

Apollinaris, Romae, 1928-

Archiv für katholisches Kirchenrecht, Vols. I-VI, Innsbruck, 1857-1861; Vols. VII-CX, Mainz, 1862.

Gregorianum, Romae, 1920-

Homiletic and Pastoral Review, The, New York, 1900-

Irish Ecclesiastical Record, The, Dublin, 1864-
Jus Pontificium, Romae, 1921-
Nouvelle Revue Théologique, Tournai, 1869-
Periodica de re canonica et morali utili praesertim Religiosis et Missionariis, Brugis, 1905-
Revue des Sciences Ecclésiastiques, Arras, 1860-1906.
Theologie und Glaube, Paderborn, 1909-
Theologische Quartalschrift, Tübingen, 1819-
Theologisch-praktische Quartalschrift, Linz, 1832-
Theologische Revue, Münster i. W., 1902-
Zeitschrift für katholische Theologie, Innsbruck, 1877-

UNIVERSITAS CATHOLICA AMERICAE

WASHINGTON, D. C.

FACULTAS IURIS CANONICI

1930

No. 58

DEUS LUX MEA

TITULI

QUOS

AD DOCTORATUS GRADUM

IN

UTROQUE IURE

Apud Universitatem Catholicam Americae

CONSEQUENDUM

PUBLICE PROPUGNABIT

CLEMENS VINCENTIUS BASTNAGEL

SACERDOS DIOECESIS INDIANAPOLITANAE

IURIS UTRIUSQUE LICENTIATUS

HORA IX A. M. DIE XXIII MAII A. D. MCMXXX

TITULI

DE IURE CANONICO

XXXI.	Canones 726-730	De Simonia.
XXXII.	Canones 951-976	De Ministro Sacrae Ordinationis.
XXXIII.	Canones 968-991	De Subiecto Sacrae Ordinationis.
XXXIV.	Canones 1012-1018	De Matrimonio in Genere.
XXXV.	Canones 1019-1034	De iis quae Matrimonii Celebrationi Praemitti Debent.
XXXVI.	Canones 1035-1057	De Impedimentis in Genere.
XXXVII.	Canones 1058-1066	De Impedimentis Impedientibus.
XXXVIII.	Canones 1067-1080	De Impedimentis Dirimentibus.
XXXIX.	Canones 1081-1093	De Consensu Matrimoniali.
XL.	Canones 1094-1103	De Forma Celebrationis Matrimonii.
XLI.	Canones 1104-1107	De Matrimonio Conscientiae.
XLII.	Canones 1108-1117	De Tempore et Loco Celebrationis Matrimonii, et de Matromonii Effectibus.
XLIII.	Canones 1118-1132	De Separatione Coniugum.
XLIV.	Canones 1133-1143	De Matrimonii Convalidatione, et de Secundis Nuptiis.
XLV.	Canones 1552-1571	De Iudiciis, de Foro Competenti, et de Variis Tribunalium Gradibus et Speciebus.
XLVI.	Canones 1572-1596	De Tribunali Ordinario Primae et Secundae Instantiae.
XLVII.	Canones 1597-1607	De Ordinariis Apostolicae Sedis Tribunalibus et de Tribunali Delegato.
XLVIII.	Canones 1608-1645	De Disciplina in Tribunalibus Servanda.
XLIX.	Canones 1646-1666	De Partibus in Causa.
L.	Canones 1667-1705	De Actionibus et Exceptionibus.
LI.	Canones 1706-1725	De Causae Introductione.
LII.	Canones 1726-1741	De Litis Contestatione et Instantia.
LIII.	Canones 1742-1746	De Interrogationibus Partibus in Iudicio Faciendis.
LIV.	Canones 1747-1769	De Probationibus.
LV.	Canones 1825-1836	De Praesumptionibus.
LVI.	Canones 1960-1992	De Causis Matrimonialibus.
LVII.	Canones 1993-1998	De Causis contra Sacram Ordinationem.
LVIII.	Canones 2195-2213	De Delictis.
LIX.	Canones 2214-2240	De Poenis in Genere.
LX.	Canones 2241-2254	De Censuris in Genere.
LXI.	Canones 2257-2267	De Excommunicatione.
LXII.	Canones 2268-2277	De Interdicto.
LXIII.	Canones 2278-2285	De Suspensione.
LXIV.	Canones 2286-2305	De Poenis Vindicativis.
LXV.	Canones 2306-2313	De Remediis Poenalibus et Poenitentiis.

DE IURE ROMANO

LXVI. De Fontibus Iuris Romani.
LXVII. De Periodis Iuris Romani.
LXVIII. De Evolutione Iuris Romani.
LXIX. De Codificatione Iustiniana.
LXX. De Interpolationibus.
LXXI. De Criteriis Interpolationes Cognoscendi.
LXXII. De Variis Interpretationis Scholis.
LXXIII. De Persona.
LXXIV. De Statu Libertatis.
LXXV. De Personis in Mancipii Causa.
LXXVI. De Personis in Servitute.
LXXVII. De Legibus Aelia Sentia, Fufia Caninia, Iunia Norbana.
LXXVIII. De Statu Civitatis.
LXXIX. De Capitis Diminutione.
LXXX. De Statu Familiae.
LXXXI. De Patria Potestate.
LXXXII. De Adoptione et Adrogatione.
LXXXIII. De Iustis Nuptiis.
LXXXIV. De Tutela et Cura.
LXXXV. De Rerum Acquisitionis Modis.
LXXXVI. De Iure Dominii.
LXXXVII. De Iure Possessionis.
LXXXVIII. De Iure in Re Aliena.
LXXXIX. De Successione Universali.
XC. De Legatis.
XCI. De Lege Falcidia.
XCII. De Bonorum Possessione.
XCIII. De Senatus Consulto Tertulliano.
XCIV. De Senatus Consulto Orphitiano.
XCV. De Constitutione Anastasii.
XCVI. De Obligationibus.
XCVII. De Contractibus.
XCVIII. De Delictis.
XCIX. De Lege Aquilia.
C. De Actionibus.

Vidit Facultas:

PHILIPPUS BERNARDINI, S.T.D., J.U.D., Decanus.
LUDOVICUS H. MOTRY, S.T.D., J.C.D., a Secretis.
VALENTINUS T. SCHAAF, O.F.M., J.C.D.
FRANCISCUS J. LARDONE, S.T.D., J.U.D.

Vidit Rector Magnificus Universitatis:

JACOBUS HUGO RYAN, Ph.D., S.T.D., LL.D., Litt.D.

BIOGRAPHICAL NOTE

Clement Vincent Bastnagel was born on December 15, 1896, in Posey County, Indiana. He attended the public and parochial schools between the years 1902 and 1910. In 1912 he entered St. Meinrad's Preparatory Seminary. After a course of eleven years he was ordained at St. Meinrad's Major Seminary for the Diocese of Indianapolis on May 22, 1923. During the next four years he was engaged in the service of his diocese in the capacity of a parochial assistant. In the fall of 1927 he was sent by his bishop to the Catholic University of America to pursue a graduate course of studies in the School of Canon Law.

CATHOLIC UNIVERSITY OF AMERICA

CANON LAW STUDIES

1. FRERIKS, REV. CELESTINE A., C.PP.S., J.C.D., Religious Congregations in Their External Relations, 121 pp., 1916.

2. GALLIHER, REV. DANIEL M., O.P., J.C.D., Canonical Elections, 117 pp., 1917.

3. BORKOWSKI, REV. AURELIUS L., O.F.M., J.C.D., De Confraternitatibus Ecclesiasticis, 136 pp., 1918.

4. CASTILLO, REV. CAYO, J.C.D., Disertacion Historico-canonica sobre la Potestad del Cabildo en Sede Vacante o Impedida del Vicario Capitular, 99 pp., 1919 (1918).

5. KUBELBECK, REV. WILLIAM J., S.T.B., J.C.D., The Sacred Penitentiaria and Its Relations to Faculties of Ordinaries and Priests, 129 pp., 1918.

6. PETROVITS, REV. JOSEPH J. C., S.T.D., J.C.D., The New Church Law on Matrimony, X-461 pp., 1919.

7. HICKEY, REV. JOHN J., S.T.B., J.C.D., Irregularities and Simple Impediments in the New Code of Canon Law, 100 pp., 1920.

8. KLEKOTKA, REV. PETER J., S.T.B., J.C.D., Diocesan Consultors, 179 pp., 1920.

9. WANNENMACHER, REV. FRANCIS, J.C.D., The Evidence in Ecclesiastical Procedure Affecting the Marriage Bond, 1920. (Not Printed.)

10. GOLDEN, REV. HENRY FRANCIS, J.C.D., Parochial Benefices in the New Code, IV-119 pp., 1921. (Printed 1925).

11. KOUDELKA, REV. CHARLES J., J.C.D., Pastors, Their Rights and Duties According to the New Code of Canon Law, 211 pp., 1921.

12. MELO, REV. ANTONIUS, O.F.M., J.C.D., De Exemptione Regularium, X-188 pp., 1921.

13. SCHAAF, REV. VALENTINE THEODORE, O.F.M., S.T.B., J.C.D., The Cloister, X-180 pp., 1921.

14. BURKE, REV. THOMAS JOSEPH, S.T.B., J.C.D., Competence in Ecclesiastical Tribunals, IV-117 pp., 1922.

15. LEECH, REV. GEORGE LEO, J.C.D., A Comparative Study of the Constitution "Apostolicae Sedis" and the "Codex Juris Canonici," 179 pp., 1922.

16. MOTRY, REV. HUBERT LOUIS, S.T.D., J.C.D., Diocesan Faculties according to the Code of Canon Law, II-167 pp., 1922.

17. MURPHY, REV. GEORGE LAWRENCE, J.C.D., Delinquencies and Penalties in the Administration and the Reception of the Sacraments, IV-121 pp., 1923.

18. O'REILLY, REV. JOHN ANTHONY, S.T.B., J.C.D., Ecclesiastical Sepulture in the New Code of Canon Law, II-129 pp., 1923.

19. MICHALICKA, REV. WENCESLAS CYRILL, O.S.B., J.C.D., Judicial Procedure in Dismissal of Clerical Exempt Religious, 107 pp., 1923.

20. DARGIN, REV. EDWARD VINCENT, S.T.B., J.C.D., Reserved Cases According to the Code of Canon Law, IV-103 pp., 1924.

21. GODFREY, REV. JOHN A., S.T.B., J.C.D., The Right of Patronage According to the Code of Canon Law, 153 pp., 1924.

22. HAGEDORN, REV. FRANCIS EDWARD, J.C.D., General Legislation on Indulgences, II-154 pp., 1924.

23. KING, REV. JAMES IGNATIUS, J.C.D., The Administration of the Sacraments to Dying Non-Catholics, V-141 pp., 1924.

24. WINSLOW, REV. FRANCIS JOSEPH, A.F.M., J.C.D., Vicars and Prefects Apostolic, IV-149 pp., 1924.

25. CORREA, REV. JOSE SERVELION, S.T.L., J.C.D., La Potestad Legislativa de la Iglesia Catolica, IV-127 pp., 1925.

26. DUGAN, REV. HENRY FRANCIS, M.A., J.C.D., The Judiciary Department of the Diocesan Curia, 87 pp., 1925.

27. KELLER, REV. CHARLES FREDERICK, S.T.B., J.C.D., Mass Stipends, 167 pp., 1925.

28. PASCHANG, REV. JOHN LINUS, J.C.D., The Sacramentals According to the Code of Canon Law, 129 pp., 1925.

29. PIONTEK, REV. CYRILLUS, O.F.M., S.T.B., J.C.D., De Indulto Exclaustrationis necnon Saecularizationis, XIII-289 pp., 1925.

30. KEARNEY, REV. RICHARD JOSEPH, S.T.B., J.C.D., Sponsors at Baptism According to the Code of Canon Law, IV-127 pp., 1925.

31. BARTLETT, REV. CHESTER JOSEPH, A.M., LL.B., J.C.D., The Tenure of Parochial Property in the United States of America, V-108 pp., 1926.

32. KILKER, REV. ADRIAN JEROME, J.C.D., Extreme Unction, V-425 pp., 1926.

33. MCCORMICK, REV. ROBERT EMMET, J.C.D., Confessors of Religious, VIII-266 pp., 1926.

34. MILLER, REV. NEWTON THOMAS, J.C.D., Founded Masses According to the Code of Canon Law, VII-93 pp., 1926.

35. ROELKER, REV. EDWARD G., S.T.D., J.C.D., Principles of Privilege According to the Code of Canon Law, XI-166 pp., 1926.

36. BAKALARCZYK, REV. RICHARDUS, M.I.C., J.U.D., De Novitiatu, VIII-208 pp., 1927.

37. PIZZUTI, REV. LAWRENCE, O.F.M., J.U.L., De Parochis Religiosis, 1927. (Not Printed.)

38. BLILEY, REV. NICHOLAS MARTIN, O.S.B., J.C.D., Altars According to the Code of Canon Law, XIX-132 pp., 1927.

39. BROWN, BRENDAN FRANCIS, A.B., LL.M., J.U.D., The Canonical Juristic Personality with Special Reference to its Status in the United States of America, V-212 pp., 1927.

40. CAVANAUGH, REV. WILLIAM THOMAS, C.P., J.U.D., The Reservation of the Blessed Sacrament, VIII-101 pp., 1927.

41. DOHENY, REV. WILLIAM J., C.S.C., A.B., J.U.D., Church Property: Modes of Acquisition, X-118 pp., 1927.

42. FELDHAUS, REV. ALOYSIUS H., C.PP.S., J.C.D., Oratories, IX-141 pp., 1927.

43. KELLY, REV. JAMES PATRICK, A.B., J.C.D., The Jurisdiction of the Simple Confessor, X-208 pp., 1927.

44. NEUBERGER, REV. NICHOLAS J., J.C.D., Canon 6 or the Relation of the Codex Juris Canonici to the Preceding Legislation, V-95 pp., 1927.

45. O'KEEFFE, REV. GERALD MICHAEL, J.C.D., Matrimonial Dispensations, Powers of Bishops, Priests, and Confessors, VIII-232 pp., 1927.

46. QUIGLEY, REV. JOSEPH, A.M., A.B., J.C.D., Condemned Societies, 139 pp. 1927.

47. ZAPLOTNIK, REV. IOANNES LEO, J.C.D., De Vicariis Foraneis, X-142 1927.

48. DUSKIE, REV. JOHN ALOYSIUS, A.B., J.C.D., The Canonical Status of the Orientals in the United States, VIII-196 pp., 1928.

49. HYLAND, REV. FRANCIS EDWARD, J.C.D., Excommunication, Its Nature, Historical Development and Effects, VIII-181 pp., 1928.

50. REINMANN, REV. GERALD JOSEPH, O.M.C., J.C.D., The Third Order Secular of Saint Francis, 201 pp., 1928.

51. SCHENK, REV. FRANCIS J., J.C.D., The Matrimonial Impediments of Mixed Religion and Disparity of Cult. XVI-318 pp., 1929.

52. COADY, REV. JOHN JOSEPH, S.T.D., J.U.D., A.M., The Appointment of Pastors, VIII-150 pp., 1929.

53. KAY, REV. THOMAS HENRY, J.C.D., Competence in Matrimonial Procedure, VIII-164 pp., 1929.

54. TURNER, REV. SIDNEY JOSEPH, C.P., J.U.D., The Vow of Poverty, XLIX-217 pp., 1929.

55. KEARNEY, REV. RAYMOND A., A.B., S.T.D., J.C.D., The Principles of Delegation, VII-149 pp. 1929.

56. CONRAN, REV. EDWARD JAMES, A.B., J.C.L., The Interdict, 1930.

57. O'NEILL, REV. WILLIAM H., J.C.L., Papal Rescripts of Favor, 1930.

58. BASTNAGEL, REV. CLEMENT VINCENT, J.U.L., The Appointment of Parochial Adjutants and Assistants, 1930.

59. FERRY, REV. WILLIAM A., A.B., J.C.L., Stole Fees, 1930.

60. COSTELLO, REV. JOHN MICHAEL, A.B., J.C.L., Domicile and Quasi-Domicile, 1930.

61. KREMER, REV. MICHAEL NICHOLAS, A.B., S.T.B., J.C.L., Church Support in the United States, 1930.

www.ingramcontent.com/pod-product-compliance
Lightning Source LLC
LaVergne TN
LVHW050253080826
844660LV00012B/634

* 9 7 8 0 8 1 3 2 2 2 4 7 9 *